The Healthcare Community and Australian Immigration Detention

Ryan Essex

The Healthcare Community and Australian Immigration Detention

The Case for Non-Violent Resistance

Ryan Essex
The Institute for Lifecourse Development
University of Greenwich
London, UK

ISBN 978-981-15-7536-5   ISBN 978-981-15-7537-2   (eBook)
https://doi.org/10.1007/978-981-15-7537-2

Cover illustration: © John Orsbun / Alamy Stock Photo

This Palgrave Macmillan imprint is published by the registered company Springer Nature Singapore Pte Ltd.
The registered company address is: 152 Beach Road, #21-01/04 Gateway East, Singapore 189721, Singapore

For Lindsay and Lianne

Preface

Inverbrackie, Curtin and Villawood

In December 2010 the Australian government announced the opening of the Inverbrackie Alternate Place of Detention. It was one of many centres that opened throughout 2010 and 2011 in response to an increasing number of asylum seeker boat arrivals. Inverbrackie was former military housing, about 35 km outside of Adelaide and a little over 1 km outside of the town of Woodside. Unsurprisingly, there was substantial community opposition.[1] Woodside sits within one of the more conservative electorates in Australia. This opposition however was not just about Inverbrackie, nor were these anxieties isolated to Woodside. These issues struck at the heart of the Australian psyche. While the "land of the fair go"[2] for some, when it came to relatively few desperate people seeking help, we were seemingly happy to look away, dismiss their claims and attack those who argued otherwise. These "boat people" held up a mirror and forced us to confront who we thought we were.

I was not to know any of this when I began working for International Health and Medical Services at Inverbrackie in March 2011. I naively thought that things couldn't be as bad as they sounded, that I could make

---

[1] For further discussion about this, see Curtis and Mee (2012).
[2] For further discussion about this, see Bolton (2003).

a difference. Inverbrackie allowed me to operate under this illusion for a while. On the surface, it was a relatively nice centre. It was rural, surrounded by green farmland and rolling hills. The fence surrounding the centre was small, even the least athletic of us could climb over. Curiously, nobody escaped or even attempted to. Inverbrackie had a number of other facilities that gave the impression of normality. A pre-school, social activities, communal areas and a small shop which, at the time, was under construction. Children were picked up daily and taken to school; parents were taken to do the shopping a couple of times a week. People lived in refurbished housing, sometimes having to share. They were free to walk around the centre, which was comparatively bigger than others. On the surface, this gave the impression that things were fine; they obviously weren't. Life was institutionalized, there were headcounts, day-to-day life was managed, rules were arbitrary and inconsistent. The environment also did little to buffer against those who were particularly vulnerable; adults and children were hospitalized with serious mental health concerns; despair was never far from the surface.

I never planned to write a book, so I can't give a blow-by-blow account of my time working in immigration detention, but there remain some things that stand out.

For the most part, Inverbrackie was calm. This however was frequently interrupted by moments of panic. Actual or threatened self-harm, protest or even some kind of "unacceptable behaviour" prompted military-like responses. More often than not this was related to some kind of frustration that had boiled over. For those detained the question of when they would be released almost always lingered at the forefront of their minds. This was a question, to which there was rarely an answer. This lack of certainty combined with a slow and opaque process ensured frustration was inevitable.

Perhaps the thing I remember the most were the kind, resilient people in Inverbrackie. I talked to those who had survived the Sri Lankan civil war, which indiscriminately targeted civilians and that killed at least 100,000. Many who were detained had left family behind. Some were still in contact, many had died, some were the only survivors, and others were in denial and never called home to find out.

By the end of 2011, Australia's immigration detention centres (IDCs) were full, with record numbers of boat arrivals; the government had nowhere to put people. "Surge capacity" was a term used to describe the upper limit of people that could be detained. Gyms, common areas and really any other place where you could fit a bed were converted into dormitories.

Curtin Immigration Detention Centre (IDC) detained single adult men on an unused military base. It had a notorious reputation, opened by the Howard government in 1995, closed and re-opened again in 2010. Curtin was in a beautiful but inhospitable part of Australia, over 2000 km from the nearest city and about 40 km out of the small town of Derby. It wasn't unusual for temperatures to exceed 40 degrees Celsius most of the year, and there was little respite, with no rain for months on end. The location of Curtin worked as a type of detention beyond detention. The week before I arrived in late 2011, there was an escape attempt; the fence was pushed down by 40 men. This was more an act of frustration however; most didn't go much further than the fence line; they all knew they wouldn't have got anywhere and were unlikely to survive more than a few days.

Resistance was a recurring theme in Curtin. Many acts went unnoticed. Breaking arbitrary rules and small acts of disobedience were common. Many more acts were public. We had anywhere between 10 and 20 people on suicide watch. This list was populated almost exclusively with men who had become increasingly despairing about their situation. In the week after my arrival, there was a mass hunger strike, which over three days culminated into about 20 men self-harming in protest. It became quite clear, quite quickly, that what could be labelled as "maladaptive" in other settings was completely functional in this environment.

During my time at Curtin, a majority of the men detained had waited two years or more with little to no news about their claims for protection or when they would be released. Between emergencies, life in Curtin was monotonous. Despair and hopelessness manifest in a number of ways. This not only resulted in protest but also in a range of medical complaints, aches, pains and constant migraines. Towards the end of my seven months at Curtin, I was unsure as to why anybody turned up for their mental health appointments. People didn't need mental health support; they just needed someone there, someone who they saw as separate from the system. The problem was clear, and there was little we could do about it. At about the same time we began writing letters to the department of immigration, outlining our concerns for each person and recommending "less restrictive environments". Vague language was the norm to soften what may have been construed as "advocacy". The immigration department had already started moving people to the community; however, this appeared to be more because centres had reached their capacity. When they did move people, this still appeared to be completely arbitrary. In my final weeks, all but a few of the men I knew had been moved to the community. There was one man who remained, he was stateless, he kept a low profile while in detention, and he was very likely to be granted refugee status at some point. I had written to the immigration department outlining my concerns multiple times. In my final days and in my frustration I approached a senior department of immigration employee, who had been supportive of the mental health team in the past. I re-iterated what I had already written multiple times. He sent my concerns to Canberra, and we received news that this man would be moved to the community the next day. It seemed that occasionally you could still get things done, not through therapeutic work but by cultivating a rapport with the people who could make a tangible difference—the department of immigration.

In immigration detention, life was divided into compounds. In 2012, Villawood IDC had several distinct compounds that had been thrown together over the course of several decades. Originally opened as migrant housing in the 1940s, Villawood was converted to a detention centre in the 1970s. A range of different accommodation and security measures had been put in place to meet whatever need the government had at the time. It stood in contrast to Curtin's purpose-built, four-metre-high, double electrified fences and sterile shipping container infrastructure. The design flaws throughout Villawood not only made it a relatively unpleasant environment, but they allowed people to escape and scale buildings to protest in full view of the public. The centre was also quite flammable. This had been tested nine months earlier, when up to 100 people rioted, setting a large part of the centre alight. The medical centre was destroyed by the fire and a number of exploding oxygen cylinders.

When I arrived in early 2012, nine months after the riot, we were relegated to a few small cells and interview rooms that were converted into a "medical centre" to serve the needs of anywhere up to 400 people.

Villawood had a different population from most other centres. It detained people who had overstayed their visa, those who had had their visa cancelled on character grounds (in 2012 this was usually people who had served a custodial sentence for longer than 12 months) and those who had arrived in Australia seeking asylum, both by plane and by boat. It was also used to accommodate people who had in some way been "disruptive" while detained elsewhere, those who needed to be detained in a high security setting or those who were being deported. This meant there were a lot of people in Villawood who had nothing left to lose. If I had any doubts about the cruelty of these policies, these were put to rest during my time in here. While I could count some small victories in Curtin, having had a number of people moved to the community, this was not the case at Villawood. It was the last stop for many. If you stood any chance of being released to the community, you would often be waiting for years. Small requests were often denied, and even though we had allies in the immigration department, they too had little power to effect change. While the medical team was often involved in all major meetings across the centre, your position became obvious after attending one or two. Security and administrative concerns would always trump health and welfare. Medical opinion carried weight only when it suited the department's objectives or supported the day-to-day operation of the centre.

Resistance was once again another recurring theme. Those who had been detained for years had their own type of dark humour. There were many who stood stoic and defiant. Many knew exactly where the line of "acceptable" behaviour was, when to cross the line, and if caught, how to minimize the fallout. There were the arbitrary rules and then there was what actually happened out of sight, day to day.

There were four deaths at Villawood in the years I worked there. One stays with me, Ahmad Ali Jafari. I met Ahmed shortly after arriving in Curtin; he was moved to the community in early 2012, just after I had left Curtin. We crossed paths again after he was detained about six months later and brought to Villawood. Ahmed remained hopeful about being granted refugee status in Australia but became increasingly despairing as time went on. The immigration department had detained him as they believed he had criminal convictions overseas. He denied this, and from what I knew of him, it seemed unlikely. He got the documents that cleared him a few months later and these were provided to the department. A number of other staff and I advocated for his release for months. There was no good reason for him to remain in detention. He was detained for almost 12 months before he died from a heart attack on 20 June 2013, unnecessarily and unjustly detained in Villawood. He was 26 years old.

Research and the Border Force Act

While I contemplated leaving, I continued to work in detention for the next 18 months. I felt compelled to start to write about my experiences and in particular the issues facing healthcare workers within centres. There were too many stories that needed to be told and too many issues that needed to be brought to light. This book is based on my PhD, which I completed with Sydney Health Ethics at the University of Sydney, partly while I was still working in detention.

The first 12 months of this research were unremarkable. I drafted a research proposal, conducted a literature review and had put in for ethics approval to interview healthcare workers who had worked in immigration detention centres. The idea was simple: have people speak about their experiences, about the limitations in providing healthcare and about the impact of detention; have people tell their stories and, importantly, identify ways in which the healthcare community should respond to these issues. At the time I submitted an application to the University of Sydney's Human Research Ethics Committee, there was no restriction on healthcare professionals speaking about their experiences in immigration detention centres. The Human Research Ethics Committee were however concerned about the introduction of a new law, the Border Force Act (2015) which was coming into effect on 1 July 2015. This legislation criminalized the disclosure of any information related to immigration detention centres by current or former staff, an offence which carried up to two years' imprisonment. Both myself and those who I intended on recruiting would have fallen under the Act and would have been potentially liable to prosecution. Consultation with the University of Sydney's Office of General Counsel all but confirmed this. The advice I received noted the broad nature of what may be considered "protected information". I was told that everything from "highly sensitive" to "highly mundane" matters would be captured under the Act. Thus, any disclosure from participants would likely be considered "protected information" as would the proposed recruitment strategy and the structure of participant interviews, as both involved information gained from my employment in immigration detention. Both myself and the interviewees could face a two-year gaol term for any disclosure that resulted from the study. Furthermore, the University could also be held liable. The Office of General Counsel concluded that the only way to proceed with this research was to "(a) not interview a current or past Australian Border Force employee or (b) to seek the approval of the Department [of Immigration and Border Protection] to conduct interviews, which would likely curtail any free inquiry". At that point, I abandoned plans to conduct interviews; it was also perhaps the beginning of this book.

A great deal happened around the introduction of this legislation, something which I will discuss in greater detail in Chap. 3. However, the introduction of the Border Force Act and the healthcare communities' response proved formative in shaping my thoughts on how we should respond to these policies. The Border Force Act was eventually amended 15 months later in 2016 and again in 2017 to exclude health professionals and clarify what type of disclosures would be covered under the legislation. It was not healthcare as usual that achieved these amendments. There were no "free speech" advocates, who came out in opposition to these policies. It was the healthcare community who spoke out for themselves, who took a risk in declaring they would not be silenced. Many whistleblowers were made in the months following the introduction of the Border Force Act and many continued to publicly break the law.

Australian Immigration Detention, Today and into the Future

Since leaving immigration detention, I have watched on. I can only begin to distil the misery throughout this book. There have been countless reports of self-harm and suicide, including multiple self-immolations. A number of investigations have revealed widespread physical and sexual abuse perpetrated against men, women and children. There have also been many more deaths, many of whom I had come in contact with at some point while working in centres. In response to all of this, the Australian government has dismissed, ignored or attempted to cover up. While most of this has happened offshore, the Australian government has maintained a hardline approach onshore. Some have now been detained for over a decade while the government has continued to deport those who have been living in the Australian community.

While we should count some small victories, if anything over the last few years, policies have become increasingly cruel. While the government maintains that this is necessary to "stop the boats", the hypocrisy of this has been laid bare. What silencing healthcare staff has to do with asylum seekers thinking twice before making the journey to Australia or how denying journalists access to centres deters people smuggling remains a mystery. While these policies are dressed up as deterrence, they are also far more than this. They are callous, deliberate and engineered to dehumanize.

This book brings together a decade of work. Australian immigration detention and related policies have changed drastically over this time as have the number of people arriving by boat, seeking asylum. This book and my experiences have been shaped over five prime ministers and countless shifts in policy. In 2011, when I started working in detention, offshore processing wasn't policy and boat arrivals were in the tens of thousands. Today, boat arrivals have virtually ceased, and the government continues to pursue resettlement for those left in offshore centres. While it seems Australia will maintain these policies into the foreseeable future, in a decade these policies may look very different. While the question of how the healthcare community responds will remain important, into the future the answer may be very different to what is outlined here.

In saying this, however, some things introduced in this book will have enduring value. Throughout history, equality, rights and justice have had to be fought for. Controversial and confrontational action undertaken by the healthcare community in response to injustice has been common, and it seems that such action is only going to have increasing importance for the global healthcare community. Migration throughout Europe and North America has become increasingly contentious with governments taking increasingly harsh measures to stop people crossing borders. Immigration detention has also proliferated, increasingly becoming the go-to option for many states. Across the globe, at a time which has been characterized by the growth of populism and xenophobia, governments or those seeking power have openly attacked the rights of migrants and those defending them. One does not have to look far for a repentant literature that attempts to make sense of atrocities in which the healthcare community has played a part. It is never good enough to spectate; in such circumstances and if we are to effect change, we need to move beyond evidence and reasoned argument; we need to undermine and resist what creates and sustains these injustices.

London, UK   Ryan Essex

References

Australian Border Force Act 2015. (2015).

Bolton, T. (2003). Land of the fair go—an exploration of Australian identity. *AQ: Journal of Contemporary Analysis*, 16–40.

Curtis, F., & Mee, K. J. (2012). Welcome to Woodside: Inverbrackie alternative place of detention and performances of belonging in Woodside, South Australia, and Australia. *Australian Geographer, 43*(4), 357–375.

Acknowledgements

This book has come together over the course of a decade and with the support of many. First and foremost, I need to thank Chris Jordens and Angus Dawson at Sydney Health Ethics, the University of Sydney. This book would not exist without their knowledge and guidance. I also need to thank all within the Institute for Lifecourse Development at the University of Greenwich for supporting me and giving me the time and space to finish this book.

More generally, there are too many names to mention, but thank you to everyone who have offered their support over nearly a decade, those who I worked with in detention, those who I have written with and all others who have sat down with me, provided advice or answered my emails.

Thanks to those who have opposed Australian immigration detention and particularly those people who have taken the risk to resist, your actions have inspired much of this book. To those who have suffered at the hands of Australia's policies, thank you for your stoicism. I hope this book contributes to change so others do not have to suffer needlessly.

Finally, I would like to thank my family. In particular, I would like to thank my parents for their years of support and my wife, Mani, who has been infinitely patient in waiting for this book to come together.

Contents

List of Figures

1

Introduction

For three decades Australia has maintained a policy of mandatory, indefinite immigration detention and a range of related measures throughout the Asia-Pacific region. These policies have not come about by accident, their intent has long been made clear by the Australian government. The harm created and perpetuated by these policies has been engineered as a means to deter others who might otherwise seek Australia's assistance. In practice this means tens of thousands of men, women and children have been detained in squalid conditions and exposed to violence, riots, physical and sexual assaults, self-harm and suicidal behaviour as a means to achieve these ends. For those who are detained, the consequences of these policies are nothing short of devastating.

The healthcare community has had a close relationship with these policies. Healthcare has been provided within Australian immigration detention for decades. The near futility of doing so has been well documented. Outside of detention, healthcare professionals and healthcare bodies have advocated for change, with the healthcare community forming a small part of a larger chorus of criticism that has involved lawyers, artists, academics and concerned citizens.

© The Author(s) 2020
R. Essex, *The Healthcare Community and Australian Immigration Detention*,
https://doi.org/10.1007/978-981-15-7537-2_1

Despite these controversies, despite the well-documented harms and despite rarely leaving the headlines for close to three decades, the Australian government has only hardened in its resolve to deter further arrivals, shutting down cooperative efforts, attacking those critical of these policies and attempting to cover up the despair within centres.

How should the healthcare community respond? This question is not new, and I am sure it has weighed heavily on many. In this book I want to challenge decades of thinking on this issue and argue that the healthcare community should incorporate non-violent resistance into future efforts that seek change. This approach recognizes that change will not come through consensus or collaboration alone but instead seeks to leverage the power of the healthcare community to demand change. Non-violent resistance could include a range of action, including strikes, whistleblowing and principled disobedience[1]; all aimed at expressing opposition to or undermining these policies. The broader argument I make in this book, which could also be applied elsewhere, is that when faced with major injustices such as human rights violations and when conventional avenues to pursue change have been shut down, the healthcare community should undermine and resist what creates and sustains these injustices.

This book which started off as PhD, originally sought to investigate the ethics of healthcare in Australian immigration detention. As you will see, discussions about the ethics of healthcare now occupy less than a chapter. I provide few answers on how individual healthcare professionals should act when working within immigration. This book also says little about consensus, mediation or negotiation. This book is focused on broader political change in how we approach the issue of refugees and asylum seekers in Australia. In doing so I cover some ground and despite being thorough I have had to make some trade-offs in what I discuss; many of the issues throughout this book are not settled, they deserve ongoing debate. A further trade-off that has weighed heavily was the need to tread a path between what was ideal and what was feasible. While debates about what is ideal should continue, this book was written knowing that many remain detained. It was written knowing that urgent,

---

[1] These will be defined and discussed from Chap. 6 onwards.

pragmatic solutions are needed. An overview of each chapter is discussed below.

In Chap. 2 I will outline Australia's policy of mandatory immigration detention and related regional measures aimed at denying and deterring boat arrivals. I outline a brief history of immigration detention, from its introduction in 1992 to the present day. While immigration detention could be criticized for a range of reasons, I will focus on two particularly important issues, the impact of these policies on health and wellbeing and on human rights.

In Chap. 3 I will provide an overview of the administrative and contractual arrangements related to healthcare delivery in detention centres. I will highlight testimony from healthcare professionals, refugees and asylum seekers and consider statements from professional healthcare bodies. In addition to providing an overview of the healthcare arrangements in detention I seek to do two things in this chapter. First, show that the delivery of healthcare in immigration detention is next to futile; and second, highlight disparity between testimony, the contractual arrangements and statements made by professional healthcare bodies. I will also consider some major controversies that have occurred and how the healthcare community have responded to these, outlining the action taken in response to the Border Force Act, the Medevac legislation and the case of Baby Asha.

While Chap. 3 inevitably began to touch on some of the ethical issues raised by the delivery of healthcare in detention, I will consider these issues in more depth in Chap. 4. I will first consider whether Australia's policy of mandatory immigration detention and the actions it has taken throughout the Asia-Pacific region can be justified. This is an important question as it will, at least to some degree, determine whether we can justify non-violent resistance as a response. I will argue that Australia's present policies are profoundly unjust. However, while drastic reform is needed and justified, some caution is warranted as we also need to carefully consider the regional implications of such reform. That is, in seeking reform domestically, changes to Australia's policies are likely to have repercussions throughout the Asia-Pacific region, which could again lead to asylum seeker boat arrivals, which could in turn lead to deaths at sea. I will conclude this chapter by outlining the literature that has considered the ethics of healthcare within immigration detention centres (IDCs), touching upon some key concepts and discussions in relation to the delivery of healthcare within centres.

In Chap. 5 I will sketch how we should begin to approach the issue of reform. First, I will outline an alternate approach to Australian immigration detention and ultimately what we should demand when engaging in action that seeks change. In proposing reform, I suggest a minimum standard needed to protect the health, wellbeing and rights of asylum seekers in Australia. I draw on human rights to do this and the recognition that health is dependent on human rights first being upheld and that human rights cannot be upheld in Australian immigration detention. I thus call for major systemic reform, consistent with the human rights instruments to which Australia is signatory. I will then consider the major constraints on achieving this reform or any type of reform for that matter. To do this I will start with Nethery's (2010) thesis which argues that to understand why Australia persists with these policies, we need to consider a range of historical, social and political factors. I will also discuss a number of contemporary political constraints on reform. Finally, I will offer some reflections on why current approaches to immigration detention by the healthcare community are poorly equipped to challenge these constraints. This of course is not take away from those who have advocated for change for the last three decades. It is simply to say that we can and should do more, a case I will make in the next chapter.

In Chap. 6 I will make the case for a new way of thinking and acting in response to Australian immigration detention. As the title of this book has already given away, this approach employs a disruptive and adversarial non-violent action. I will first consider debates about the role of healthcare professionals in social and political change, arguing that the healthcare community should play a role in shaping social and political change more generally, particularly when faced with egregious injustices. Next, I will define what I mean by non-violent resistance. For the purposes of this book, non-violent resistance is a strategy that seeks to oppose, subvert and undermine Australian immigration detention (and related policies) through action that is often unorthodox, adversarial or disruptive. Such a strategy recognizes that change will not come through consensus or collaboration and instead leverages the power of the healthcare community to demand change. A range of action could be considered non-violent resistance, such as strikes, boycotts, whistleblowing and principled disobedience. While this book is also primarily concerned with "how" we should respond, in this chapter I will also deal with the question of "why" the healthcare community should engage in non-violent resistance.

In the next three chapters I will consider three forms of action and question whether they are justified. In Chap. 7 I will consider whether strike action is justified. A strike is important to consider for two reasons. First, given the nature of the system and the almost futile delivery of healthcare within in, it would not be unreasonable to resign or decline to participate in the system. Second, unlike the other forms of action discussed in this book, a strike has already been debated amongst the healthcare community—I hope to expand on these discussions here. I will start by outlining what I mean by a strike. I will then outline the discussions that have been had in relation to strike action in response to Australian immigration detention. Starting with a framework proposed by Selemogo (2013) I will then discuss the most important points when considering strike action. Amongst a number of other considerations I argue that the health and wellbeing of detainees should weigh heavily in any decision making and for this reason I don't believe a strike can be justified, nor would it be feasible. This of course does not mean we should accept the status quo or should dismiss a strike completely, it should be seen amongst a repertoire of other action. Furthermore, depending on shifts in future policy, such action may be justified. I will conclude by discussing some other avenues for action for those working within detention centres.

Unlike a strike, whistleblowing in response to Australian immigration detention hasn't just been debated, and there have been numerous whistleblowers from the healthcare community who have come forth after working in detention centres. In Chap. 8 I will consider whether whistleblowing by healthcare professionals can be justified in response to Australian immigration detention. I will first outline what I mean by whistleblowing and consider whistleblowing as it has occurred in response to Australian immigration detention. I will then consider whether whistleblowing is justified. Drawing on the work of Ceva and Bocchiola (2020) I will provide an overview of two major theories related to whistleblowing, extrema ratio and deontic approaches. I will then consider how this applies to Australian immigration detention, arguing that given the clear and egregious failings of Australian immigration detention, whistleblowing is justified, with some constraints, namely that disclosures are honest, communicated clearly and based on evidence. In addition to this, healthcare professionals will need to carefully weigh up the risks associated with whistleblowing, particularly to those detained, but also to themselves.

In Chap. 9 I will discuss whether principled disobedience is justified. While there is a degree of overlap with whistleblowing, one of the major differences between principled disobedience and the action discussed in previous chapters is that principled disobedience deliberately seeks to break the law. I will start by outlining precisely what is meant by principled disobedience, civil disobedience and the relatively new concept of uncivil disobedience. I go on to consider principled disobedience as it has occurred in response to Australian immigration detention. I will then consider justifications that have been offered for principled disobedience. Unlike strike action and whistleblowing, it is somewhat difficult to be as specific with principled disobedience as it could take a number of forms. I however conclude that there is a prima facie case for both civil and uncivil disobedience in response to Australian immigration detention.

Important Facts, Figures and Terms

Before moving on there is a need to outline some important facts, figures and terms that I will discuss throughout this book. Many may already be familiar with these issues, for those who are not, the below section outlines some of the more fundamental aspects of Australia's policies and will help give weight to my arguments in later chapters. While some of the figures below are presented with little context, Chap. 2 will shed some light here, when I outline a brief history of Australian immigration detention.

Australia's Humanitarian Programme

Over the last three decades Australia has resettled tens of thousands of refugees through its humanitarian programme. This programme has two components: an onshore and offshore component. The offshore component is generally comprised of those who have already been recognized as refugees by the United Nations High Commissioner for Refugees (UNHCR) and awaiting resettlement in overseas locations. The onshore component is comprised of those who had arrived in Australia with or without a valid visa and then applied for protection. It is this group who will be the focus of this book. The onshore and offshore components were linked in 1996, meaning that for every visa issued onshore (e.g., to somebody who arrived by boat) there would be one less available for those offshore. Australia has generally resettled between 10,000 and 20,000 people a year since 1975 (Phillips, 2017a). These statistics are summarized in Fig. 1.4.

Who Is Detained?

Under Australian law anyone without a valid visa can be detained. That is, a person could arrive without a visa, their visa could expire or it could be cancelled. While most of this book will have relevance for anyone who is detained, it will focus on those who attempt to make the journey to Australia by sea without a visa, that is, those who travel to Australia by boat. There are a number of reasons for this. First, almost all of those who travel to Australia by boat are asylum seekers; between 1976 and 2015 over 80% of those who arrived by boat were found to be refugees (Refugee Council of Australia; RCOA, 2016).[2] Second, Australia has agreed to be bound by a number of international legal and human rights instruments which create clear obligations in relation to the treatment of refugees and asylum seekers. Third, the most punitive policies, such as offshore

---

[2] For the other 20%, little is known; however, there is evidence to suggest that at different times and under different governments, some have been allowed to stay in Australia on humanitarian ground, while others have been returned to their countries of origin.

immigration detention, target those who travel by boat. Fourth and finally, boat arrivals, despite their relatively small numbers, have been one of the most controversial contemporary political issues in Australia for a number of years.

I will often use the terms asylum seeker and refugee interchangeably. This is because Australia has detained both groups. Many who have travelled to Australia by boat were already recognized as refugees while overseas, while others have been granted refugee status in Australia but have either been re-detained or denied the right to move to the community on either security or character[3] grounds. For the purposes of this book, I use the term "detainee" to refer to anyone who is detained. The terms refugee and asylum seeker should be interpreted in line with their international legal definitions (1967; United Nations [UN] General Assembly, 1951). An asylum seeker is someone who has fled their country and applied for protection as a refugee. According to the UN Convention Relating to the Status of Refugees (1951, art. 1), a refugee is any person who

> owing to well-founded fear of being persecuted for reasons of race, religion, nationality, membership of a particular social group or political opinion, is outside the country of his nationality and is unable or, owing to such fear, is unwilling to avail himself of the protection of that country; or who, not having a nationality and being outside the country of his former habitual residence as a result of such events, is unable or, owing to such fear, is unwilling to return to it.

Types of Detention Centre

Over three decades the Australian government has managed several different "types" of detention centres. The first distinction worth making here is those centres offshore and those onshore. As noted above since 2012 the Australian government has managed centres on Manus Island

---

[3] Australia has character requirements for all visas; that is, anybody who applies for a visa must be of good character. Generally, most people who are denied a visa on character grounds have been convicted of a criminal offence; however, this also gives the immigration minister substantial discretionary power to cancel or deny visas.

(Papua New Guinea) and Nauru. Almost all available evidence suggests that centres offshore are far worse than those maintained onshore, this is for a variety of reasons, many of which will become apparent in subsequent chapters. Also, for clarity throughout this book I will more often than not refer to immigration detention generally. When I do this, I am speaking about all types of detention.

The Australian government has also managed at least four different types of centre onshore: Alternative Places of Detention (APODs), Immigration Transit Accommodation (ITA), Immigration Residential Housing (IRH) and Immigration Detention Centres (IDCs). Offshore, centres, while technically IDCs have also been referred to as Regional Processing Centres. APODs, ITA and IRH were used to detain children and those considered vulnerable, usually due to illness. They feature a number of superficial improvements to IDCs and were described in the Australian Human Rights Commission Forgotten Children Report (AHRC, 2014) as follows:

> The facility [Sydney Detention Centre][4] contains four duplex houses, each of which has three bedrooms, two bathrooms, shared kitchen, living and dining areas and a garage area that can be used for visits. The houses face a common area which contains grassy space and a small garden. There is a children's playground, a basketball half-court and a small undercover recreation area. It is next to Villawood Detention Centre. The facilities are highly preferable to other detention facilities in Australia. However, Sydney Detention Centre is still a locked detention facility where people are not free to come and go. (p. 174)

> The Inverbrackie Detention Centre in Adelaide comprises 75 houses … Unless the houses are occupied by a large family they are usually shared with other families. These houses provide a friendlier environment for children. Families have some privacy and while they may share a kitchen space, they are able to cook and eat together. Nevertheless, there are reminders that Inverbrackie and Sydney are detention centres. There are four head counts per day and people are not free to leave the fenced communities. (p. 130)

---

[4]Although referred to as Sydney IRH by the Australian government, the Forgotten Children Report refers to this centre as Sydney Detention Centre.

It is worthwhile noting here that the Australian government has re-categorized immigration detention centres depending on its needs at the time, effectively meaning that IDCs have been "converted" to APODs[5] with little to no oversight.

The Location of Detention Centres

The location of major detention centres is shown in Fig. 1.1.

Number of Boat Arrivals and Detainees

The first asylum seekers to travel to Australia by boat after World War II arrived in 1976. Until the late 1990s less than 1000 people a year arrived. There was a spike in arrivals in the early 2000s, with 4175 people arriving in the 1999–2000 financial year. Arrivals ceased almost completely by 2002. Australia didn't have to deal with a significant number of arrivals until 2009–2010 when 5609 people arrived by boat. The number of arrivals peaked in 2012–2013 with 25,173 arrivals, which again ceased by 2015–2016. Between 1976 and 2015, 69,602 people arrived by boat (RCOA, 2016). These numbers are shown in Fig. 1.2.

The population held in onshore detention has fluctuated, with about 5–10,000 people detained each year between 2000 and 2010. Numbers increased significantly between 2010 and 2016 with almost 40,000 people detained in 2012–2013. As noted above, these numbers do not just represent boat arrivals who have been detained, it also includes others who have been detained without a visa. The numbers displayed in Fig. 1.3 include detainees who have been held for short periods of time (weeks or months) and those who have been detained for longer periods over multiple years. In 2018, for example, those who arrived by boat were detained for an average of 826 days (RCOA, 2019b).

---

[5] For example, the Commonwealth Ombudsman (2013) commented on this during the investigation into self-harm in immigration detention, noting that at different times, centres on Christmas Island and in Pontville, Tasmania were re-classified from IDCs to APODs.

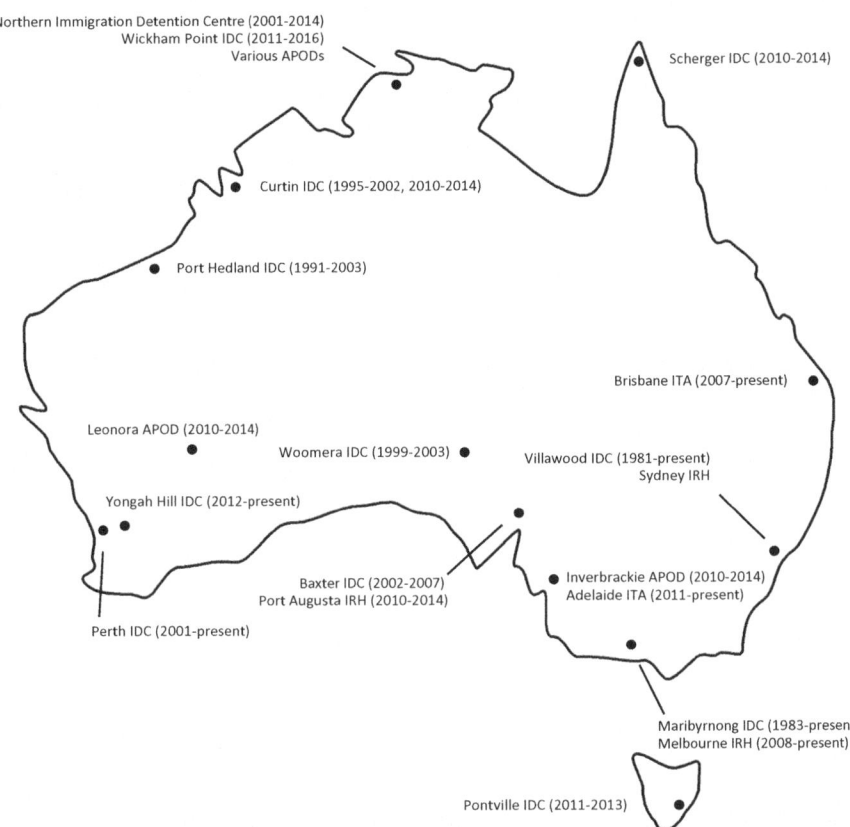

Manus RPC (2001-2004, 2012-2017)
East Lorengau Refugee Transit Centre (2017-Present)
West Lorengau Haus (2018-Present)
Hillside Haus (2018-Present)

Christmas Island IDC, various APODs
(2001-2018, 2019 -present)

Nauru RPC (2001-2008, 2012-present)

Northern Immigration Detention Centre (2001-2014)
Wickham Point IDC (2011-2016)
Various APODs

Scherger IDC (2010-2014)

Curtin IDC (1995-2002, 2010-2014)

Port Hedland IDC (1991-2003)

Brisbane ITA (2007-present)

Leonora APOD (2010-2014)

Woomera IDC (1999-2003)

Villawood IDC (1981-present)
Sydney IRH

Yongah Hill IDC (2012-present)

Baxter IDC (2002-2007)
Port Augusta IRH (2010-2014)

Perth IDC (2001-present)

Inverbrackie APOD (2010-2014)
Adelaide ITA (2011-present)

Maribyrnong IDC (1983-present)
Melbourne IRH (2008-present)

Pontville IDC (2011-2013)

Fig. 1.1 Locations of major Australian immigration detention facilities and years of operation. (Note. The list of centres above is not complete. The opening and closure of detention centres is not well publicized. This figure also cannot account for the location of people transferred from offshore, many of whom were held in hotels)

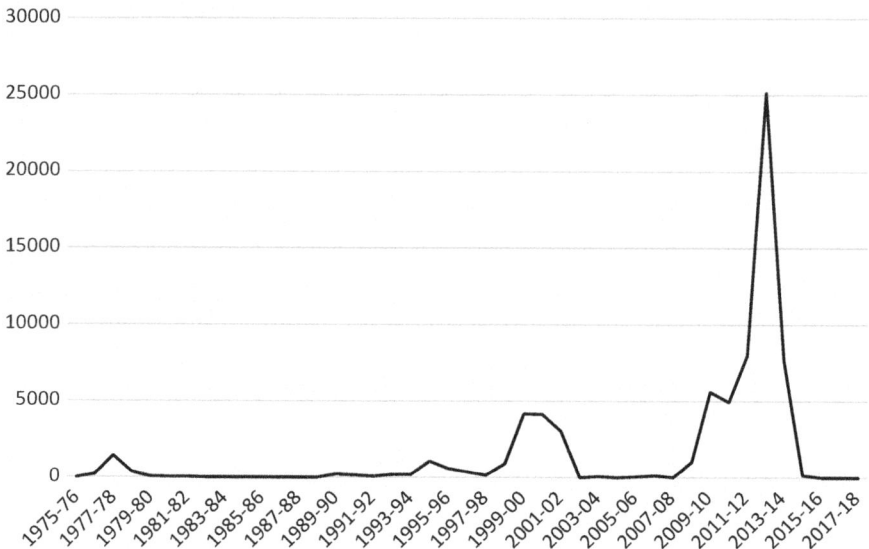

Fig. 1.2 Boat arrivals in Australia. (Note. For clarity, I have only taken into account arrivals who made it to an Australian territory. A number of boats have failed to make it to Australia or been turned back at sea)

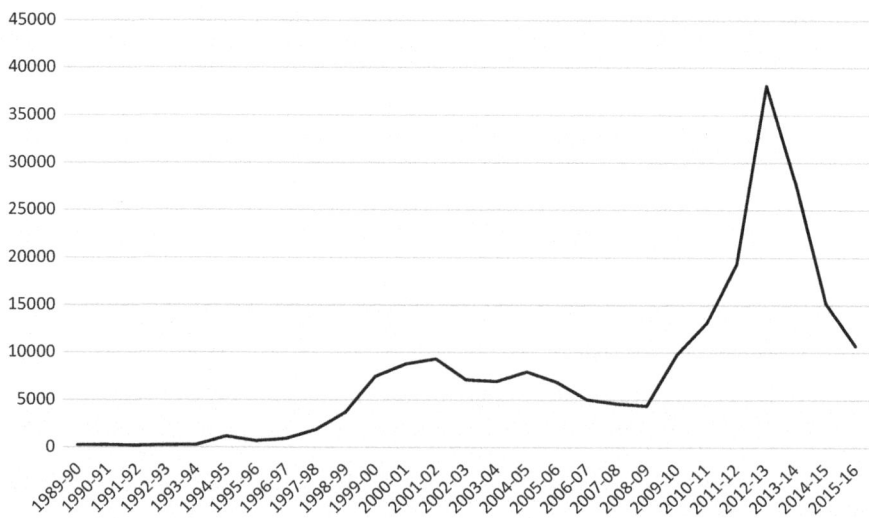

Fig. 1.3 Onshore immigration detention population. (Note. Data adapted from Phillips (2017c). These numbers include those held in community detention and will also include other groups who do not hold a valid visa or who have had their visa cancelled. This graph does not include those detained offshore)

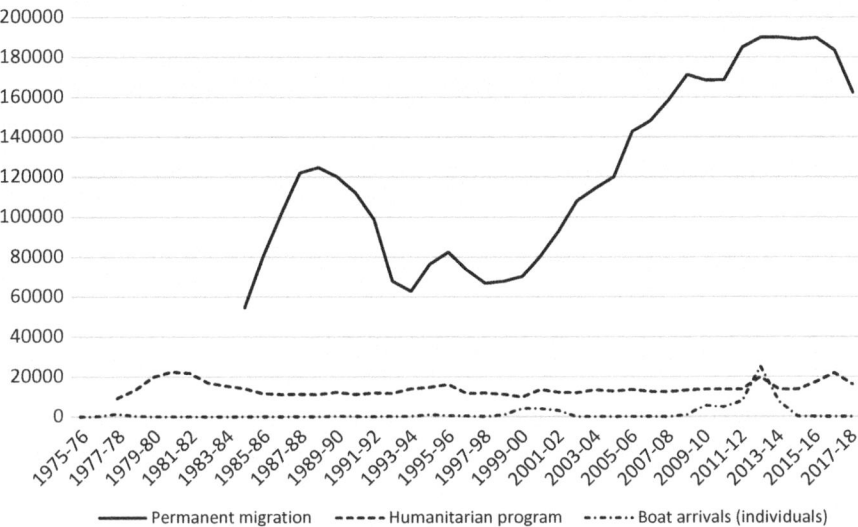

Fig. 1.4 Migrant, humanitarian and boat arrivals in Australia. (Note. Figure adapted from data found in Department of Home Affairs [2019] and Phillips [2017b]. Since 1996 those who arrived in Australia seeking asylum (including boat arrivals) were included in visa grants for the humanitarian programme, that is, if a substantial number of visas were issued to boat arrivals, for example, fewer would be issued for those offshore, awaiting resettlement [Karlsen, Phillips, & Koleth, 2011]. Boat arrivals and visa grants under the humanitarian programme are also not directly comparable year by year. Many boat arrivals waited years to be granted a visa and as will be discussed in this chapter, many others were not granted an Australian visa and sent offshore. Numbers taken from Phillips [2017b] exclude boat crew members [where recorded]. The figures cited here for Australia's migration programme are conservative. In reality, the total migration programme [permanent and long-term temporary visa grants] is much larger than the 190,000 figure often cited. The Australian Bureau of Statistics forecast total migration arrivals for the year ending 30 September 2014 to be 511,500, with a net overseas migration for the same period as 246,300 [Douglas, Higgins, Keski-Nummi, McAdam, & McLeod, 2014])

While Australian government has detained tens of thousands of men, women and children over the last three decades, asylum seekers and refugees account for a small proportion of Australia's overall migration intake. Even when compared to Australia's humanitarian programme, the number of people who arrive by boat is small. These numbers are displayed in Fig. 1.4, which compares Australia's overall migration and humanitarian intake with the number of people who arrived by boats each year.

As noted, the above figures do not account for people detained offshore on Manus Island and Nauru. Between 2001 and 2008, 1637 people were detained on Manus Island and Nauru (Phillips, 2017c). Since re-opening in 2012, 4177 people have been detained. As of 30 September 2019, there were 562 people left in Nauru and in Manus Island, and another 47 being detained by the Papua New Guinean government (RCOA, 2019a).

The Financial Cost of Detention

There is no comprehensive estimate of the financial costs of immigration detention and its related policies; however, we can begin to piece together costs reported in numerous inquiries, hearings and throughout the literature.

Together the best available estimates suggest that between 2008 and 2020 the cost of Australian immigration detention has been about 20 billion dollars (Asylum Seeker Resource Centre, Save the Children, & GetUp, 2019; Australian Parliamentary Joint Select Committee on Australia's Immigration Detention Network: Final Report, 2012). Offshore processing was far more expensive than all other forms of detention, costing in excess of $573,000 per person per year. Detention onshore cost $346,000 per person per year while it cost the government $10,221 per person per year for those living in the community (Asylum Seeker Resource Centre et al., 2019).

In relation to healthcare, International Health and Medical Services (IHMS)[6] has held successive contracts for healthcare onshore and offshore. These were valued at over 1.6 billion dollars between 2009 and 2014 (Farrell, 2015). Since this time, IHMS has held further contracts valued in the hundreds of millions. These figures are obviously incomplete, and

---

[6] IHMS was the detention healthcare provider. I will discuss their role and contractual arrangements in Chap. 3.

there have been numerous other companies who have provided health and social services in recent years. However, it is safe to say that over the last three decades billions have been spent on healthcare alone.

Other Key Terms

The Australian Immigration Department has taken a number of forms and has been referred to as the Department of Immigration and Citizenship, Department of Immigration and Border Protection (DIBP), Department of Immigration and Multicultural Affairs, among other names. Most recently this department has been renamed the Department of Home Affairs. Regardless of how this department has been labelled it has had almost sole responsibility for the day-to-day operation of Australia's IDCs and for the implementation of government policy on immigration. I will refer to this department as the immigration department or department of immigration throughout this book.

I will also refer to the healthcare community in a number of ways. I use the term "healthcare professional" to refer to individual healthcare professionals. I will most frequently however use the term "the healthcare community". With this reference, I mean everybody, that is, those who have worked within detention, those who have not and professional healthcare bodies. I believe everybody has a role here and in many ways, it is unhelpful to parse out who may be more complicit or responsible than others. The healthcare community have stood in close proximity to these policies and, regardless of their involvement, all have a responsibly to protect the rights of those who are vulnerable. If non-violent resistance is to have an impact, consensus isn't needed nor would it be possible, but action will need to be at least somewhat collective endeavour. As I noted in the introduction above, this book has little to say about how individual healthcare professionals should mediate the dilemmas they face when working in detention.

References

Asylum Seeker Resource Centre, Save the Children, & GetUp. (2019). *At what cost? The human and economic cost of Australia's offshore detention policies.* Retrieved from https://www.asrc.org.au/wp-content/uploads/2013/04/1912-At-What-Cost-report.pdf

Australian Parliamentary Joint Select Committee on Australia's Immigration Detention Network: Final Report. (2012). Canberra. Author.

Australian Human Rights Commission. (2014). *The forgotten children: National inquiry into children in immigration detention.* Retrieved from https://www.humanrights.gov.au/our-work/asylum-seekers-and-refugees/publications/forgotten-children-national-inquiry-children

Ceva, E., & Bocchiola, M. (2020). Theories of whistleblowing. *Philosophy Compass, 15*(1), e12642.

Commonwealth Ombudsman. (2013). *Suicide and self-harm in the immigration detention network.* Canberra. Author.

Department of Home Affairs. (2019). *Historical migration statistics.* Retrieved from https://www.homeaffairs.gov.au/research-and-statistics/statistics/visa-statistics/live/historical-migration

Douglas, B., Higgins, C., Keski-Nummi, A., McAdam, J., & McLeod, T. (2014). Beyond the boats: Building an asylum and refugee policy for the long term. Retrieved from http://www.kaldorcentre.unsw.edu.au/publication/beyond-boats-building-asylum-and-refugee-policy-long-term

Farrell, P. (2015). IHMS, the healthcare giant at the heart of Australia's asylum system—Explainer. *The Guardian.* Retrieved from http://www.theguardian.com/australia-news/2015/jul/21/ihms-the-healthcare-giant-at-the-heart-of-australias-asylum-system-explainer

Karlsen, E., Phillips, J., & Koleth, E. (2011). Seeking asylum: Australia's humanitarian program. *Parliamentary Library of Australia.* Retrieved from https://www.aph.gov.au/binaries/library/pubs/bn/sp/seekingasylum.pdf

Nethery, A. (2010). Immigration detention in Australia. (Doctoral dissertation, Deakin University, Victoria, Australia). Retrieved from http://dro.deakin.edu.au/view/DU:30032385

Phillips, J. (2017a). Australia's humanitarian program: A quick guide to the statistics since 1947. *Parliamentary Library of Australia.* Retrieved from https://www.aph.gov.au/About_Parliament/Parliamentary_Departments/Parliamentary_Library/pubs/rp/rp1617/Quick_Guides/HumanitarianProg

Phillips, J. (2017b). Boat arrivals and boat 'turnbacks' in Australia since 1976: A quick guide to the statistics. *Parliamentary Library of Australia.* Retrieved from https://www.aph.gov.au/About_Parliament/Parliamentary_ Departments/Parliamentary_Library/pubs/rp/rp1617/Quick_Guides/ BoatTurnbacks

Phillips, J. (2017c). Immigration detention in Australia: A quick guide to the statistics. *Australian Parliamentary Library.* Retrieved from https://www.aph. gov.au/About_Parliament/Parliamentary_Departments/Parliamentary_ Library/pubs/rp/rp1617/Quick_Guides/ImmigrationDetention

RCOA. (2019a). *Offshore processing statistics.* Retrieved from https://www.refu- geecouncil.org.au/operation-sovereign-borders-offshore-detention-statistics/

RCOA. (2019b). *Statistics on people in detention in Australia.* Retrieved from https://www.refugeecouncil.org.au/detention-australia-statistics/

Refugee Council of Australia. (2016). *Economic migrants or refugees? Analysis of refugee recognition rates for boat arrivals, 1976–2015.* Retrieved from https:// www.refugeecouncil.org.au/economic-migrant-or-refugee/

Selemogo, M. (2013). Criteria for a just strike action by medical doctors. *Indian Journal of Medical Ethics, 11*(1), 35–38.

United Nations General Assembly. (1951). *Convention relating to the status of refugees.*

United Nations General Assembly. (1967). *Protocol relating to the status of refugees.*

2

A Brief History and Overview of Australian Immigration Detention

Overview

Australia's policy of mandatory immigration detention has been one of the most contentious contemporary political issues for almost three decades. In this chapter I will provide a brief outline of the history and consequences of these policies, providing a context for many of the issues I will discuss throughout this book. While I will attempt to give a fairly broad history and overview, I will largely focus on issues that are particularly relevant to how the Australian healthcare community should shape its response to these policies. First, I will briefly discuss the global and regional context in which Australian immigration detention operates, I will then outline a brief history of Australian immigration detention. I go on to argue that to fully appreciate the consequences of these policies, which are far more than a (potentially indefinite) deprivation of liberty, they should be seen first and foremost as a deterrent to others that would otherwise seek asylum in Australia. I will then go on to quantify the impact of these policies, focusing on their impact on the health and human rights of asylum seekers and refugees.

© The Author(s) 2020
R. Essex, *The Healthcare Community and Australian Immigration Detention*,
https://doi.org/10.1007/978-981-15-7537-2_2

The Global and Regional Context

While this book will not deal with global or regional issues, it is necessary to have a basic understanding of the regional context in which Australian immigration detention operates. For our purposes and in thinking about a response to these policies, the global and regional context is important for at least two major reasons.[1] First to begin to highlight some of the structural causes of irregular migration, that is, why people seek asylum in the first place. If we are to address these issues, we cannot operate under the illusion that the problem starts when people board boats to travel to Australia. The Australian government has for many decades now, framed these issues as a problem that starts when people board a boat (usually in Indonesia), and has maintained that policies engineered to deter, are the only way to address this issue. This of course is not the case. Second, this context is needed to begin to think about policy alternatives, as I will argue in later chapters, in demanding change, thought will need to be given to its possible impact across the Asia-Pacific region.

Globally in 2018 there were 78.4 million people of concern to the UNHCR. Of these people, 20.4 million were refugees, 3.5 million were asylum seekers and 41.4 million were internally displaced persons (IDPs). The Asia-Pacific region was home to 9.5 million people of concern, including 4.2 million refugees, 176,000 asylum seekers, 2.7 million IDPs and 2.2 million stateless persons (UNHCR, 2019). The 45 countries included in this region stretch from Iran in the west, Kazakhstan and Mongolia in the north, to Australia and the Pacific Islands in the south and east. Only 20 of the 45 countries and territories in the Asia-Pacific region have acceded to the 1951 Convention Relating to the Status of Refugees (UN, 1951) and its 1967 Protocol (UN General Assembly, 1967). Countries surrounding Australia, like Malaysia and Indonesia who are major hosts of refugees and asylum seekers, are not parties to the Refugee Convention or its Protocol and do not have procedures in place

---

[1] It is beyond the scope of this book to go into the global and regional circumstances in any further detail; however, there is a well-established literature that deals with these issues (e.g., Dastyari & Hirsch, 2019; Hirsch, 2017).

for determining refugee status or ensuring that the rights of refugees and asylum seekers are protected.

Those seeking to travel to Australia can only do so by air or sea. As an island continent which shares no borders, Australia is one of the few countries in the world that has a relative degree of control over the movement of people in and out of its territories. While asylum seekers and refugees have travelled to Australia by both air and sea, majority of the measures discussed below almost exclusively target those seeking to travel by sea usually on small, unsafe boats. For those who attempt the dangerous journey by boat, most attempt to cross a narrow 350 km stretch of water between Indonesia and Christmas Island, a remote Australian territory. The number of people who attempt to reach Australia by boat is relatively low when compared with marine crossings overseas[2] and compared with Australia's overall level of migration. These figures were outlined above in the introduction.

Despite the relatively small number of people attempting to enter Australia by boat and its geographic isolation, which itself acts as a natural deterrent, Australia has invested heavily in efforts to control migration throughout the Asia-Pacific region, implementing policies aimed to both deter and deny those seeking safety. In addition to continuing to enforce more routine non-arrival measures such as visa restrictions (Gibney, 2006), efforts have included the Bali process[3] and the Bali Declaration on People Smuggling (UNHCR, 2018), diplomatic initiatives geared to curb uncontrolled migration throughout the region. Australia has also collaborated on policing and intelligence efforts throughout the region and invested in technology and infrastructure, including immigration detention centres (Larking, 2017; Nethery, Rafferty-Brown, & Taylor, 2013; Spinks, Karlsen, Brew, Harris, & Watt, 2013; Taylor, 2008). Foreign aid has also been used strategically, funding the International Organization for Migration and the UNHCR to process and support asylum seekers and refugees living in the community in Indonesia, Nauru, Papua New Guinea and Cambodia (Kneebone, 2014; Larking, 2017;

---

[2] As a comparison, there were over 1 million undocumented migrants who crossed the Mediterranean in 2015.

[3] https://www.baliprocess.net.

Nethery et al., 2013; Taylor, 2008). As a result of these and many more measures, over the last two decades increasingly restrictive policies designed to limit movement have been adopted throughout the Asia-Pacific region (Wesley, 2007) and as detailed in the introduction, Australia has spent billions to implement and maintain this approach.

The most important point in all of this is to understand that Australian immigration detention is, in many ways, the last obstacle asylum seekers face. Furthermore, migration throughout the Asia-Pacific region is far more complex than the picture often painted in the media and by successive governments, opportunistic individuals who would like to circumvent Australia's migration controls by boarding a boat.[4] In reality, many safe means to migrate have been shut down or restricted. A major consequence of this is that over 1400 people have been confirmed dead or missing at sea, with the majority occurring between late 2009 and late 2013 (The Border Crossing Observatory, n.d.). Put simply, people would avoid risking their lives at sea if other options were open to them in seeking safety and security.

A Brief History of Australian Immigration Detention

Refugee Resettlement in Australia Post-World War II

Despite a historically racist and exclusionary approach to migration Australia has resettled millions of migrants and over 800,000 refugees since federation in 1901 (Refugee Council of Australia [RCOA], 2016). Following World War II Australia played a significant role in resettling those displaced by the war, settling tens of thousands of people a year from Europe. In addition to its annual intake under the humanitarian programme, Australia has also entered into a variety of other agreements in response to other international crises, including providing refuge for

---

[4] I will discuss how the government has framed this issue in more depth in Chaps. 4 and 5.

14,000 Hungarians who fled their country after the 1956 uprising and 6000 Czechs who fled after the 1968 Prague uprising (Hugo, 2002). Most recently and in response to the war in Syria, the Australian government resettled an additional 12,000 Syrian refugees.

The Vietnam War, which concluded in 1975, resulted in the first asylum seekers from Vietnam, Cambodia and Laos. It was estimated that in the two decades after the war, there were over 3 million departures (Robinson, 1998). Of these people, relatively few attempted to travel to Australia, and it was not until 1976 that the first boats began arriving on Australian shores (Hugo, 2002). This was the first time since World War II that asylum seekers had arrived without any prior assessment or formalities undertaken in an overseas location. From 1976 onwards there were 56 boat arrivals, with 2100 asylum seekers onboard, the last of which arrived in 1981. At the time, there was little controversy about whether these people were "genuine" and arrivals were generally held in "loose detention"[5] in Sydney and their claims processed immediately (Millbank, 2001). As the last boats were arriving in the 1980s public sentiment began to shift, with increasing questions about the legitimacy of those who were arriving. In 1989 boats again began to arrive, mainly from Cambodia. Arrivals were held for a number of weeks near Broome and subsequently moved to detention in Sydney. For many placed in detention, the process was protracted with many spending a number of years waiting for the outcome of their protection applications (Betts, 1993).

During the 20 years after the Vietnam War Australia was a major resettlement country, on a per capita basis, accepting more refugees for resettlement than any other country. In total, Australia resettled 137,000 Indochinese refugees between 1975 and 1995 (Robinson, 1998). Those who arrived by boat accounted for a small proportion of the total number of refugees settled during this time. In total, between 1976 and 1992, approximately 70 boats carrying 2500 people made it to Australian shores (Phillips & Spinks, 2012).[6]

---

[5] That is, although not allowed to leave, centres were unfenced.

[6] For further discussion about Australia's history of refugee resettlement, see Neumann (2015).

The Introduction of Immigration Detention: 1992–2001

From 1989 onwards, the number of individuals detained in immigration detention slowly increased but it was not until 1992 that mandatory detention was introduced by the Keating government (receiving bipartisan support at the time) through the Migration Amendment Act (1992). The reasons for introducing mandatory detention were given at the time by Gerry Hand. In his speech at second reading, the then Minister for Immigration stated,

> The Government is determined that a clear signal be sent that migration to Australia may not be achieved by simply arriving in this country and expecting to be allowed into the community … this legislation is only intended to be an interim measure. The present proposal refers principally to a detention regime for a specific class of persons. As such it is designed to address only the pressing requirements of the current situation. However, I acknowledge that it is necessary for wider consideration to be given to such basic issues as entry, detention and removal of certain non-citizens. (Hand, 1992)

In 1994, the Migration Reform Act (1992) extended mandatory detention to all "unlawful non-citizens" and removed the 273-day time limit on detention. Unlawful non-citizens included those who overstayed their visa, attempted to enter Australia without a visa or those who had their visa cancelled. Even though this gave the government the power to detain all unlawful citizens, those who were not considered a flight or security risk were often eligible for a bridging visa, which allowed them to reside in the community while their status was being determined. The same leniency wasn't extended to those who arrived by boat, the rationale for this being that boat arrivals had not submitted themselves to the correct processes and the fact that a number of boat arrivals had escaped detention (57, between 1991 and 1993) (Joint Standing Committee on Migration, 2008).

The Pacific Solution: 2001–2012

Between 1999 and 2001, those arriving by boat increased significantly with over 10,000 people reaching Australian shores (Phillips, 2017). This was accompanied by increasing political hysteria and subsequent pressure to respond to the increasing number of arrivals.

The catalyst for the most punitive elements of Australia's approach and the incident which has set the tenor for policy ever since occurred in August 2001 when 433 asylum seekers sent a distress call from their sinking ship. Those onboard were subsequently rescued by a Norwegian freight ship, the Tampa. The asylum seekers requested to be taken to Christmas Island; however, the Tampa was refused entry to Australian waters. A brief standoff ensued until the Captain of the Tampa defied the orders and entered Australian waters. The ship was intercepted by Special Air Service soldiers to prevent it from reaching land.

On 1 September 2001, Australia announced that it had found a "solution" to the Tampa crisis. The government, led at the time by then Prime Minister John Howard, entered into an agreement with Nauru, a small Pacific island and former Australian dependent territory. In exchange for an initial sum of US$10 million in aid, Nauru agreed to house asylum seekers while their claims were being processed. The UNHCR would assess the claims of the asylum seekers on Nauru and Australia's "Pacific Solution" was born (Brouwer & Kumin, 2003). Shortly after, a centre was also opened on Manus Island, a territory of Papua New Guinea. In addition the Howard government introduced a number of measures aimed at deterring arrivals including temporary protection visas (TPVs)[7] and restricting family reunion visas for those who had arrived by boat (Ruddock, 1999). It also took steps to limit the ability of asylum seekers to make an application for protection while watering down other legal

---

[7] Temporary protection visas have also been widely criticized. While they allow refugees to live in the Australian community, they offer, as implied in their name, temporary protection. They have been shown to have significant impact on the health and wellbeing of refugees. For more, please see Momartin et al. (2006).

protections. The government also began boat turn-backs, for the first time, turning asylum seekers around at sea before reaching the Australian mainland.

During the years of the Pacific Solution, 1637 asylum seekers, including those rescued by the Tampa, were sent to offshore processing centres on Nauru and Manus Island (Spinks & Phillips, 2011). Of those detained on Nauru and Manus Island, 1153 (70%) of individuals were found to be refugees and owed protection. The majority of these people were settled in Australia, with the remainder settled in a number of third countries (Spinks & Phillips, 2011). Boat arrivals decreased dramatically as did the political and popular hysteria after the implementation of the Pacific Solution.

The Howard government was defeated in the Australian federal election in 2007 after 11 years in power. The newly elected government, led by then Prime Minister Kevin Rudd, kept a number of pre-election promises to implement significant changes to mandatory detention with the last detainees removed from Nauru in February 2008. While this was welcomed by advocates and human rights groups, a number of measures aimed at deterring boat arrivals were retained. Mandatory immigration detention continued on mainland Australia and no steps were taken to repeal the restrictions already placed on applications for asylum or the legal reforms made by the previous government. Between 2008 and 2012 the number of boat arrivals increased sharply. The government responded to the increase in arrivals by opening a number of new centres onshore while increasing the capacity of existing centres. Increasing numbers of boat arrivals along with increasing deaths at sea placed mounting pressure on the government to tighten its policies once again (Billings, 2013).

With a change in leadership, the then Prime Minister Julia Gillard continued to respond to increasing arrivals by proposing offshore processing in East Timor and a "people swap" deal with Malaysia, a deal which would see Australia transfer 800 people who had arrived by boat with 4000 refugees in Malaysia. All proposals collapsed, and with detention centres at capacity, the government was left with little choice to begin to move people into the community[8] (Phillips & Spinks, 2013). In June 2012 the government announced the Expert Panel on Asylum Seekers (2012), with the panel releasing its report in August 2012. All recommendations in the report were accepted, including the resumption of offshore processing. Under the new arrangements, those who arrived after 13 August 2012 could be transferred to Manus Island and Nauru for processing where they would be detained in temporary camps pending the construction of permanent facilities. These measures did little to deter further arrivals.

Another change in leadership returned Kevin Rudd to the Prime Ministership in June 2013. Now an election issue and with mounting pressure to take action on boat arrivals, Rudd announced that those who travelled to Australia by boat from 19 July 2013 would no longer be assessed and resettled in Australia, in his words:

> As of today asylum seekers who come here by boat without a visa will never be settled in Australia. Under the new arrangement signed with Papua New Guinea today—the Regional Settlement Arrangement—unauthorised arrivals will be sent to Papua New Guinea for assessment and if found to be a refugee will be settled there. Arriving in Australia by boat will no longer mean settlement in Australia. Australians have had enough of seeing people drowning in the waters to our north. Our country has had enough of people smugglers exploiting asylum seekers and seeing them drown on the high seas. We are sick of watching our servicemen and women risking their lives in rescues in dangerous conditions on the high seas. Regional processing arrangements in Papua New Guinea will be significantly expanded and people will be sent to Manus Island as soon as health checks are complete and appropriate accommodation is identified. (Rudd, 2013)

Operation Sovereign Borders: 2013–Present

Despite the increasingly hardline approach pursued by the Rudd government, they lost the election, with the issue of boat arrivals playing a major

---

[8] Those who were moved to the community were generally placed on Bridging Visa E (BVEs). While preferable to held detention, many remained on BVEs for years, with little support or security. For further discussion, please see Essex (2013).

role in this defeat. In September 2013, the newly elected government, led by then Prime Minister Tony Abbott, introduced "Operation Sovereign Borders", a military-led operation, aimed at deterring and denying asylum seekers through offshore immigration detention and a range of other activities, including the interception and turn-back of boats. Like the Howard government in the early 2000's boat turn-backs were again official government policy. That is, if asylum seeker boats were either found in Australian waters or outside of Australian waters, they were intercepted and turned around at sea without having their refugee status assessed. From 2001 to 2003, five boats with 614 people were intercepted and turned back at sea. Between 2013 and 2018, the government turned back 33 boats with 810 people onboard (Spinks, 2018). Numbers are outlined in Fig. 2.1.

While we now have an idea of the number of boats that have been turned back, at the time, this was largely carried out in secret with the government declining to comment about "on-water matters"; furthermore questions remain about the accuracy of these figures (The Kaldor Centre, 2019). The Australian government has even been accused of

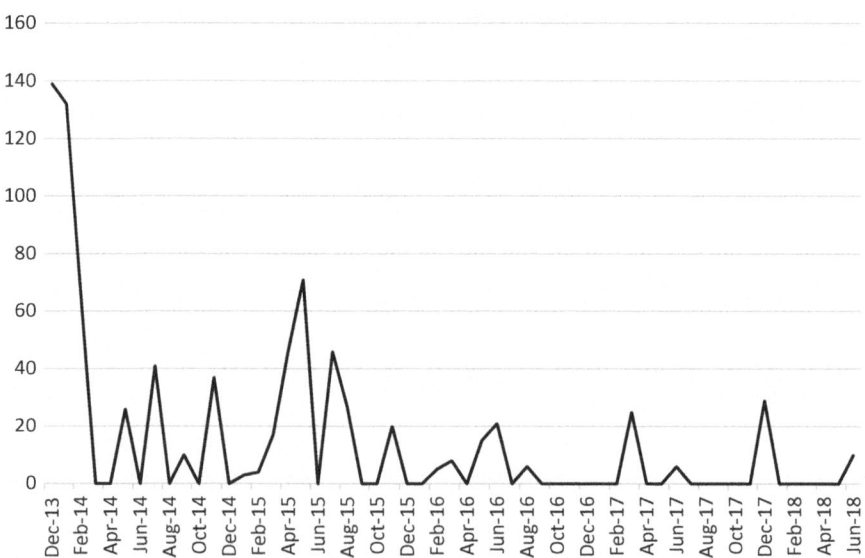

Fig. 2.1 Number of people on boats that were turned back, 2013–2018

paying people smugglers to turn their boats around, with substantial evidence suggesting that at least one crew was paid to return to Indonesia (Phipps, 2015). Although boat arrivals were already in decline before the introduction of Operation Sovereign Borders over the next 12–24 months, they continued to decrease and all arrivals virtually stopped under the Abbott government.

To this day these measures have remained in place. This of course was not the end of the story for the people who were detained. Since the reopening of offshore centres there have been multiple riots and unrest, violence has been common and sexual and physical assault frequently reported and subsequently dismissed or covered up by the government (Australian Parliamentary Select Committee, 2015). Some key events since 2013 are worth mentioning.

Shortly after the reopening of Nauru in July 2013 tensions boiled over with asylum seekers rioting. Over $60 million dollars of damage was reported and four people were hospitalized with minor injuries. A subsequent review concluded that the riot occurred as the result of increasing frustration related to their uncertain time faced in detention and inconsistent and inaccurate messaging about this. The review was highly critical of the immigration department and said there was a "lack of decisive operational leadership" (Hamburger, 2013).

In February 2014, a series of protests by detainees on Manus Island escalated into a riot, which resulted in the death of an asylum seeker and injuries to 70 others. Of those injured one asylum seeker suffered a gunshot wound, while another lost an eye. Multiple people were attacked and beaten by locals and security staff. It was later revealed that Reza Barati, a 23-year-old Iranian asylum seeker, was murdered after being struck in the head, with the attacks described as a "brutal beating by several assailants" (Cornall, 2014). In April 2016, two detention centre workers were sentenced to 10 years in jail for Barati's murder (Doherty & Davidson, 2016).

By late 2015, the legitimacy of offshore processing was challenged in the Australian High Court. In October 2015, the Nauru government announced that they would be processing all remaining asylum seekers who would no longer be confined within the detention centre. This was announced only days before an Australian High Court challenge, with the opening of the centre forming a key part of the government's defence (Davidson & Hurst, 2015; Hurst, 2015). A number of months later, in April 2016, Papua New Guinea's Supreme Court ruled that the immigration detention centre on Manus Island was illegal (Tlozek & Anderson, 2016). Between this ruling and the closure of the centre on Manus Island, there were a number of noteworthy incidents. In April 2017, Papua New Guinean Defence Force staff at the neighbouring Naval Base fired over 100 rounds into the compound. The local police later blamed the shooting on "drunken soldiers" with nine asylum seekers and staff injured (Doherty, 2017b). Peter Dutton, Australia's former Immigration Minister, sought to diminish the seriousness of the shooting, and to date, there has been little said about accountability or repercussions related to this incident. In September 2017, the first group of refugees from Manus Island left for the US under the resettlement deal that was struck in 2016 (Tlozek, 2017).

The Manus Island centre was formally "closed" on 31 October 2017; however, asylum seekers refused to leave and expressed concerns about their safety in the community. Given the violence directed at asylum seekers over the last number of years, these fears were well founded. More than 300 men were removed by force by Papua New Guinean Police on 24 November 2017. The term closure is somewhat misleading for both Manus and Nauru, these islands continue to serve as "open air prisons". Asylum seekers cannot not leave the islands unless resettled, with all continuing to face uncertain and unsafe futures.

While the government has continued to resettle people on Manus Island and Nauru and while in February 2019 they announced that all children were removed from Nauru (Guardian staff with agencies, 2019), this came after years of pressure. In August 2019, 51 asylum seekers, all of whom were not deemed to be refugees or who had not had their cases assessed, were arrested and taken to Bomana immigration centre, an Australian-funded facility, which was annexed from a Port Moresby prison. As of January 2020, 18 people remained in Bomana; others who were detained signed agreements to be voluntarily returned to their country of origin. Conditions within the centre were described as worse than those in Australian run centres, and despite having spent several years on Manus Island, many former detainees have said it was Bomana which broke them and prompted them to return home (Davidson, 2020). At the time of writing, the last reliable report of numbers on Manus and Nauru was from September 2019, where it was reported that 562 people remain (RCOA, 2019). To this day, Australia has dismissed an offer from New Zealand's to resettle people from Manus Island and Nauru (Murphy, 2019).

Deterrence and Australian Immigration Detention

To understand the consequences of Australia's policy, it is first necessary to understand that immigration detention is far more than a (potentially indefinite) deprivation of liberty. Immigration detention in Australia has been explicitly engineered as a deterrent.[9] While it could be argued that Australian immigration detention fulfils a number of other purposes, its evolution since 1992 and expansion of regional measures have been driven almost exclusively by the desire to deter and deny further arrivals, and particularly those who travel to Australia by boat. While over the decades the necessity for shifts in policy have been framed differently, as issues of national security, sovereignty and even as humanitarian concerns, almost all are engineered to immobilize or to use the government's words, "stop the boats".

Deterrence was given as a reason to introduce immigration detention. As you might recall above, when introducing immigration detention in 1992, the then Minister for Immigration made the point that "a clear signal be sent that migration to Australia may not be achieved by simply arriving in this country and expecting to be allowed into the community". Before introducing the Pacific Solution, then Prime Minister John Howard infamously declared that "we will decide who comes to this country and the circumstances in which they come" (Howard, 2001). The then Minister for Immigration Philip Ruddock, who also engineered the Pacific Solution, maintained that after its introduction that

---

[9] Deterrence has become the go-to response for almost all wealthy nations globally, for more on this see Gammeltoft-Hansen and Tan (2017).

detention arrangements which have been a very important mechanism for ensuring that people are available for processing and available for removal, and thereby a very important deterrent in preventing people from getting into boats which we know can be life taking. (ABC Radio National, 2002)

Since the Howard government's election win on the back of the introduction of the Pacific Solution, almost every election since has at been partially fought (and often won) on who is perceived to be able to better secure Australia's borders and "stop the boats". Scott Morrison, the current Prime Minister and former Minister for Immigration, made the case that "[o]nly the Coalition can be trusted to implement strong border protection policies focused on deterrence, rather than accommodation" (cited in Pickering & Weber, 2014).

Since the introduction of Operation Sovereign Borders, the government has also openly promoted "regional deterrence" and "regional deterrence frameworks" (Morrison, 2013) with subsequent leaders and ministers maintaining that deterrence is necessary (Remeikis & Murphy, 2019).

Deterrence also plays out in how these policies are administered. For years now the Australian government has resisted measures or suggestions that would lead to a "softening" of Australia's approach.[10] In practice this has meant tens of thousands of men, women and children have been detained in squalid conditions and exposed to violence, riots, physical and sexual assaults, self-harm and suicidal behaviour as a means to deter others (Australian Parliamentary Select Committee, 2015). Not only did these policies aim to deter further arrivals, they were also geared to break people and have them agree to be returned home.[11] This was not only achieved through the conditions of detention, but the government also offered up to $25,000 cash incentives to asylum seekers to return home (Holmes & Doherty, 2017). An asylum seeker was quoted in Amnesty International's Until When Report:

The system the Australian government has designed for refugees and asylum seekers, has a kind of evil and devastating effect. It can ruin the very

[10] Such as a resettlement deal with New Zealand or transferring those who are unwell to Australia discussed above and below.
[11] See the discussion above about Bomana for a particularly stark example of this.

inner strength of human spirit. To the outsider, Fariborz [Karami] took his own life [on Nauru in June 2018], but the truth is the system took his life. There is no alternative explanation, and we must hold the Australian government accountable for this action … It feels like it is Australia's ultimate goal to put every vulnerable refugee and asylum seeker into an inescapable corner … We have now lost seven lives from the hell of Manus and five from Nauru. All were full of life. I don't know how many more lives they want in the name of this policy. (Amnesty International, 2018)

The deliberate aim of these policies, to deter and deny, has not been lost on others. Amnesty International's Island of Despair report concluded,

The inescapable conclusion is that the abuse and anguish that constitutes the daily reality of refugees and asylum-seekers on Nauru is the express intention of the Government of Australia. In furtherance of a policy to deter people arriving in Australia by boat, the Government of Australia has made a calculation in which intolerable cruelty and the destruction of the physical and mental integrity of hundreds of children, men and women, have been chosen as a tool of government policy. (Amnesty International, 2016)

All of this has resulted in condemnation, both domestically and internationally, and led many to describe Australia's approach towards refugees and asylum seekers as state-sanctioned child abuse (Owler, 2016), cruel and degrading (Mendez, 2015), a crime against humanity (Doherty, 2017a) and likened to torture (Berger, 2016; Boochani, 2016; Doherty & Hurst, 2015; Essex, 2016; Isaacs, 2015; Perera & Pugliese, 2015; Sanggaran & Zion, 2016).

The Health and Human Rights Consequences of Australian Immigration Detention

This push to deter, which has rightly been criticized in its own right, has also had a number of devastating consequences. Below I will focus on two major criticisms that are particularly relevant in considering how the healthcare community should respond, the health and human rights consequences of these policies. Even given the scope of this book, the wide ranging and sustained criticism of these policies for over 20 year means that discussing them here will have to be somewhat summary. In outlining the impact of immigration detention on health and wellbeing, I will largely focus on the available empirical research; I won't discuss the many interviews, news articles, inquiries and testimonies that also attest to immigration detention's cruelty.[12] Similarly my focus on human rights will not and could not be exhaustive. Criticisms have come from both domestic and international health and human rights bodies for almost three decades. I also don't feel that the studies and criticisms discussed here give full insight into the "daily humiliations" (Amnesty International, 2016), misery, indignity and dehumanization suffered by those detained. For these reasons the following sections need to be taken in context with the rest of this book. In saying this, however, the below discussion should be sufficient to make the point that Australian immigration detention violates almost every major human rights instrument and has a devastating impact on health and wellbeing.

The Health Consequences of Australian Immigration Detention

Despite the intense scrutiny and controversy that has surrounded onshore and offshore immigration detention, empirical research has been somewhat limited, largely due to restrictions placed on access by the Australian government (this will be discussed in more detail in Chap. 5). Of the studies that exist, all point to immigration detention as being uniquely damaging and having a dramatic impact on health and wellbeing.

A survey conducted by an Iraqi doctor detained at Villawood immigration detention centre in collaboration with a psychologist working there revealed that among those who had been detained for over 9 months, 58% reported exposure to pre-migration trauma including torture, and 28% reported the murder or disappearance of immediate family members. A majority of the sample displayed chronic depressive symptoms (85%) and pronounced suicidal ideation (65%). Mental state was observed to deteriorate as the length of time in detention increased.

---

[12] Although throughout this book, inquiries, testimonies, and so on, will be used for other reasons.

Symptoms included impairment in concentration, pervasive fear and mistrust, repeated instances of self-harm and, in some cases, psychosis. Of the 33 detainees observed, only one displayed no symptoms (Sultan & O'Sullivan, 2001).

In a study of families detained in a remote onshore immigration detention centre, Steel et al. (2004) conducted telephone interviews without the knowledge of the immigration department or contractors. They concluded that all adults and children met diagnostic criteria for at least one psychiatric disorder. Among 14 adults, they identified 26 disorders. Among 20 children, they identified 52 disorders. Retrospective comparisons indicated that adults displayed a threefold and children a tenfold increase in psychiatric diagnoses subsequent to detention. The study also noted that trauma was common within immigration detention. All adults and children were distressed about their situation, had intrusive images of events that had occurred in detention, and had feelings of sadness and hopelessness.

Other evidence has come from asylum seekers treated in the Australian community. Mares and Jureidini (2004) examined the practical and ethical issues that arose in the assessment of 16 adults and 20 children who were held in detention and referred to a child and adolescent mental health service. They concluded that there were very high levels of mood disturbance and post-traumatic stress related symptoms. All children had at least one parent with a psychiatric illness. Of the ten children aged 6–17 years, all fulfilled criteria for both post-traumatic stress disorder (PTSD) and major depression with suicidal ideation. Eight of the ten children, including three pre-adolescents, had made significant attempts at self-harm. Seven had symptoms of an anxiety disorder and half reported persistent severe somatic symptoms. The majority (80%) of pre-school-age children were identified with developmental delay or emotional disturbance. The authors concluded that a number of these issues were attributable to their experiences in detention.

In a study funded by the immigration department, Green and Eagar (2010) conducted an analysis of the health records of 720 people who were detained.[13] This study revealed that there was a clear association

---

[13] This study does not specify whether the population was detained in onshore or offshore detention; however, only a small number of participants were classified as boat arrivals; thus, majority, if not all, were likely to have been detained onshore.

between length of detention and poor health. Those detained for over 24 months were found to have particularly poor physical and mental health. Asylum seekers also had more health problems than others held in detention. Other researchers have also turned to medical records to gain insight into the impact of detention. Bull, Schindeler, Berkman, and Ransley (2013) reviewed 419 Commonwealth Ombudsman reports over a four-year period relating to individuals who had been in immigration detention for longer than 24 months.[14] Rates of physical and mental illness were extremely high. In 252 cases (of which 179 were professionally confirmed), 65% reported problems with physical health and 60% reported mental health problems. Approximately 21% reported problems with both mental and physical health. Two-thirds of those with mental health problems showed signs of depression, which was the most common diagnosis. Approximately 40% of people had experienced suicidal ideation. About 30% experienced sleep difficulties and anxiety respectively, and a quarter reported PTSD and actual self-harm. There was a direct link with health and length of time detained, although this was not just unidirectional[15] with one quarter of cases having mental and physical health concerns explicitly linked to difficulties engaging in the migration process and delays in final refugee determinations. This extended the period of detention between three and five months. In 54% of cases detention was identified as either causing, being among the causes of, or exacerbating health problems, both mental and physical.

The AHRC Forgotten Children Report (2014) examined children's health and wellbeing and the impact of onshore and offshore immigration detention. It found that "[t]he mandatory and prolonged immigration detention of children is in clear violation of international human rights law" and that immigration detention was having "profound negative impacts on the mental and emotional health of children" (p. 29). In relation to offshore detention on Nauru, the report found that "[c]hildren detained indefinitely on Nauru are suffering from extreme levels of physical, emotional, psychological and developmental distress" (p. 13). In a

---

[14] This study also does not specify whether the population is detained onshore or offshore.

[15] That is, length of detention resulted in generally worse mental health, with generally worse mental health resulting in longer periods detained.

follow-up study, Young and Gordon (2016) re-examined the data collected by the AHRC in relation to 25 onshore detention centres. They concluded that length of time detained was associated with higher self-reported depression scores, with females more vulnerable to length of time in detention. Approximately half of the individuals were identified as having symptoms of PTSD on scales rated by healthcare professionals. One-third of the children, adolescents and adults suffered with clinical symptoms requiring tertiary outpatient assessment. This investigation confirmed the long-established impact that immigration detention has on children and families. For example, almost 10 years earlier, a healthcare professional told the People's Inquiry into Immigration Detention (Australian Council of Heads of Schools of Social Work [ACHSSW], 2006, p. 49):

> You couldn't really design an environment more destructive to child development than immigration detention. The parents are all crippled by their experiences to a point where every case that we are involved in was notified to the local state welfare child protection services and in every case the child protection services found that abuse was proven. Sometimes that was all at the hands of the detention centre, but also often it was at the hands of the parents who we have no reason at all to believe were anything less than competent parents at the time that they arrived in the country, but by virtue of the detention experience they've had they have been so damaged that they are either incapable of caring for their children or were actively damaging them. I guess the other main abuse that the children were subject to was the witnessing of unrelenting violence, not just the spectacular stuff that happened during the riots but people cutting themselves and writing their names in blood and the kinds of comments that their parents were making to them, like you know "I'm dead, do your best to be a good girl and get on with your life," that kind of stuff.

The Médecins Sans Frontières (2018) (MSF) Indefinite Despair Report begins to give insight into the impact of offshore detention on Nauru. Unlike most other reports, it does not just look at the consequences of these policies but also contains data on the exposure to traumatic events while detained and their impact on mental health. In total, 191 refugee and asylum seekers (92%) reported facing difficulties in Nauru, which likely exacerbated their feelings of vulnerability and mental health problems. Among the stressors experienced, 134 (64%) felt that they could not control the events in their lives and similarly 134 (64%) had fears for the future, 73 (35%) cited a lack of daily activities and 28 (13%) expressed distress resulting from being separated from a family member due to medical transfer overseas.[16] This report goes on to outline the rates of mental illness on the island. Morbidity was recorded based on diagnoses given by an MSF psychiatrist or psychologist assessing the patient. Up to six diagnoses were recorded for each patient throughout the period of therapy at point of assessment and during follow-up. Among the 208 refugee and asylum seekers assessed by MSF, 129 (62%) were diagnosed with moderate to severe depression. The second highest diagnosis was anxiety disorder (25%), followed by PTSD (18%), mild depression (11%), complex trauma (6%) and resignation syndrome (6%), also known as traumatic withdrawal syndrome. Some patients had isolated symptoms (5%), psychosis (4%), acute stress (4%) or somatoform disorder (3%). Of the 39 refugee and asylum seeker children seen by MSF, 17 (44%) were diagnosed with moderate to severe depression. Children were also reported to have suffered from serious mental health conditions including resignation syndrome (26%), complex trauma (18%) and PTSD (15%). This report importantly provides data to further substantiate what has long been reported, a deterioration of refugees and asylum seekers over time. For the 74 refugees and asylum seekers seen over time, 15 (20%) remained stable, while 51 (69%) deteriorated and only 8 (11%) showed improvement in their daily functioning.

Finally, a number of investigations have examined self-harm and suicidal behaviour in immigration detention. Men's and women's rates of suicidal behaviours in Australian immigration detention centres were estimated to be approximately 41 and 26 times the national average, respectively (Dudley, 2003).[17] The Commonwealth Ombudsman (2013) found that between January 2011 and February 2013 there were 4313 incidents of actual, threatened and attempted serious self-harm recorded in immigration detention facilities in Australia. In the 2012–2013

---

[16] The data below was collected over the course of multiple consultations with patients, who did not necessarily disclose everything that had happened to them, meaning there is a likelihood of under-reporting of exposure to traumatic events, in particular those associated with stigma (such as sexual violence).

[17] This study does not specify whether the population was detained in onshore or offshore detention.

financial year, there were 846 incidents of self-harm across the immigration detention network. This report found links between mental illness, self-harm and a number of aspects of the detention environment and immigration policy. This included levels of previous trauma, fears for family who may have been left behind, isolation, the detention environment itself, including a lack of autonomy, disempowerment and overcrowding. Furthermore, the detention environment itself promotes self-harm beyond the individual with groups of people who are often experiencing frustration, distress and/or mental illness causing a "contagion" effect, resulting in the spread of "maladaptive behaviours" (Commonwealth Ombudsman, 2013). Hedrick, Armstrong, Coffey, and Borschmann (2019) utilized health records to analyse episodes of self-harm between August 2014 and July 2015, comparing this against the average estimated adult population figures for that period. There were 949 self-harm episodes reported in total. Rates of self-harm ranged from 5 per 1000 asylum seekers in community-based arrangements to 260 per 1000 asylum seekers in offshore detention in Nauru. Rates were highest among asylum seekers in offshore and onshore detention facilities, and lowest among asylum seekers in community-based arrangements and community detention. As a comparison, rates in the Australian community between 2012 and 2013 were 1.2 per 1000 people, meaning rates of self-harm in onshore and offshore detention were up to 216 times higher. All of the above investigations acknowledge a number of limitations, mainly related to data not being available or incomplete, making comparisons difficult between rates of self-harm and suicidal behaviour in immigration detention and the general community. In addition to this, at least 1997 deaths related to Australia's policies have been recorded from 2000 to 2017 (The Border Crossing Observatory, n.d.). Of these deaths, 49 have occurred within Australian immigration detention centres, and 32 have been due to suicide or suspected suicide.[18] While those who died after forced return to their country of origin are recorded, these deaths are likely to be underreported because of difficulties in obtaining data.

---

[18] Not all suicides occurred within immigration detention centres; some occurred in the community or upon forced return to country of origin.

The Human Rights Consequences of Australian Immigration Detention

Before discussing the human rights consequences of these policies, it is worth noting the human rights commitments Australia has made. Australia was a founding member of the UN and played a prominent role in the negotiation of the UN Charter in 1945. Australia was also one of eight nations involved in drafting the Universal Declaration of Human Rights (UN General Assembly, 1948). Australia has agreed to be party to all major human rights treaties including the Convention relating to the Status of Refugees (UN General Assembly, 1951), Protocol relating to the Status of Refugees (UN General Assembly, 1967), International Covenant on Civil and Political Rights (ICCPR) (UN General Assembly, 1966a), International Covenant on Economic, Social and Cultural Rights (UN General Assembly, 1966b), Convention against Torture and Other Cruel, Inhuman or Degrading Treatment or Punishment (UN General Assembly, 1984), and Convention on the Rights of the Child (CRC) (UN General Assembly, 1989a).

Additionally, Australia has ratified the Optional Protocol to the Convention against Torture and Other Cruel, Inhuman or Degrading Treatment or Punishment (OPCAT) (UN General Assembly, 2002), the Protocol to Prevent, Suppress and Punish Trafficking in Persons, Especially Women and Children (UN General Assembly, 2000d), and the Protocol against the Smuggling of Migrants by Land, Sea and Air (UN General Assembly, 2000c). Australia has also ratified the first two optional protocols to the Convention on the Rights of the Child (UN General Assembly, 2000a, 2000b) and the Second Optional Protocol to the International Covenant on Civil and Political Rights (UN General Assembly, 1989b). Australia has also ratified the Convention on the Law of the Sea (UN General Assembly, 1982), which establishes the structure of maritime territory and the rights and obligations of states. It has acceded to the International Convention on Maritime Search and Rescue (International Maritime Organization, 1979), which establishes State duties in relation to establishing search and rescue services, and the International Convention for the Safety of Life at Sea (International Maritime Organization, 1974), which builds on the norms that States and other actors have an explicit duty to meet for those in distress at sea. Australia has thus committed to, at a minimum,[19] respect and cooperate on human rights internationally and in certain circumstances, protect human rights extraterritorially (OHCHR, 2015). These commitments stand in stark contrast to the rights-related criticisms aimed at mandatory detention. Some major reports and investigations will be discussed below.

In late 2014, the UN High Commissioner for Human Rights raised concerns about Australia's policies of offshore processing and boat turn-backs, noting that these were "leading to a chain of human rights violations, including arbitrary detention and possible torture following return to home countries" (Al Hussein, 2014). Shortly after, the UN Committee Against Torture (2014) released its periodic review which again cited concerns about offshore processing. In 2015 the Special Rapporteur on Torture and Other Cruel, Inhuman or Degrading Treatment or Punishment found that Australia's policy of offshore processing had systemically violated the Convention Against Torture (UN General Assembly, 1984), violating the right "to be free from torture or cruel, inhuman or degrading treatment" (Mendez, 2015, p. 8). During Australia's second Universal Periodic Review by the Human Rights Council, over 50 states raised concerns about Australia's policies. Mandatory indefinite detention, the detention of children, offshore processing and boat turn-backs were all criticized (UN Human Rights Council, 2016). In 2016 the UN called on Australia to end the practice and processing of people offshore, after the Nauru files[20] were released (*The Guardian Australia*, 2016; UN, 2016). Most recently, in July 2019, the UN subcommittee on the prevention of torture announced it would visit Australia and Nauru to conduct random inspections in places of detention to investigate human rights abuses. This will be the first time Australia will be subject to the UN inspections, after ratifying the OPCAT in 2017. Investigators will be given unlimited access at random to any facility in the country (Beech, 2017).

---

[19] Given Australia's active role in the development of many of these instruments and standing in the international community, a reasonable argument could be put forth as to why it should do more than the "minimum".

[20] The Nauru files were the largest collection of documents to be leaked in relation to Australian immigration detention (*The Guardian Australia*, 2016). These documents detailed the conditions within detention along with a number of "incident" reports. I will discuss the Nauru files again when considering whistleblowing in Chap. 8.

Beyond these criticisms, some have suggested that these policies constitute a crime. The most comprehensive review comes from Henderson (2014) who concluded that following an element-by-element analysis, that there would be a prima facie case under the statute of the International Criminal Court (ICC) for the crimes against humanity of severe deprivation of liberty and persecution. Similarly, in 2017, a report from Global Legal Action Network and the Stanford International Human Rights Clinic was submitted to the ICC urging them to open an investigation into Australian immigration detention centres. In 2020, the ICC found that offshore detention could constitute a breach of international law, acknowledging that detention appeared to amount to "cruel, inhuman, or degrading treatment". There was no further action taken however as the ICC did not find that immigration detention was a crime against humanity and thus was not within its jurisdiction (Stayner, 2020).

References

Al Hussein, Z. R. a. (2014, September 8). *United Nations high commissioner for human rights, 'opening statement'.* Speech delivered at the 27th Session of the United Nations Human Rights Council, Geneva. Retrieved from http://www.ohchr.org/EN/NewsEvents/Pages/DisplayNews.aspx?NewsID=14998

Amnesty International. (2016). Island of despair: Australia's "processing" of refugees on Nauru. Retrieved from https://www.amnesty.org.au/island-of-despair-nauru-refugee-report-2016/

Amnesty International. (2018). *Until when? The forgotten men of Manus island.* Retrieved from https://www.amnesty.org/en/documents/asa34/9422/2018/en/

Australian Broadcasting Corporation Radio National. (2002, August 1). *Radio national breakfast, interview on the treatment of children in detention.* Retrieved from https://webarchive.nla.gov.au/awa/20030422081404/http://www.minister.immi.gov.au/media/transcripts/transcripts02/radio-national_010802.htm

Australian Council of Heads of Schools of Social Work. (2006). *We've boundless plains to share: The first report of the people's inquiry into detention.* Australian Council of Heads of Schools of Social Work.

Australian Human Rights Commission. (2014). The forgotten children: National inquiry into children in immigration detention. Retrieved from https://www.humanrights.gov.au/our-work/asylum-seekers-and-refugees/publications/forgotten-children-national-inquiry-children

Australian Parliamentary Select Committee. (2015). *Taking responsibility: conditions and circumstances at Australia's Regional Processing Centre in Nauru.* Select Committee on the Recent allegations relating to conditions and circumstances at the Regional Processing Centre in Nauru. Retrieved from https://www.aph.gov.au/Parliamentary_Business/Committees/Senate/Regional_processing_Nauru/Regional_processing_Nauru/Final_Report

Beech, A. (2017). OPCAT: Australia makes long-awaited pledge to ratify international torture treaty. *Australian Broadcasting Corporation News.* Retrieved from http://www.abc.net.au/news/2017-02-09/australia-pledges-to-ratify-opcat-torture-treaty/8255782

Berger, D. (2016). Australia's torture of asylum seekers. *British Medical Journal, 354:*i4606

Betts, K. (1993). Refugee-status procedures and the boat people. *People and Place, 1*(3), 9–15.

Billings, P. (2013). Irregular maritime migration and the Pacific solution mark II: Back to the future for refugee law and policy in Australia? *International Journal on Minority and Group Rights, 20*(2), 279–305.

Boochani, B. (2016). This is Manus Island. My prison. My torture. My humiliation. *The Guardian.* Retrieved from https://www.theguardian.com/commentisfree/2016/feb/19/this-is-manus-island-my-prison-my-torture-my-humiliation

Brouwer, A., & Kumin, J. (2003). Interception and asylum: When migration control and human rights collide. *Refuge, 21*(4), 6–24.

Bull, M., Schindeler, E., Berkman, D., & Ransley, J. (2013). Sickness in the system of long-term immigration detention. *Journal of Refugee Studies, 26*(1), 47–68.

Commonwealth Ombudsman. (2013). *Suicide and self-harm in the immigration detention network.* Retrieved from http://www.ombudsman.gov.au/reports/investigation/2013

Cornall, R. (2014). *Review into the events of 16–18 February at the Manus regional processing centre.* Retrieved from https://www.homeaffairs.gov.au/reports-and-publications/reviews-and-inquiries/departmental-reviews/manus-regional-processing-centre

Dastyari, A., & Hirsch, A. (2019). The ring of steel: Extraterritorial migration controls in Indonesia and Libya and the complicity of Australia and Italy. *Human Rights Law Review, 19*(3), 435–465.

Davidson, H. (2020). Leaked photos of Papua New Guinea prison reveal 'torture' of 18 asylum seekers cut off from world. *The Guardian*. Retrieved from https://www.theguardian.com/world/2020/jan/15/leaked-photos-of-papua-new-guinea-prison-reveal-torture-of-18-asylum-seekers-cut-off-from-world

Davidson, H., & Hurst, D. (2015). Nauru says it will process remaining 600 refugee claims within a week. *The Guardian Australia*. Retrieved from https://www.theguardian.com/australia-news/2015/oct/05/nauru-says-it-will-process-remaining-600-refugee-claims-within-a-week

Doherty, B. (2017a). International Criminal Court told Australia's detention regime could be a crime against humanity. *The Guardian*. Retrieved from https://www.theguardian.com/australia-news/2017/feb/13/international-criminal-court-told-australias-detention-regime-could-be-a-against-humanity

Doherty, B. (2017b). Manus Island shooting left nine injured, immigration department admits *The Guardian*. Retrieved from https://www.theguardian.com/australia-news/2017/may/22/manus-island-shooting-left-nine-injured-immigration-department-admits

Doherty, B., & Davidson, H. (2016). Reza Barati: men convicted of asylum seeker's murder to be free in less than four years. *The Guardian*. Retrieved from https://www.theguardian.com/australia-news/2016/apr/19/reza-barati-men-convicted-of-asylum-seekers-to-be-free-in-less-than-four-years

Doherty, B., & Hurst, D. (2015). UN accuses Australia of systematically violating torture convention. *The Guardian*. Retrieved from https://www.theguardian.com/australia-news/2015/mar/09/un-reports-australias-immigration-detention-breaches-torture-convention

Dudley, M. (2003). Contradictory Australian national policies on self-harm and suicide: The case of asylum seekers in mandatory detention. *Australiasian Psychiatry, 11*(Supplement), S102–S108.

Essex, R. (2013). Asylum seeker health and bridging visas: History repeating. *Australian and New Zealand Journal of Public Health, 37*(6), 506–508.

Essex, R. (2016). Torture, healthcare and Australian immigration detention. *Journal of Medical Ethics, 42*(7), 418–419.

Expert Panel on Asylum Seekers. (2012). *Report of the expert panel on asylum seekers*. Canberra: Department of the Prime Minister and Cabinet.

Gammeltoft-Hansen, T., & Tan, N. F. (2017). The end of the deterrence paradigm? Future directions for global refugee policy. *Journal on Migration and Human Security, 5*(1), 28–56.

Gibney, M. J. (2006). A thousand little Guantanamos: Western states and measures to prevent the arrival of refugees. In K. E. Tunstall (Ed.), *Migration, Displacement, Asylum: The Oxford Amnesty Lectures, 2004*, 139–160.

Green, J. P., & Eagar, K. (2010). The health of people in Australian immigration detention centres. *Medical Journal of Australia, 192*(2), 65–70.

Guardian Staff with Agencies. (2019). Final four children held on Nauru to be resettled with their families in US. *The Guardian.* Retrieved from https://www.theguardian.com/australia-news/2019/feb/03/final-four-children-held-on-nauru-to-resettled-with-families-in-us

Hamburger, K. (2013). *Executive report of the review into the 19 July 2013 incident at the Nauru regional processing centre.* Retrieved from https://www.homeaffairs.gov.au/reports-and-pubs/files/executive-report-nauru-2013.pdf

Hand, G. (1992, May 5). Migration amendment bill 1992, second reading speech. Retrieved from http://parlinfo.aph.gov.au/parlInfo/search/display/display.w3p;query=Id%3A%22chamber%2Fhansardr%2F1992-05-05%2F0031%22

Hedrick, K., Armstrong, G., Coffey, G., & Borschmann, R. (2019). Self-harm in the Australian asylum seeker population: A national records-based study. *SSM-Population Health, 8,* 100452.

Henderson, C. (2014). Australia's treatment of asylum seekers: From human rights violations to crimes against humanity. *Journal of International Criminal Justice, 12*(5), 1161–1181.

Hirsch, A. L. (2017). The borders beyond the border: Australia's extraterritorial migration controls. *Refugee Survey Quarterly, 36*(3), 48–80.

Holmes, O., & Doherty, B. (2017). Australia offers to pay Rohingya refugees to return to Myanmar. *The Guardian.* Retrieved from https://www.theguardian.com/world/2017/sep/19/australia-offers-pay-rohingya-refugees-return-myanmar

Howard, J. (2001). *Election campaign policy launch speech.* Retrieved from https://pmtranscripts.pmc.gov.au/release/transcript-12332

Hugo, G. (2002). From compassion to compliance? Trends in refugee and humanitarian migration in Australia. *GeoJournal, 56*(1), 27–37.

Hurst, D. (2015). Nauru centre opening has 'dramatic effect' on detention challenge, court told. *The Guardian.* Retrieved from https://www.theguardian.com/australia-news/2015/oct/07/nauru-open-centres-asylum-seeker-fighting-offshore-detention-high-court

International Maritime Organization. (1974). *International convention for the safety of life at sea,* 1 November 1974, 1184 UNTS 3.

International Maritime Organization. (1979). *International convention on maritime search and rescue,* 27 April 1979, 1403 UNTS.

Isaacs, D. (2015). Are healthcare professionals working in Australia's immigration detention centres condoning torture? *Journal of Medical Ethics, 42,* 413–415.

Joint Standing Committee on Migration. (2008). *Joint Standing Committee on Migration, Immigration detention in Australia: a new beginning: criteria for release from detention, First report of the inquiry into immigration detention.* Retrieved from http://www.aph.gov.au/Parliamentary_Business/Committees/ House_of_Representatives_Committees?url=mig/detention/report.htm

Kneebone, S. (2014). The Bali process and global refugee policy in the Asia–Pacific region. *Journal of Refugee Studies, 27*(4), 596–618.

Larking, E. (2017). Controlling irregular migration in the Asia-pacific: Is Australia acting against its own interests? *Asia & the Pacific Policy Studies, 4*(1), 85–103.

Mares, S., & Jureidini, J. (2004). Psychiatric assessment of children and families in immigration detention—Clinical, administrative and ethical issues. *Australian & New Zealand Journal of Public Health, 28*(6), 520–526.

Médecins Sans Frontières. (2018). *Indefinite despair: The tragic mental health consequences of offshore processing on Nauru.* Retrieved from https://msf.org.au/article/statements-opinion/indefinite-despair-mental-health-consequences-nauru

Mendez, J. E. (2015). *Special Rapporteur on torture and other cruel, inhuman or degrading treatment or punishment, observations on communications transmitted to governments and replies received. United Nations Human Rights Council, 28th Session, Agenda Item 3. UN Doc A/HRC/28/68/Add.1 (5 March 2015) 8.* Retrieved from http://www.ohchr.org/EN/HRBodies/HRC/RegularSessions/Session28/Documents/A_HRC_28_68_Add.1_en.docF

Migration Amendment Act. (1992).

Migration Reform Act. (1992).

Millbank, A. (2001). The detention of boat people, current issues brief. *Austrlaian Parliamentary Library.* Retrieved from http://www.aph.gov.au/About_Parliament/Parliamentary_Departments/Parliamentary_Library/Publications_Archive/CIB/cib0001/01CIB08#rationale

Momartin, S., Steel, Z., Coello, M., Aroche, J., Silove, D., & Brooks, R. (2006). A comparison of the mental health of refugees with temporary versus permanent protection visas. *Medical Journal of Australia, 185*, 357–361.

Morrison, S. (2013). Malaysia visit reboots cooperation on regional deterrence. Retrieved from https://webarchive.nla.gov.au/awa/20141215055736/http://www.minister.immi.gov.au/media/sm/2013/sm209088.htm

Murphy, K. (2019). Jacinda Ardern tells Scott Morrison New Zealand remains open to resettling Nauru refugees. *The Guardian.* Retrieved from https://www.theguardian.com/australia-news/2019/dec/05/jacinda-ardern-tells-scott-morrison-new-zealand-remains-open-to-resettling-nauru-refugees

Nethery, A., Rafferty-Brown, B., & Taylor, S. (2013). Exporting detention: Australia-funded immigration detention in Indonesia. *Journal of Refugee Studies, 26*(1), 88–109.

Neumann, K. (2015). *Across the seas: Australia's response to refugees: A history.* Collingwood, Victoria: Black Inc.

Owler, B. (2016). *Speech to AMA forum on health of asylum seekers.* Retrieved from https://ama.com.au/media/ama-speech-prof-owler-ama-asylum-seeker-health-forum

Perera, S., & Pugliese, J. (2015). Offshore detention 'black sites' open door to torture. *The Conversation.* Retrieved from https://theconversation.com/offshore-detention-black-sites-open-door-to-torture-46400

Phillips, J. (2017). Boat arrivals and boat 'turnbacks' in Australia since 1976: A quick guide to the statistics. *Parliamentary Library of Australia.* Retrieved from https://www.aph.gov.au/About_Parliament/Parliamentary_Departments/Parliamentary_Library/pubs/rp/rp1617/Quick_Guides/BoatTurnbacks

Phillips, J., & Spinks, H. (2012). Boat arrivals in Australia since 1976. *Parliamentary Library of Australia.* Retrieved from https://www.aph.gov.au/about_parliament/parliamentary_departments/parliamentary_library/pubs/bn/2012-2013/boatarrivals

Phillips, J., & Spinks, H. (2013). Immigration detention in Australia. *Parliamentary Library of Australia.* Retrieved from https://www.aph.gov.au/About_Parliament/Parliamentary_Departments/Parliamentary_Library/pubs/BN/2012-2013/Detention

Phipps, C. (2015). Did Australia pay people-smugglers to turn back asylum seekers? *The Guardian.* Retrieved from https://www.theguardian.com/world/2015/jun/17/did-australia-pay-people-smugglers-to-turn-back-boats

Pickering, S., & Weber, L. (2014). New deterrence scripts in Australia's rejuvenated offshore detention regime for asylum seekers. *Law & Social Inquiry, 39*(4), 1006–1026.

Refugee Council of Australia. (2016). *Refugee arrivals to Australia since federation.* Retrieved from https://www.refugeecouncil.org.au/getfacts/statistics/aust/historical/refugee-arrivals-australia-since-federation/

Refugee Council of Australia. (2019). *Offshore processing statistics.* Retrieved from https://www.refugeecouncil.org.au/operation-sovereign-borders-offshore-detention-statistics/

Remeikis, A., & Murphy, K. (2019). Scott Morrison ramps up border protection rhetoric with attack on Labor. *The Guardian.* Retrieved from https://www.theguardian.com/australia-news/2019/feb/11/scott-morrison-ramps-up-border-protection-rhetoric-with-attack-on-labor

Robinson, C. W. (1998). *Terms of refuge: The Indochinese exodus & the international response.* London, New York: Zed Books.

Rudd, K. (2013). *Australia and Papua New Guinea regional settlement arrangement.* Retrieved from http://pandora.nla.gov.au/pan/79983/20130830-1433/ www.pm.gov.au/press-office/australia-and-papua-new-guinea-regional-settlement-arrangement.html

Ruddock, P. (1999). *Ruddock announces tough new initiatives, media release.* Retrieved from https://parlinfo.aph.gov.au/parlInfo/search/display/display. w3p;query=Id:%22media/pressrel/YOG06%22

Sanggaran, J.-P., & Zion, D. (2016). Is Australia engaged in torturing asylum seekers? A cautionary tale for Europe. *Journal of Medical Ethics, 42*(7), 420–423.

Spinks, H. (2018). Boat 'turnbacks' in Australia: A quick guide to the statistics since 2001. *Australian Parliamentary Library.* Retrieved from https://www. aph.gov.au/About_Parliament/Parliamentary_Departments/Parliamentary_ Library/pubs/rp/rp1819/Quick_Guides/BoatTurnbacksSince2001

Spinks, H., & Phillips, J. (2011). Tampa: Ten years on. *FlagPost.* Retrieved from http://parliamentflagpost.blogspot.com/2011/08/tampa-ten-years-on.html

Spinks, H., Karlsen, E., Brew, N., Harris, M., & Watt, D. (2013). Australian Government spending on irregular maritime arrivals and counter-people smuggling activity. *Australian Parliamentary Library.* Retrieved from https:// www.aph.gov.au/About_Parliament/Parliamentary_Departments/ Parliamentary_Library/pubs/rp/rp1314/PeopleSmuggling

Stayner, T. (2020). Offshore detention conditions may constitute a breach of international law, but Australia won't be prosecuted. *SBS News.* Retrieved from https://www.sbs.com.au/news/offshore-detention-conditions-may-constitute-a-breach-of-international-law-but-australia-won-t-be-prosecuted

Steel, Z., Momartin, S., Bateman, C., Hafshejani, A., Silove, D. M., & Everson, N. (2004). Psychiatric status of asylum seeker families held for a protracted period in a remote detention Centre in Australia. *Australian and New Zealand Journal of Public Health, 28*(6), 527–536.

Sultan, A., & O'Sullivan, K. (2001). Psychological disturbances in asylum seekers held in long term detention: A participant-observer account. *Medical Journal of Australia, 11*, 593–596.

Taylor, S. (2008). Australia's border control and refugee protection capacity building activities in the Asia-Pacific region. In A. Babacan & L. Briskman (Eds.), *Asylum seekers: International perspective on interdiction and deterrence* (pp. 63–81). Newcastle, United Kingdom: Cambridge Scholars Publishing.

The Border Crossing Observatory. (n.d.). *Australian border deaths database.* Retrieved from https://www.monash.edu/arts/border-crossing-observatory/ research-agenda/australian-border-deaths-database

The Guardian. (2016). *The Nauru files*. Retrieved from https://www.theguardian. com/news/series/nauru-files

The Kaldor Centre. (2019). *Australia's refugee policy: An overview*. Retrieved from https://www.kaldorcentre.unsw.edu.au/publication/australias-refugee-policy-overview

Tlozek, E. (2017). Manus Island: First refugees leave PNG for US under swap deal. *Australian Broadcasting Corporation News*. Retrieved from https://www. abc.net.au/news/2017-09-26/22-refugees-leave-manus-island-for-us-swap-deal/8988424

Tlozek, E., & Anderson, S. (2016). PNG's Supreme Court rules detention of asylum seekers on Manus Island is illegal. *Australian Broadcasting Corporation News*. Retrieved from http://www.abc.net.au/news/2016-04-26/png-court-rules-asylum-seeker-detention-manus-island-illegal/7360078

United Nations. (2016). *Australia and Nauru must end offshore detention; investigate claims of abuse*. UN rights office. Retrieved from https://news.un.org/en/story/2016/08/536522-australia-and-nauru-must-end-offshore-detention-investigate-claims-abuse-un

United Nations General Assembly. (1948). *Universal declaration of human rights*.

United Nations General Assembly. (1951). *Convention relating to the status of refugees*.

United Nations General Assembly. (1966a). *International covenant on civil and political rights*.

United Nations General Assembly. (1966b). *International covenant on economic, social and cultural rights*.

United Nations General Assembly. (1967). *Protocol relating to the status of refugees*.

United Nations General Assembly. (1982). *Convention on the law of the sea*.

United Nations General Assembly. (1984). Convention against torture and other cruel, inhuman or degrading treatment or punishment.

United Nations General Assembly. (1989a). *Convention on the rights of the child*.

United Nations General Assembly. (1989b). *Second optional protocol to the international covenant on civil and political rights, aiming at the abolition of the death penalty*.

United Nations General Assembly. (2000a). *Optional protocol to the convention on the rights of the child on the involvement of children in armed conflict*.

United Nations General Assembly. (2000b). *Optional protocol to the convention on the rights of the child on the sale of children, child prostitution and child pornography*.

United Nations General Assembly. (2000c). *Protocol against the smuggling of migrants by land, sea and air, supplementing the United Nations convention against transnational organized crime.*

United Nations General Assembly. (2000d). *Protocol to prevent, suppress and punish trafficking in persons, especially women and children.*

United Nations General Assembly. (2002). *Optional protocol to the convention against torture and other cruel, inhuman or degrading treatment or punishment.*

United Nations Human Rights Council. (2016, January 13). *Report of the working group on the universal periodic review: Australia, 31st sess, agenda Item 6: universal periodic review.* UN Doc A/HRC/31/14, 26–29. Retrieved from http://daccess-ods.un.org/access.nsf/Get?Open&DS=A/HRC/31/14&Lang=E

UNHCR. (2018). *UNHCR global report 2017—Asia and the Pacific regional summary.* Retrieved from https://www.unhcr.org/uk/publications/fundraising/5b30ba6a7/unhcr-global-report-2017-asia-pacific-regional-summary.html

UNHCR. (2019). *Global report 2018.* Retrieved from https://www.unhcr.org/en-us/5e4ff98f7.pdf

United Nations Committee against Torture. (2014, December 23). *Concluding observations on the combined fourth and fifth periodic reports of Australia.* UN Doc CAT/C/ AUS/CO/4-5. Retrieved from http://tbinternet.ohchr.org/Treaties/CAT/Shared%20Documents/AUS/CAT_C_AUS_CO_4-5_18888_E.pdf

United Nations Office of the High Commissioner for Human Rights. (2015). *Who will be accountable? Human rights and the post-2015 development agenda.* Retrieved from http://www.ohchr.org/Documents/Publications/WhoWillBeAccountable_summary_en.pdf

Wesley, M. (2007). *The Howard paradox: Australian diplomacy in Asia, 1996–2006.* Sydney: ABC Books.

Young, P., & Gordon, M. S. (2016). Mental health screening in immigration detention: A fresh look at Australian government data. *Australasian Psychiatry, 24*(1), 19–22.

3

The Delivery of Healthcare in Australian Immigration Detention

Overview

While Chap. 2 provided an overview of Australian immigration detention and related policies, their development and controversies, discussions about healthcare, its limitations and issues were notably absent. In
this chapter I will focus on healthcare, what has been said about it and
some of the major controversies surrounding its delivery. First, I will
outline the contractual and administrative arrangements for healthcare
services in onshore and offshore detention. I will then discuss what
healthcare professionals, asylum seekers and professional healthcare
bodies have said about its delivery. In doing this I want to show two
things: the disparity between the testimony of healthcare professionals
and detainees, the contractual arrangements for healthcare and statements made by professional healthcare bodies. I also want to highlight
the near futility in the delivery of healthcare within centres. Finally,
healthcare professionals have also played an active role in pushing for
broader social and political change outside of detention. I will also discuss some major controversies that have occurred outside of detention
centres and how the healthcare community have responded to these.

© The Author(s) 2020
R. Essex, *The Healthcare Community and Australian Immigration Detention*,
https://doi.org/10.1007/978-981-15-7537-2_3

While this chapter will inevitably begin to touch on some of the obvious conflicts and ethical issues raised in detention, I will discuss these at length in the next chapter.

Healthcare in Australian Immigration Detention

The Australian government has provided health services within immigration detention, both onshore and offshore through contracted providers, local hospitals and other contracted allied health professionals. International Health and Medical Services (IHMS), a subsidiary of International SOS, has held most major contracts related to the delivery of health services since 2004 (Australian National Audit Office, 2016), and since 2007, it has been primarily responsible for the delivery of care in detention centres both onshore and offshore. The mission statement for IHMS declares that healthcare will be delivered "consistent with that available to the wider Australian community" and "without any form of discrimination, with appropriate dignity, humanity, cultural and gender sensitivity, and respect for privacy and confidentiality" (Australian Parliamentary Joint Select Committee on Australia's Immigration Detention Network, 2012, p. 82).

Today, IHMS delivers healthcare within detention and to those held in community detention[1] onshore and to those on Nauru. It previously delivered healthcare on Manus Island until April 2018 when the Australian government did not renew its contract (Amnesty International, 2018). The contract for healthcare was subsequently handed to Pacific International Hospital (PIH), a hospital operator in Port Moresby, Papua New Guinea, in May 2018 (Knaus & Davidson, 2019). Smaller contracts have also been awarded to various organizations. MSF was contracted by the Nauru government to deliver mental health services to locals and to the asylum seeker and refugee population at the end of 2017, but was removed from the island a little over 12 months later after the relationship deteriorated with

---

[1] See community detention explanation in previous sections.

the Nauruan government who later stated that MSF had "conspired against us".

Similar to IHMS' mission statement, its contract for health services delivered in onshore detention aims to provide "a standard of care broadly comparable with that available within the Australian community" and includes objectives such as providing healthcare that is "open, accountable and transparent"[2] and that "empowers detainees with the means to manage and respond to their own health needs" (Australian National Audit Office, 2016, p. 23). The contract for healthcare services offshore is similar in that it calls for healthcare that is "open, accountable and transparent" and to a standard "that as far as possible (but recognising any unavoidable limitations deriving from the circumstances of Manus Island and Nauru) [is] broadly comparable with health services available within the Australian community"[3] (de Boer, 2013, p. 2). While at the time of writing a contract has yet to be finalized with Pacific International Hospital, it is understood that the government has asked for services comparative to those provided by IHMS (Knaus & Davidson, 2019).

The Australian National Audit Office (2016, p. 16) Delivery of Health Services in Onshore Immigration Detention Report provides an overview of what the delivery of healthcare services should look like day-to-day under these arrangements:

> Primary health care, including nurse and general practitioner consultations, is provided at clinics located within the detention facilities. Most detainees receive prescribed medication at set medication distribution times. Mental health, dental and optical consultations are also to be provided within detention facilities. Access to external specialists, hospitals and other allied health services, is facilitated by IHMS referral arrange-

---

[2] Promoting healthcare as open and accountable while limiting the availability of financial information and contracts is one of many inconsistencies that characterize official discourse around healthcare in detention centres.

[3] The qualification about the "circumstances" on Manus Island and Nauru provides a further way to dodge the other stated aims of providing healthcare to a standard comparable to that found in the Australian community. More broadly, these statements, objectives and contractual arrangements are clearly incompatible with the government's more general approach to immigration detention which I outlined in Chap. 2.

ments. Detainee access to health services in facilities is structured according to set procedures. Detainees are required to submit a written request to see a nurse or doctor. Consultation hours are generally from 9am to 5pm, Monday to Friday. Outside of these hours, IHMS operates a telephone nursing service that detention centre officers can access on a detainee's behalf. Emergency services attend detention facilities outside consultation hours when necessary.[4]

While the dry contractual language above seems unremarkable, as can be imagined from my discussion in Chap. 2, healthcare has been far from what is outlined in these documents. On this point, one final issue worth discussing here is the relationship between healthcare providers and the government. While there has always been friction between contractors and while this has occasionally played out publicly as was the case with MSF, many organizations have also been complicit in malpractice and in covering up complaints and abuse. IHMS has rightly received most of the attention as it relates to this point. Leaked documents have revealed that IHMS failed to meet targets, included incorrect data in reports and admitted it was "inevitable" fraud would occur while trying to meet government standards (Farrell, Jabour, & Evershed, 2015). Furthermore, IHMS have been reprimanded or caught out a number of times for contractual violations or malpractice including failing to run police checks on staff on Manus Island (Farrell, 2017). A number of healthcare workers have also pointed out the somewhat obvious conflict of interest, between IHMS commercial interests and in maintaining an acceptable standard of care (Christmas Island Medical Officer's Letter of Concern, 2013). Dr. David Isaacs, a Professor of Pediatric Infectious Diseases, visited Nauru as a paediatric specialist. After he spent 5 days on Nauru seeing children in consultation, he felt compelled to highlight the appalling conditions. He describes what happened upon returning to Australia:

---

[4] Further specifics on the day-to-day delivery of healthcare can be found in other reports such as Australian Parliamentary Joint Select Committee on Australia's Immigration Detention Network (2012).

On our return to Australia, we were nervous about writing a media opinion piece, but our sense of outrage and our promise to the families trumped guilt at breaking our contract and fear of reprisal. A prominent human rights lawyer advised us it was legitimate to break a contract to reveal 'iniquity' and what we had witnessed was undoubtedly iniquitous. We decided to provide IHMS with a detailed report of suggested changes but also decided to publish an opinion piece and do subsequent media interviews. We met senior IHMS staff to discuss our report. They expressed disappointment we had gone to the media and felt betrayed. We said we thought IHMS tried hard in the camp and had done excellent work propping up Nauru health care services outside the camp (IHMS asked us to consult on some children at the Republic of Nauru Hospital), but we thought IHMS should protest more about conditions. The IHMS staff said their Government contract forbade them criticising Government policy and they preferred to work for change from within the system. The meeting ended with each of us acknowledging our respect for but disagreement with the others' position. (Isaacs, 2015b, p. 354)

Testimony from Healthcare Professionals, Refugees and Asylum Seekers

The testimony of healthcare professionals and asylum seekers contrasts sharply with the bureaucratic, contractual language above. As a whole, it shows a dysfunctional system where conflicts between patients' interests and the immigration department undermine almost every aspect of healthcare. Evidence and testimony suggest that at best, treatment is only marginally effective, at worst it is futile. While this is only a selection below, there is next to no testimony that says anything even remotely positive about the delivery of healthcare.

Dr. Peter Young, Psychiatrist and former Medical Director of IHMS, wrote and spoke extensively about his experiences in managing healthcare services across the detention network and his dealings with the immigration department. At the time he was the most senior figure who had worked in the system to condemn it. Here he discusses the impact of the government's policy of deterrence, the impact this had on healthcare and why treatment was largely ineffective:

You can't mitigate the harm, because the system is designed to create a negative mental state. It's designed to produce suffering. If you suffer, then it's punishment. If you suffer, you're more likely to agree to go back to where you came from. By reducing the suffering you're reducing the functioning of the system and the system doesn't want you to do that ... Everybody knows that the harm is being caused and the system carries on. Everybody accepts that this is the policy and the policy cannot change. And everybody accepts that the only thing you can do is work within the parameters of the policy. (Marr & Laughland, 2014)

A number of other healthcare professionals have discussed how they delivered treatment and negotiated the day-to-day restrictions they faced. Guy Coffey, a Clinical Psychologist and Lawyer, wrote about his experiences treating detained refugees and asylum seekers in the community, while working for Foundation House (formerly the Victorian Foundation for Survivors of Torture). He discusses a range of issues, present throughout his writing however is the tension in how he mediated the restrictions placed on his role:

Treatment recommendations may fail to consider patients' broader interests and may be confined by policy goals within the detention environment. In other words, treatment recommendations may be formulated for "what is possible" given the current circumstances rather than what is in a patient's best interests. In many cases, the action needed to assist in mental health treatment and recovery is it quite obvious, with the best option for most patients being that they are removed from the detention environment. The tensions though, in how far one takes recommending alternative arrangements, are obvious. Not to do so is to remain silent about a significant and perhaps determinative effect on the detainee's prognosis. Some might argue that it is to collude with the convenient lie that extended detention can be psychologically benign. Conversely, making recommendations about services that are not available, or regularly insisting on the need for the detainee to be released, risks detracting from the measures that can be taken immediately. It is an approach that runs the risk of having recommendations dismissed as advocacy, of alienating the IDC management and the Department and therefore jeopardising the relationship between the IDC and the mental health service, and of leaving the IDC health staff feeling helpless. (Coffey, 2006, p. 76)

Dr. Nick Martin, a General Practitioner who was a senior medical officer on Nauru, discussed similar concerns about advocacy and the issues this raised in relation to putting the interests of his patients first:

Activism was stamped on incredibly quickly. It was seen as the greatest crime to be considered an advocate; it was to invite a swift cancellation of your visa and non-renewal of your contract. What was meant by 'advocate' was never explained. It seemed to me that our primary concern had to be the patient, and to push for the best appropriate treatment for them. If that was advocacy then surely it was what we did every day as doctors or nurses. (Martin, 2018)

Others have concluded that the delivery of healthcare within immigration detention is simply futile. Christine Rufener, a former mental health activities manager for MSF, described what she called the "Nauru paradox":

I found myself at a loss: why try to help a person regain a sense of hope, only for them to spend their days sitting with nothing to do and almost nowhere to go ... The same place they were in last week, last month, last year ... the past five years. We could help them manage their symptoms but for people whose hopes have been systematically and repeatedly dashed over five years, it seemed that rebuilding any sense of hope could potentially do more harm than good. (Rufener, 2018)

Almost 15 years ago, a healthcare professional provided a testimony at the People's Inquiry into Immigration Detention (ACHSSW, 2006, p. 44), stating,

You could have the Rolls Royce of mental health services in Baxter and I don't think it would make a scrap of difference, because the environment is so toxic that you can't treat anything meaningfully. I think that half a dozen of the most damaged people that I've ever seen are the adults that I've seen in Baxter and Woomera, both parents and single men. The thing is that it is all caused by being in detention. Provided you get them in time, you take these people out of detention and they're not depressed any more. Of course the interpretation of that from DIMA is to say they're putting it on,

"Isn't it convenient for them, the thing that was going to cure them from their depression is taking them out of detention." The reason it's going to cure them is because detention is a place that drives people mad and yeah, they want to get out of the place that is driving them mad.

Similarly, Harold Bilboe, a Psychologist who formerly worked at Woomera detention centre, was quoted during the first National Inquiry into Children in Detention (HREOC, 2004, p. 423):

No matter how much I worked with the clients, I couldn't change the cause of the behaviour, the course of their stress, it's like having a patient coming into the hospital with a nail through the hand and you are giving them pethidine injections for pain but you don't remove the nail. That's exactly what is happening in Woomera. You've got people down there with nails through their hands, we're holding them, we're not treating the cause. So, the trauma, the torture, the infection is growing. We are not treating it, we're just containing it. Eventually when those people return to their homelands, if they don't get temporary visas, they are going to carry that with them.

To this day, healthcare professionals have continued to struggle with these issues. Reflecting on his time on Nauru, Dr. Nick Martin questioned how he could deliver care in a system that was designed to harm people:

At what point do you throw your hands up, admit defeat, accept that the system can't be beaten? The monolith of the government was behind this, inflexible, unswerving, shameless. What could I do? Send off yet another email? Hadn't someone defined insanity as the art of doing the same thing over and over expecting a different response? Something like that. Christ, this was soul destroying. (Martin, 2018)

Many of my own experiences reflect those discussed above. In detention, you were never quite clear on the nature of your role, who you were serving and how to navigate the often conflicting demands placed on you. Like many of the authors above, the clear answer, the only way to act in the best interests of your patients was to advocate for their release.

Sometimes the conflicts I was faced with were obvious. For example, when the immigration department asked for unnecessary assessments or asked for interventions that would do nothing more than quell justified frustrations or protest. More often than not however, these conflicts were subtle. There were expectations about my role, held by the immigration department and security contractors. About its limits and what I could and could not do. Also like many of those above, advocacy was an art. What advocacy entailed was never quite clear. It was clear, however, that I could advocate only to the extent that the immigration department and security contractors allowed me to. This applied even to simple requests such as a change in accommodation or new clothing. I could be put in my place quickly if the immigration department chose to do so. While my "advocacy" was never punished, it almost always amounted to nothing. If the system wasn't trying to aggressively shut me down, requests or concerns that I raised would be lost in a faceless, non-accountable bureaucracy.

While far less testimony from detained refugees and asylum seekers can be found, what has been published is often disturbing and highlights further problems in the delivery of healthcare. The two examples below come from testimony provided by detainees to the People's Inquiry and subsequently reported by Briskman, Zion, and Loff (2010, p. 1099). They discuss two different instances of medical involvement in forced deportations:

I heard my name on the speaker, and I was escorted to meet the immigration officers. I said let me talk to my lawyer and they said no. They locked me in the isolation place. I was feeling very scared. Then I start to harm my hand. If my hand is injured they will take me to clinic. If they take me to clinic the other detainees will see me, they will ring my lawyer. Then I found maybe 16, 17 officers around me. They hold my legs together and they bend the big belt and kicked my chin and bound my hands together. They stood over my body and the nurse have an injection and Valium tablets. I said I don't want an injection. I don't want tablets. They tried to do it maybe twenty minutes. I was very angry, screaming and they couldn't. My muscle was very tight because I was frightened. And then they forced me.

The doctor entered the cell carrying an injection with four tablets, asking me to choose either the injection or the tablets. I refused both. The doctor offered the security officers to do their job and he and the officers laid me down on the floor and sit on my back, took my pants down. Then I accepted to receive the tablets. They didn't work, so they force me to take a fifth tablet at the airport. They got me on the airplane with a wheelchair accompanied by a nurse, two companions and three other ACM officers, with three types of handcuffs and ties of leather, plastic and steel around my hand and belly that gathered my arms to my trunk.

Criticism has continued to this day. Behrouz Boochani, an Iranian refugee held on Manus Island for over 5 years, condemned Australia's policies, including IHMS:

There is no hope in Manus prison's medical centre, which is run by IHMS. How many people have they treated successfully in these five years? Salim[5] had nowhere else to turn; he returned to IHMS for help over and over again, at least to collect some pain relief. It was a like seeking asylum from your torturer … IHMS has always been under the command of immigration. The institution is part of a predetermined political strategy which smothers sick refugees and tosses them into a horrific bureaucratic maze. They not only leave refugees untreated, they also aggravate the minor pains of healthy refugees and force them to return to the countries they fled. (Boochani, 2018)

The above testimony from healthcare professionals, refugees and asylum seekers highlights the numerous and pervasive issues that impact healthcare; the parlous conditions within detention, complicity with these policies, the conflicting loyalties faced by healthcare professionals, the near futility in the delivery of healthcare, the negotiation of advocacy and more broadly disagreements about how to respond to these issues.

---

[5] Salim was a Rohingya refugee who died in an apparent suicide on Manus Island.

Statements from Professional Healthcare Bodies

All major professional healthcare bodies have position statements or guidelines in relation to Australian immigration detention. Each sets out to do at least one of two things. The first is to make explicit the position of the professional body on issues as they relate to refugee and asylum seekers in Australia, and the second is to provide clinical and ethical guidance related to the standard of care that should be provided within detention. While these documents vary in scope and content, they have a number of common themes. All call for significant reform of Australian immigration detention. Some call for its abolition (Royal Australian College of Physicians, RACP, 2015). Others call for an end to the detention of children (Australian Psychological Society, APS, 2011). Some call for the use of detention as a last resort only, and only for limited periods of time (Australian Medical Association, AMA, 2015). Others base their calls for reform on existing human rights instruments (Public Health Association of Australia, PHAA, 2015). All acknowledge the damage that Australian immigration detention does (AMA, 2015; APS, 2011; PHAA, 2015; RACP, 2015; Royal Australian and New Zealand College of Psychiatrists, RANZCP, 2016). The APS (2011) have notably framed their position statement more broadly than others, encouraging psychologists to engage in broader social and political action along with promoting the rights, health and wellbeing of asylum seekers and refugees.

While the RACP (2015) refrains from providing specific guidance or recommendations, the AMA (2015) and RANZCP (2016) attempt to provide clinical and ethical guidance for healthcare professionals and attempt to define a standard of care which should be provided. Each report seeks to resolve the conflicts faced by healthcare professionals by calling for them to place the interests of the patient above all other obligations (AMA, 2015; RANZCP, 2016).[6] They go on to outline a number of standards and guidelines in relation to healthcare. Consistent with the contractual and administrative arrangements discussed above, the standards and guidance outlined in these statements have either explicitly or

---

[6] As do the Medical Board of Australia (2014) and the World Medical Association (2006).

implicitly been promoted as a standard equivalent to that found in the broader Australian community. For example, according to the AMA (2015, p. 3) position statement:

> Health and medical services in immigration detention centres should only be provided by organisations, in facilities accredited to Australian standards, that have the full capacity to provide an appropriate range of health and medical care to all detainees as needed, and according to best practice standards in health care delivery (as would apply in the general community). Adherence to these standards should be guaranteed through a process of ongoing monitoring of detainees' health by an independent statutory body of clinical experts with powers to acquire information and investigate conditions in centres as it determines.

This statement goes on to exhort healthcare professionals to maintain a range of other standards, as would be expected to apply in community settings, such as confidentiality, reporting abuse or maltreatment, advocating for patient welfare and not participating in punishment or other activities that could lead to harm. While the RANZCP (2016) statement does not explicitly call for a standard of healthcare that is equivalent to that found in the broader Australian community, it puts forth a number of similar standards such as putting patients first, advocating for patients and maintaining confidentiality. The only professional body to question the utility of defining a standard of care and of providing advice for healthcare professionals working within detention has been the RACP (2015, p. 17):

> The RACP acknowledges the significant ethical issues related to providing care in detention, and the tension in defining a standard of care … While the Australian Department of Immigration and Border Protection has stated that "asylum seekers are provided with a standard of care broadly comparable to health services within the Australian community", there are multiple constraints to providing healthcare in held detention, and people in detention are highly likely to have physical and mental health issues that require additional and specialised services. Further, health providers cannot address health issues caused by held detention while people remain in held detention.

Outside of these statements and government rhetoric the idea of equivalency can be found elsewhere. The Public Interest Advocacy Centre (2018, p. 4), for example, calls "for health care to be provided to people in immigration detention in Australia at the same standard as is available in the Australian community: fair and humane treatment for people who are especially vulnerable, and consistent with our fundamental duty of care to those we detain".[7] Similarly, Dudley (2016, p. 15) calls to transfer "healthcare from immigration to Federal and/or State health departments, with resources augmented to adequate standard, would strengthen clinical independence and quality, minimise healthcare's being securitised and politicised, and uphold ethical codes".

What Other Action Has Been Taken by Healthcare Professionals and Professional Bodies?

If the conversations were left at what I have described above, I would be somewhat misrepresenting the healthcare community and their response to these policies. There has long been opposition both within and outside of detention centres and action has gone beyond that which has occurred within detention centres. I will focus on three cases below and the response from the healthcare community; I will also talk about other actions, such as a strike action and whistleblowing in upcoming chapters. While I hope this gives an idea of the breadth of action that has been taken in response to these policies, again, it isn't exhaustive. There has been persistent opposition from the healthcare community for decades.

---

[7] The report also states, "While PIAC does not support the approach of mandatory immigration detention and maintains grave concerns about the time for which people are detained, the focus of this report is on ensuring people in immigration detention have access to the medical care and treatment they need, at a standard consistent with the Australian community" (p. 8).

The Border Force Act

The Border Force Act (2015) was introduced as part of Operation Sovereign Borders. It came into effect on 1 July 2015 with bipartisan support. Part 6 of the Act, entitled "Secrecy", set out provisions related to disclosure of "protected information". Under the act all staff (past and present) who work(ed) with or within immigration detention were considered "entrusted persons". Any information obtained during their time working in immigration detention was deemed to be "protected information" and any "record or disclosure" of this information was punishable by up to two years' imprisonment. This essentially meant that anybody who had worked in immigration detention centres, past or present, couldn't speak about any aspect of their employment. This included health professionals and raised particular concerns about the ability to report abuse within centres. While the government was quick to reassure the public and the healthcare community that the Border Force Act would not prevent staff from reporting matters of public interest or child abuse, these reassurances meant little. While there were narrow avenues for disclosure under whistleblower protection laws, these generally did not provide protection outside of Australia, and when they did, they only did so only in very specific circumstances. This effectively meant that if staff wanted to report abuse within centres or talk about any aspect of their employment for that matter, they would have to make complex legal decisions with few guarantees of protection, even if the disclosure was in the public interest (Hoang, 2015). It didn't seem far-fetched at the time, with increasing combative stance from the government and increasingly opaque policies the very least that would happen was that anybody who tested the law would be prosecuted as a means to silence others.

Recognizing the potential impact of the Border Force Act, the healthcare community took immediate action. That day before this legislation came into effect, over 40 "entrusted people" including doctors, nurses, social workers and teachers signed an open letter challenging the government to prosecute them (Farrell, 2015). The letter said,

We have advocated, and will continue to advocate, for the health of those for whom we have a duty of care, despite the threats of imprisonment, because standing by and watching sub-standard and harmful care, child abuse and gross violations of human rights is not ethically justifiable … We are aware that in publishing this letter we may be prosecuted under the Australian Border Force Act and we challenge the Department to prosecute so that these issues may be discussed in open court and in the full view of the Australian public.

This was followed by a number of protests from healthcare professionals around the country (Australian Associated Press, 2015) and condemnation from the AMA and other health and medical bodies (Safi & Farrell, 2015). Many more healthcare professionals took advantage of the protection offered by parliamentary inquiries to continue to speak out, while others openly broke the law, continuing to write and speak out in defiance of the Act (Australian Parliamentary Select Committee, 2015; Briskman & Zion, 2014; Isaacs, 2015a; Sanggaran, 2015; Zwi & Mares, 2015). With such defiance, arguably one of the law's major (unintended) impacts was to prompt more people into action to disclose their experiences working in detenteion centres. In saying this, the Border Force Act undeniably had an immediate impact. For example, in September 2015, the UN Special Rapporteur on the Human Rights of Migrants, Francois Crépeau, postponed his planned visit to Australia due to a lack of cooperation from the government who would not grant immunity to those who spoke with the UN, leaving them liable to prosecution (Crépeau, 2015).

In July 2016, Doctors 4 Refugees[8] filed a case in the High Court, challenging the Act. It was not until 30 September 2016 that the government quietly and with little explanation amended the Border Force Act, exempting health professionals from the legislation, seemingly to head off this challenge in the High Court (Doherty, 2016b). Further amendments were made in 2017, which watered down the secrecy provisions of the Act to only include information that could compromise Australian security, defence or international relations (Hutchens, 2017).

---

[8] https://www.doctors4refugees.org/.

There are a number of lessons that can be learnt from the healthcare communities' response to the Border Force Act. Given I will only be talking about a few different forms of action in later chapters, these are worth considering here. First, why didn't the government prosecute or attack those who broke the law? This lack of action stood in contrast to the government's attacks on the AHRC after the Forgotten Children Report (2014) and the other action designed to silence; raids on offices of contractors, and the referral of healthcare professionals to the Australian Federal Police (AFP), each of which will be discussed in Chap. 5. I can only speculate as to why this was the case and there are probably many factors, but a few things can be said with some certainty. The collective response from healthcare professionals and professional bodies strengthened their position, additionally those who spoke out often held relatively powerful positions, bolstering their demands. Furthermore, taking such action would have undermined the government's legitimacy and supposed commitment to "free speech".[9] On the other hand, the government may have also held little hope for a successful prosecution given the implied freedom of political communication protected under the Australian constitution (Meagher, 2004) and because numerous high-profile lawyers had offered free legal counsel to anyone who was charged.

Medical Transfers and Medevac

Hamid Khazaei arrived on Christmas Island in August 2013 shortly after the government had re-introduced offshore processing and announced those who arrived by boat would not be resettled in Australia. Khazaei was transferred to Manus Island in September about a month on Christmas Island. Khazaei initially presented to IHMS on 23 August 2014 with flu-like symptoms and small lesion on his leg. His condition rapidly deteriorated and he was unable to be treated on Manus Island. Medical staff sought his immediate evacuation, but he was not transferred to PIH in Port Moresby until 26 August 2014. Khazaei continued to deteriorate at PIH and was transferred to the Mater Hospital in

---

[9] For example, this came at a time the government was attempting to water down the Racial Discrimination Act, under the guise of free speech (Grant, 2017).

Brisbane on 27 August 2014. He was assessed on 28 August 2014 and it was determined he had "absent brainstem reflexes consistent with a profound brain injury" (Coroners Court of QLD, 2019). He was pronounced dead on 5 September 2014.[10] The Queensland Coroner (2019) reached a number of conclusions about this case, among them, inadequate facilities and staffing in Papua New Guinea and "significant flaws in the arrangements for Mr Khazaei's transfer from the MIRPC [Manus Island Regional Processing Centre]" contributed to his death. Ultimately the coroner concluded that if he were transferred to Australian hospital within 24 hours of developing sepsis his death could have been prevented.

Hamid Khazaei was not the last death in offshore detention or even the last person who suffered unnecessarily because of the Australian government's unwillingness to transfer people to mainland Australia. The issue of medical transfers has been pressing since the re-introduction of offshore processing. Stories began emerging in 2016 about the government's refusal to transfer those who were unwell. In late 2016, a refugee on Nauru with a growing lump in her breast had her transfer for treatment postponed indefinitely (Doherty, 2016c). In 2017 it was revealed nearly 50 refugees and asylum seekers held on Nauru, including three women seeking to terminate a pregnancy, were refused or not considered for medical transfers despite medical recommendations (Doherty, 2017). In an extraordinary step to ensure asylum seekers didn't make it to Australia in September 2017, Australia signed a deal with Taiwan so refugees and asylum seekers detained offshore could be transferred for medical treatment not available on Nauru or Manus Island.[11] Beginning in 2017 and by the end of 2018 over 50 injunctions were filed in the Australian Federal Court on behalf of adults and children in offshore detention. This litigation led to the evacuation of hundreds of individuals from offshore detention (Talbot & Newhouse, 2019). By July 2019, there had been 33 transfers from Nauru to Taiwan with a similar number refusing the transfer (Ryan, 2019). Throughout this time, both the Nauruan and Australian governments continued to attempt to block

---

[10] For more details on the circumstances surrounding this case, see the Coroners Court of QLD (2019).

[11] Taiwan is also not a signatory to the 1951 Refugee Convention, meaning refugees cannot apply for asylum to prevent them from being returned to Nauru.

transfers to Australia, with the Australian government accused of ignoring advice from its own doctors for up to five years (Davidson, 2019a). In fact, almost every transfer to Australia, including those of unwell children, occurred only by court order (Davidson, 2018), and even then, both the Australian and Nauruan governments worked together to defy these orders (Davidson & Doherty, 2018).

In August 2018, Malcolm Turnbull, the then Prime Minister, stepped down after Scott Morrison successfully challenged for the Liberal party leadership. Turnbull resigned and a by-election was held in October 2018, with independent candidate Kerryn Phelps winning the once-safe Liberal seat. The loss of this seat meant that the ruling Liberal party no longer had a working majority which proved to be enough to pass the Migration Amendment [Urgent Medical Treatment] Bill (2018) or what became known as the Medevac legislation. The Medevac legislation came into effect in March 2019. The newly introduced law strengthened doctors' position to recommend transfers of those who required medical treatment in Australia. To initiate a transfer, the Medevac legislation required an assessment by two doctors and subsequent review by an independent health advice panel. The home affairs minister, Peter Dutton, retained the power to refuse transfers on security grounds. The government signalled its opposition to these laws from the time they were being debated. The Australian government took legal action in an attempt to block transfers (Davidson, 2019b) and along with the Nauruan government refused or delayed requests for transfers to Australia (Smee & Vasefi, 2019). Despite this however between March and October 2019, there were 135 transfers from Nauru and Manus Island after the Medevac legislation was passed (Reilly, 2019).

In opposing the Medevac legislation and in seeking its repeal, the government argued that Medevac would result in "weaker" border policies and those who did make it to Australia would have access to at least some legal protections. Peter Dutton, the Home Affairs Minister, went as far as suggesting that rape victims on Nauru were "trying it on":

> Let's be serious about this. There are people who have claimed that they've been raped and came to Australia to seek an abortion because they couldn't get an abortion on Nauru. They arrived in Australia and then decided they

were not going to have an abortion. They have the baby here and the moment they step off the plane their lawyers lodge papers in the federal court, which injuncts us from sending them back. (Davidson, 2019c)

The 2019 federal election saw the reconfiguration of the Australian parliament, and the Liberal government, with the support of a number of independent senators, was successful in repealing Medevac in December 2019.

The healthcare community in Australia was instrumental in pushing for the introduction of the Medevac legislation and in opposing its repeal. Bolstered by other protests and in urging the government to keep Medevac, over 5000 doctors signed an open letter with a number attending parliament to lobby the government to keep the law. Almost every major professional body also implored the government to evacuate Manus and Nauru well before the introduction of Medevac (Murphy, 2018).

Baby Asha

In February 2016 a 12-month-old asylum seeker, who came to be known as Baby Asha, was transferred from Nauru and hospitalized in Brisbane. After she received treatment, doctors at Lady Cilento Hospital in Brisbane refused to discharge her to be returned to Nauru. The media were notified of this case, which, almost overnight, became national news. This occurred at the same time the #LetThemStay campaign was launched (Hall et al., 2018), which organized protests in 12 major cities over 12 days, calling for the government to stop the transfer of 267 asylum seekers, including 54 children and 37 infants, from Australia to Nauru. A vigil mobilized outside of the hospital around the clock for 10 days, placing the government under increasing pressure to honour the doctors' refusal to discharge and to accomodate the family in the Australian community (Hall et al., 2018).

At the same time that doctors were refusing to discharge Baby Asha, the AMA held a public forum to discuss the health of asylum seekers (Owler, 2016). The AMA has, to this point, been the only professional body to hold such a forum and publicly discuss these issues. Acknowledging the devastating impact that immigration detention has had on adults and that it amounted to a "state-sanctioned form of child abuse", the AMA called for the immediate release of all children along with a moratorium on asylum seeker children being returned to immigration detention. Former President of the AMA, Dr. Brian Owler also called for the re-establishment of an independent body of experts to report on the welfare of asylum seekers and refugees, and furthermore, if satisfactory healthcare could not be provided, the governments "policies should be revisited".

After negotiations with the government, Asha was discharged to community detention about 10 days later. Despite this compromise, the then Minister for Immigration, Peter Dutton, maintained she would eventually be returned to Nauru (Doherty, 2016a; Wahlquist & Murray, 2016). The #LetThemStay campaign was labelled a success; over half of the 267 asylum seekers, including 37 babies and their parents were released into onshore community detention. Despite this, however, Baby Asha and her family were eventually returned to Nauru several months later (Hall et al., 2018).

References

Australian Council of Heads of Schools of Social Work. (2006). *We've boundless plains to share: The first report of the People's Inquiry into Detention*. Australian Council of Heads of Schools of Social Work.

Australian Human Rights Commission. (2014). The forgotten children: National inquiry into children in immigration detention. Retrieved from https://www.humanrights.gov.au/our-work/asylum-seekers-and-

Australian Medical Association. (2015). *Position statement on health care of asylum seekers and refugees - 2011*. Revised 2015. Retrieved from https://ama.com.au/position-statement/health-care-asylum-seekers-and-refugees-2011

Amnesty International. (2018). *Papua New Guinea: Refugee health crisis looming as Australia withdraws support*. Retrieved from https://www.amnesty.org/en/latest/news/2018/04/papua-new-guinea-refugee-health-crisis-looming-as-australia-withdraws-support/

Australian Psychological Society. (2011). *Psychological wellbeing of refugees and asylum seekers in Australia: A Position Statement prepared for The Australian*

Psychological Society. Retrieved from https://www.psychology.org.au/About-Us/What-we-do/advocacy/Position-Statements/Psychological-wellbeing-refugees-and-asylum-seeker

Australian Associated Press. (2015). Australian doctors rally over threat of jail for speaking about asylum seekers. *The Guardian.* Retrieved from https://www.theguardian.com/australia-news/2015/jul/11/australian-doctors-rally-over-threat-of-jail-for-speaking-about-asylum-seeekers

Australian National Audit Office. (2016). *Delivery of health services in onshore immigration detention.* ANAO Report No.13 2016–17, Performance Audit.

Australian Parliamentary Joint Select Committee on Australia's Immigration Detention Network. (2012) *Final Report.* Retrieved from https://www.aph.gov.au/Parliamentary_Business/Committees/Joint/Former_Committees/immigrationdetention/index

Australian Parliamentary Select Committee. (2015). *Select Committee on the recent allegations relating to conditions and circumstances at the Regional Processing Centre in Nauru.* Retrieved from https://www.aph.gov.au/Parliamentary_Business/Committees/Senate/Regional_processing_Nauru/Regional_processing_Nauru/Final_Report

Boochani, B. (2018). Salim fled genocide to find safety. He lost his life in the most tragic way. *The Guardian.* Retrieved from https://www.theguardian.com/commentisfree/2018/may/25/salim-fled-genocide-to-find-safety-he-lost-his-life-in-the-most-tragic-way

Border Force Act 2015 (Cth) (Austl.).

Briskman, L., & Zion, D. (2014). Dual loyalties and impossible dilemmas: Health care in immigration detention. *Public Health Ethics, 7*(3), 277–286.

Briskman, L., Zion, D., & Loff, B. (2010). Challenge and collusion: Health professionals and immigration detention in Australia. *The International Journal of Human Rights, 14*(7), 1092–1106.

Christmas Island Medical Officer's Letter of Concern. (2013). *The Guardian.* Retrieved from https://www.theguardian.com/world/interactive/2014/jan/13/christmas-island-doctors-letter-of-concern-in-full

Coffey, G. (2006). 'Locked up without guilt or Sin': The ethics of mental health service delivery in immigration detention. *Psychiatry, Psychology and Law, 13*(1), 67–90.

Coroners Court of QLD. (2019). *Inquest into the death of Hamid KHAZAEI.* 2014/3292.

Crépeau, F. (2015). *Migrants/Human rights: Official visit to Australia postponed due to protection concerns.* Retrieved from https://www.ohchr.org/EN/NewsEvents/Pages/DisplayNews.aspx?NewsID=16503&LangID=E

Davidson, H. (2018). Eleven refugee children transferred from Nauru to Australia in one day. *The Guardian*. Retrieved from https://www.theguardian.com/australia-news/2018/oct/22/australia-spends-480000-more-in-legal-fees-on-nauru-detainee-healthcare-claims

Davidson, H. (2019a). Australian government ignored refugee transfer advice from its own doctors for up to five years. *The Guardian*. Retrieved from https://www.theguardian.com/australia-news/2019/feb/07/australian-government-ignored-refugee-transfer-advice-from-its-own-doctors-for-up-to-five-years

Davidson, H. (2019b). Federal court overturns attempt to block Medevac transfer from Nauru. *The Guardian*. Retrieved from https://www.theguardian.com/australia-news/2019/jun/19/federal-court-overturn-attempt-to-block-medevac-transfer-from-nauru

Davidson, H. (2019c). Peter Dutton condemned for 'vile and offensive' Nauru rape claims. *The Guardian*. Retrieved from https://www.theguardian.com/australia-news/2019/jun/21/peter-dutton-condemned-for-vile-and-offensive-nauru-claims

Davidson, H., & Doherty, B. (2018). Nauru blocks court-ordered transfer of critically ill refugee to Australia. *The Guardian*. Retrieved from https://www.theguardian.com/world/2018/sep/06/nauru-blocks-court-ordered-transfer-of-critically-ill-refugee-to-australia

de Boer, R. (2013). Health care for asylum seekers on Nauru and Manus Island. *Australian Parliamentary Library*. Retrieved from https://www.aph.gov.au/About_Parliament/Parliamentary_Departments/Parliamentary_Library/pubs/BN/2012-2013/AsylumSeekersHealthCare

Doherty, B. (2016a). 'Baby Asha' and Nauru protests held as hospital staff oppose transfer. *The Guardian*. Retrieved from https://www.theguardian.com/australia-news/2016/feb/13/baby-asha-and-nauru-protests-held-as-hospital-staff-oppose-transfer

Doherty, B. (2016b). Doctors freed to speak about Australia's detention regime after U-turn. *The Guardian*. Retrieved from https://www.theguardian.com/australia-news/2016/oct/20/doctors-freed-to-speak-about-australias-detention-regime-after-u-turn

Doherty, B. (2016c). Refugee with growing breast lump has medical transfer from Nauru cancelled. *The Guardian*. Retrieved from https://www.theguardian.com/australia-news/2016/aug/06/refugee-with-growing-breast-lump-has-medical-transfer-from-nauru-cancelled

Doherty, B. (2017). Three pregnant refugees and nearly 50 others denied medical transfers from Nauru. *The Guardian*. Retrieved from https://www.theguardian.com/australia-news/2017/aug/21/three-pregnant-refugees-and-nearly-50-others-denied-medical-transfers-from-nauru

Dudley, M. (2016). Helping professionals and Border Force secrecy: Effective asylum-seeker healthcare requires independence from callous policies. *Australasian Psychiatry, 24*(1), 15-18.

Farrell, P. (2015). Detention centre staff speak out in defiance of new asylum secrecy laws. *The Guardian*. Retrieved from https://www.theguardian.com/australia-news/2015/jul/01/detention-centre-staff-speak-out-in-defiance-of-new-asylum-secrecy-laws

Farrell, P., Jabour, B., & Evershed, N. (2015). Fraud 'inevitable' over asylum seeker health targets, leaked documents show. *The Guardian*. Retrieved from http://www.theguardian.com/australia-news/2015/jul/21/inevitable-over-asylum-seeker-health-targets-leaked-documents-show

Grant, S. (2017). Section 18C: What's all the fuss and why does it matter? Australian Broadcasting Corporation News. Retrieved from https://www.abc.net.au/news/2017-03-21/section-18c-whats-the-fuss/8374136

Hall, S., Lenette, C., Murray, S., Chan, C., Flannery, A., & Vickery, K. (2018). # LetThemStay: Visual representations of protests and community mobilization for asylum seekers in Australia. *Journal of Critical Thought and Praxis, 7*(1), 4.

Hoang, K. (2015). Border Force Act entrenches secrecy around Australia's asylum seeker regime. *The Conversation*. Retrieved from https://theconversation.com/border-force-act-entrenches-secrecy-around-australias-asylum-seeker-regime-44136

Human Rights and Equal Opportunities Committee. (2004). *A last resort: National inquiry into children in immigration detention*. Retrieved from https://www.humanrights.gov.au/our-work/asylum-seekers-and-refugees/publications/last-resort-national-inquiry-children-immigration

Hutchens, G. (2017). Dutton retreats on offshore detention secrecy rules that threaten workers with jail. *The Guardian*. Retrieved from https://www.theguardian.com/australia-news/2017/aug/14/dutton-retreats-on-offshore-detention-secrecy-rules-that-threaten-workers-with-jail

Isaacs, D. (2015a). Are healthcare professionals working in Australia's immigration detention centres condoning torture? *Journal of Medical Ethics, 42*(7), 413–415.

Isaacs, D. (2015b). Nauru and detention of children. *Journal of Paediatrics and Child Health, 51*(4), 353–354.

Knaus, C., & Davidson, H. (2019). Company given $21.5m for Manus healthcare without a contract. *The Guardian*. Retrieved from https://www.theguardian.com/australia-news/2019/feb/22/company-given-215m-for-manus-healthcare-despite-poor-track-record

Marr, D., & Laughland, O. (2014). Australia's detention regime sets out to make asylum seekers suffer, says chief immigration psychiatrist. *The Guardian*. Retrieved from http://www.theguardian.com/world/2014/aug/05/-sp-australias-detention-regime-sets-out-to-make-asylum-seekers-suffer-says-chief-immigration-psychiatrist

Martin, N. (2018). The Nauru diaries. *Meanjin*. Retrieved from https://meanjin.com.au/essays/the-nauru-diaries/

Meagher, D. (2004). What is political communication-the rationale and scope of the implied freedom of political communication. *Melbourne University Law Review, 28*, 438.

Medical Board of Australia. (2014). *Good medical practice: A code of conduct for doctors in Australia*. Retrieved from https://www.medicalboard.gov.au/Codes-Guidelines-Policies/Code-of-conduct.aspx

Migration Amendment (Urgent Medical Treatment) Bill. (2018).

Murphy, K. (2018). AMA president calls for urgent transfer of refugee families from Nauru. *The Guardian*. Retrieved from https://www.theguardian.com/australia-news/2018/sep/20/ama-president-calls-for-urgent-transfer-of-refugee-families-from-nauru

Owler, B. (2016). *Speech to AMA forum on health of asylum seekers*. Retrieved from https://ama.com.au/media/ama-speech-prof-owler-ama-asylum-seeker-health-forum

Farrell, P. (2017). Immigration healthcare provider failed to run police checks on staff on Manus. *The Guardian*. Retrieved from https://www.theguardian.com/australia-news/2017/feb/16/immigration-healthcare-provider-failed-to-run-police-checks-on-staff-on-manus

Public Health Association of Australia. (2015). *Public health association of Australia: Policy-at-a-glance—Refugee and asylum seeker health policy*. Retrieved from https://www.phaa.net.au/documents/item/882

Public Interest Advocacy Centre. (2018). *In poor health: Health care in Australian immigration detention*. Retrieved from https://www.piac.asn.au/2018/06/13/in-poor-health-health-care-in-australian-immigration-detention/

Royal Australian College of Physicians. (2015). *Policy on refugee and asylum seeker health*. Retrieved from https://www.racp.edu.au/advocacy/policy-and-advocacy-priorities/refugee-and-asylum-seeker-health

Royal Australian and New Zealand College of Psychiatrists. (2016). *Professional practice guideline 12: Guidance for psychiatrists working in Australian immigration detention centres*. Retrieved from https://www.ranzcp.org/Files/Resources/

College_Statements/Practice_Guidelines/PPG-12-Guidance-for-psychiatrists-working-in-Austr.aspx

Reilly, A. (2019). Explainer: The Medevac repeal and what it means for asylum seekers on Manus Island and Nauru. *The Conversation.* Retrieved from https://theconversation.com/explainer-the-medevac-repeal-and-what-it-means-for-asylum-seekers-on-manus-island-and-nauru-128118

Rufener, C. (2018). The Nauru paradox: Why help patients regain hope when it is dashed systematically? *The Guardian.* Retrieved from https://www.theguardian.com/commentisfree/2018/oct/28/the-nauru-paradox-why-help-patients-regain-hope-when-it-is-dashed-systematically

Ryan, H. (2019). Australia flew a refugee with an infected cavity from an island detention camp to Taiwan. *BuzzFeed News.* Retrieved from https://www.buzzfeed.com/hannahryan/australia-taiwan-refugee-island-detention-health

Safi, M., & Farrell, P. (2015). AMA joins protest against asylum law that can jail detention centre staff. *The Guardian.* Retrieved from https://www.theguardian.com/australia-news/2015/jul/01/ama-joins-protest-against-asylum-law-that-can-jail-detention-centre-staff

Sanggaran, J.-P. (2015). Asylum seekers are being abused on our watch. It's time to put detention under surveillance. *The Guardian.* Retrieved from https://www.theguardian.com/commentisfree/2015/sep/12/asylum-seekers-are-being-abused-on-our-watch-its-time-to-put-detention-under-surveillance

Smee, B., & Vasefi, S. (2019). Nauru refugees still waiting for medical care months after 'urgent' warnings about threat to life. *The Guardian.* Retrieved from https://www.theguardian.com/world/2019/jul/15/it-is-like-a-slow-death-seriously-ill-nauru-refugees-remain-trapped-amid-delays

Talbot, A., & Newhouse, G. (2019). Strategic litigation, offshore detention and the Medevac bill. *Court of Conscience, 13,* 85.

Wahlquist, C., & Murray, W. (2016). Baby Asha: Immigration minister confirms community detention in Australia. *The Guardian.* Retrieved from https://www.theguardian.com/australia-news/2016/feb/21/baby-asha-community-detention-negotiations-follow-hospital-protests

World Medical Association. (2006). *WMA international code of medical ethics.* Retrieved from https://www.wma.net/policies-post/wma-international-code-of-medical-ethics/

Zwi, K., & Mares, S. (2015). Stories from unaccompanied children in immigration detention: A composite account. *Journal of Paediatrics and Child Health, 51*(7), 658–662.

4

The Ethics of Australian Immigration Detention

Overview

Now that we have an understanding of Australian immigration detention, its impact and the healthcare arrangements within detention, I want to consider the justification for these policies. This book is about responding to Australian government policy. It is important to ask whether these policies, as a whole or in part, can be justified. This of course will determine how we respond and is an important step in considering whether we can justify non-violent resistance. I will first briefly discuss the literature that has outlined the ethics of immigration and asylum. I will outline key debates and then apply this to consider whether Australian immigration detention can be justified. I will argue that Australia has a duty to admit refugees and asylum seekers and that its policies of deterrence are profoundly unjust. I do however argue that while drastic reform is needed, some caution is warranted as we need to carefully consider the regional implications of such reform. That is, in seeking reform domestically, changes to Australia's policies are likely to have repercussions throughout the Asia-Pacific region, which could again lead to asylum seeker boat arrivals, which could in turn lead to deaths at sea. I will then

© The Author(s) 2020
R. Essex, *The Healthcare Community and Australian Immigration Detention*,
https://doi.org/10.1007/978-981-15-7537-2_4

discuss the ethics of healthcare within immigration detention centres. I will conclude this chapter by outlining the literature that has considered the ethics of healthcare within immigration detention centres, touching upon some key concepts and discussions in relation to the delivery of healthcare within centres.

Some may be wondering why my focus in this chapter somewhat expands, why I deal with the issue of refugees and asylum seekers throughout the Asia-Pacific region here when the major focus of this book is on the healthcare communities' response to Australian immigration detention. As I will argue in Chap. 5, to achieve any reasonable standard of healthcare, we would need major systemic reform which would have implications for policy throughout the Asia-Pacific region; it is thus important we situate this discussion amongst this broader literature and begin to think about its possible implications.

Open Borders

In this book, I am trying to chart a course in less than ideal circumstances and against a number of constraints. As I outlined earlier, I have written this book knowing that urgent, pragmatic solutions are needed, so while I am concerned with what is justified, I am also concerned with what is feasible. This issue also weighs heavily throughout the literature concerned with the ethics of migration. Gibney (2004, p. 228) suggests that in demanding change we need to first recognize "how the capabilities of governments in asylum policy are (for the most part) politically constructed within a structure—the modern state—that demands that governments legitimise their actions to the members of their state". Similarly, Carens (1996) suggests a number of key "realities" which act as constraints when approaching issues of migration. First, institutional constraints relate to the modern state, with any realistic discussion of migration accepting the division of the world into states that have the ability to admit or exclude. Second, behavioural constraints relate to taking action that is realistic and not using "moral standards that no one ever meets or even approximates in their actual behaviour" (p. 158). Finally, there are also a number of political constraints; that is, any approach needs to also be politically feasible. Similarly Little and Macdonald (2015, p. 384) argue that if we are to find guidance and make change an approach is needed that is "adequately responsive to the concrete speci-ficities of the problems political actors confront, on the terms that politi-cal actors understand and recognise these problems". With this in mind I take a similar approach to Gibney (2004, p. 15) (and many others who have thought about these issues) who proposes that when thinking about the issue of asylum, that in any solution we need to think about ethical force and practical relevance. That is, any approach to these issues needs to "be informed by a convincing value or furnish a credible moral ideal" and "take account of the character and capabilities of the agents at whom it is directed, and of the probable consequences of their actions". Doing this is no easy task, but failing to do so risks resulting in "privileged spec-ulations that do little to help us reflect upon the moral choices we must make or to guide us to act responsibly in the world" (Carens, 1996, p. 168). I will thus work from the conventional assumption that demo-cratic states have the right to exercise discretionary control over immigra-tion. That is, into the foreseeable future, Australia will continue to assert its right to maintain control over its borders and keep non-arrival mea-sures such as visa checks in place. Many who are committed to open borders have taken such a position in beginning to think about solutions; Dummett (2004, pp. 121–122), for example, discusses the unlikelihood of open borders:

> No state … could at this time open its borders to all save those particular individuals—criminals and rabblerousers—from whom it must protect its citizens. No state could do this without creating an unmanageable influx. To arrive at a position in which the acceptance of immigrants was the norm, all countries would have to move together towards it. Such a move-ment would require an immediate liberalisation of immigration laws and immediate public recognition by government of the benefits of immigra-tion and the determined discouragement of xenophobic propaganda against it. It would require an end to the hypocrisy of denouncing people-smugglers as traffickers in human misery while preventing anyone from getting in by any other means, and while scouting the idea that there is any real human misery from which refugees are trying to escape.

This of course does not mean we should settle. And on this point, I have a similar views to Silverman (2013, p. 11), who argues "that the most coherent ethical position with regards to the rights of non-citizens is to continue to strive towards open borders in the long-term while pressing states to adopt and enforce minimum standards towards their immigration detainees in the short-term". In this sense and in making these assumptions, the remainder of the next two chapters is an attempt to strike a balance between what is ethical and what is feasible in the Australian context, while maintaining a commitment to the longer-term ideal of open borders.

The Ethics of Asylum and Immigration Detention

The literature concerned with the ethics of asylum discusses a range of issues: who is a refugee, how to ground the obligations states have to refugees and asylum seekers, how to allocate asylum places amongst states, what is owed to refugees and what the limits of these obligations might be. While I will discuss some principles which ground our obligations towards refugees and asylum seeker in this section, I largely discuss the last issue raised above, what is owed to refugees and what the limits of our obligations might be, particularly as this relates to entry and detention.

The literature that debates the ethics of asylum sits within a broader debate about migration more generally and between two opposing positions. The first could be labelled partiality[1]. This position views, states as unique communities, possessing a right to self-determination, which justifies the interests of citizens over those of outsiders and in restricting and setting their own criteria for admission. Broadly and while there are important differences which I will not discuss here, this approach is largely promoted by communitarians, conservatives and realists (e.g., Miller, 2005; Walzer, 1983). Those taking an opposing position, impartialists, argue that states are obliged to consider the interests or rights of

---

[1] Gibney (2004) uses this terminology. Other authors have used different terminology, for example, "border control defenders" and "free movement advocates" (Silverman, 2013).

the human community in its entirety when making decisions about entry. Such a position presents a challenge to current state practices appealing to freedom of movement and global justice. This position is mainly promoted by global liberals and utilitarians (e.g., Carens, 2013; Cole, 2000; Dummett, 2002).[2]

These polar positions aside, regardless of their position on migration, there is general agreement amongst philosophers that states have a duty to grant asylum and that at a minimum, people should not be returned to their country of origin if at risk of persecution or human rights violations. Even those who assert that states otherwise have total discretion to exclude concede this point. There are a number of good reasons for this. Carens (2013), for example, argues that there are at least three reasons why states have a duty to admit refugees. First, casual connection: if our actions have in some way contributed to the fact that refugees are no longer safe in their home country, they have a greater obligation to admit them. Second, humanitarian grounds: we have a duty to help simply because refugees are in need of safety and we have the capacity to provide it. Finally, the normative presuppositions of the state system: as states claim the exclusive authority to grant entry and the right to stay, while this works for most people, it clearly doesn't work for refugees and asylum seekers. Where a state has failed, either deliberately or through incapacity, it is up to other states to remedy because of their "claim to exercise power legitimately in a world divided into states" (Carens, 2013, p. 196).

While there is some general agreement in the literature that states should promptly and fairly process claims for asylum, offer (at least) temporary refuge to successful applicants and be willing to accept a fair number of refugees, these issues are far from settled. There remains disagreement about the precise nature and extent of these obligations. What limits could be justified? Put another way, at what point would Australia be justified in turning away refugees and asylum seekers? For Carens (2013, p. 319), the answer is simple and "almost never", and if anything, there is a case for western states to admit more refugees. Walzer (1983), who

---

[2] It is worth noting that either position alone cannot account for why states should give priority to resettling refugees and asylum seekers. Even those who advocate for open borders, a right to free movement does not necessarily say anything about the claims of the vulnerable.

otherwise maintains that states retain the right to turn away migrants, argues that states are constrained by the universal principle of mutual aid when it comes to refugees and asylum seekers, acknowledging that turning asylum seekers away would be using force against "helpless and desperate people" (pp. 22–23). For Miller (2007, p. 227), it must be left to states themselves to decide: "The final judgement must be left with the members of the receiving community who may decide that they have already done their fair share of refugee resettlement". This however conflates who ought to make the decision with what is justifiable. That is, the fact that the state has the power to turn asylum seekers away does not mean that the decision is justifiable.

Attempting to bring these positions together while considering global political realities, Gibney (2004, p. 231) argues that states should adopt the principle of humanitarianism, which holds that "states have an obligation to assist refugees when the costs of doing so are low". This "modest, sober and painstakingly realistic" (Gibney, 2004, p. 21) principle doesn't call for the repeal of all non-arrival measures or even measures that discourage dangerous travel; it can however be used to inform ethically defensible asylum practices, particularly given the political realities that face refugees and asylum seekers. I will use this position as a foundation for my arguments below. While the humanitarian principle provides a starting point to examine Australia's approach more generally, there are a number of other ethical considerations related to asylum seekers and immigration detention itself.

Unlike refugees, asylum seekers arrive on states' borders seeking protection. This raises a series of additional questions beyond simply recognizing that states have obligations to provide asylum. First, an important and difficult ethical question relates to whether states should give priority to those who are more proximal, that is, should we prioritize asylum seekers in Indonesia over others who are being persecuted farther away (Gibney, 2018). As I will discuss below, the Australian government has at times attempted to advance a similar argument. Second, a further issue as it relates to asylum seekers, is whether or what non-arrival measures are justified. While many accept that border controls such as visa checks are likely to remain, most are far less comfortable with non-arrival measures such as boat turn-backs. A further concern relates to the use of immigration detention. While there has been substantial discussion about admissions, there has been little discussion about detention's role as a means of controlling movement. Silverman (2014, p. 611) suggests that immigration detention further complicates discussions, challenging the admissions debate in at least three ways. First, the temporal and spatial assumptions of admission: that is, decisions on admission usually "take place across time and in a variety of settings". Second, rarely are the personal characteristics of refugees and asylum seekers considered. This has allowed immigration detention to be presented as fair and non-discriminatory, despite routinely singling out "men and certain minorities" for discriminatory treatment. Finally, "detention glosses over the virtually irreconcilable ethical conflicts intrinsic to the immigration admissions debate". That is:

> An unqualified right to enter would entail a wholesale rethinking of state sovereignty and the migrant-citizen-state hierarchy. It would force states to wrestle with questions of historic injustice, blame, and restitution in determining who owes what to whom. In the meantime, detention allows states to hold non-citizens—and these weighty questions—at bay. (Silverman, 2014, p. 612)

Can Australian Immigration Detention Be Justified?

Given our less than ideal circumstances and with the above discussions in mind, what should we make of Australia's response to refugees and asylum seekers? In assessing whether Australian immigration detention can be justified, it is first necessary to return to the consequences of these policies outlined in Chaps. 2 and 3. There is extensive evidence that detention has created immeasurable misery for tens of thousands of adults and children and has had a devastating impact on health and well-being. Despite being signatory to all major human rights instruments, Australia's policy of mandatory indefinite immigration detention has violated almost every major human rights commitment it has made. These policies have also denied thousands the opportunity to apply for asylum and sent many back to danger. This has all been done in the name of deterrence, in which the suffering of detainees plays a major part. For these reasons alone, Australian immigration detention and regional policies of deterrence and denial cannot be justified. Even hypothetically, I cannot foresee any situation in the future where Australia's present policies could be justified.[3]

While I could end this section here, I think there are some further important issues worth considering, particularly in relation to discussions about reform. While Australian immigration detention cannot be justified in its current form, could some form of detention be justified at all? Below I will discuss arguments which make the case for retaining at least some restriction on immigration. These arguments relate to security, whether a level of deterrence results in more overall places for refugees resettled from overseas and what I will call the humanitarian argument, that deterrence saves lives by stopping dangerous voyages by sea. I should note that before moving forward, I will try to avoid engaging with Australian government rhetoric as much as possible on these points. Again, while challenging such rhetoric is important, it is unhelpful and ultimately a distraction to what I want to achieve here, whether Australia's approach can be justified and what this means in responding to these policies.

Can some form of detention be justified on security grounds? Gibney (2004) suggests that we first should question the basis of these security concerns. While we may have reason to be concerned regarding the anonymity of asylum seekers and refugees, for example, this needs to be carefully disentangled from general concerns about their character. Furthermore, we also need to question whether there is a clear standard as to what constitutes a security threat, whether there is a clear procedure in place for investigation and whether a personal link has been established between the individual and a potential security threat. The Australian government has of course not taken the time to reflect on these things, frequently bringing the character of refugees into question

---

[3] Beyond what I discuss here, there are a multitude of further issues that could be criticized related to the administration of immigration detention and the steps the government has taken to consolidate its power, attacking a range of democratic norms within Australia. I will begin to touch on this in upcoming chapters.

and conducting security assessments that are largely secret.[4] While on this point it is worth dealing with some misconceptions about security as they relate to asylum seekers in Australia. Given the risk involved in travelling to Australia by boat, it seems highly unlikely that this would be the preferred route for those wishing to threaten Australia's national security. This position is supported by data that suggests that those who travel to Australia by boat are no more likely to offend than others (Hall, 2013). Furthermore and more generally, studies looking at migration and crime in Australia have found no link between "immigrant concentration and diversity" on rates of crime (Sydes, 2019). It also doesn't naturally follow that all potential security risks are best managed in detention; there are a range of alternatives[5] (Sampson, Chew, Mitchell, & Bowring, 2015) which could mitigate risk to the community while also better balancing the rights of the individual in question. In saying all of this, I can imagine a number of very limited circumstances where detention could be justified.[6] For example, if someone arrived seeking asylum and a clear link was established suggesting they were a threat to public safety and all other less restrictive alternatives were inappropriate, immigration detention could be justified. This doesn't mean that they should be detained indefinitely or under conditions in which detention centres currently operate. More practically, to make such a judgement, this would also require an individual assessment, oversight and transparency in terms of how this is determined.

Could deterrence of asylum seekers be justified to resettle a greater number of refugees from offshore? Similarly and as asked above, should we prioritize asylum seekers in Indonesia over others who are being persecuted farther away? While many might take issue with question itself,[7] it is worth considering as the Australian government has attempted to use this justification. In 2014, the Australian government announced that under Australia's humanitarian programme, 4400 places were set aside

---

[4] For more on this, see Saul (2012).

[5] I will discuss this in Chap. 5.

[6] My position is similar to that of the Beyond the Boats report (Douglas, Higgins, Keski-Nummi, McAdam, & McLeod, 2014), which calls for the abolition of detention except for initial health, security and identity screening.

[7] For example, the Malaysian people swap deal discussed in Chap. 2.

for people fleeing violence in Iraq and Syria. Then Immigration Minister, Scott Morrison credited the "success" of Australia's "strong border protection policies" in allowing "more places to be returned to our humanitarian programme for the world's most desperate and vulnerable people" (Morrison, 2014). Prior to making this announcement, there was a drastic decrease in boat arrivals after the government introduced Operation Sovereign Borders. While the government made out that its tough policies allowed it to do more for those in need, they would have offered asylum to the same number of people regardless.[8] Furthermore, there was nothing stopping the government resettling more people from offshore while continuing to assess the claims of asylum seekers who made their way to Australia. Finally, Australia has never made any additional effort to resettle more refugees when asylum arrivals have been low. While the government was clearly disingenuous in this case, could there be a case to restrict asylum if it resulted in Australia being able to resettle more people from offshore? I believe Australia would have to begin to resettle substantially more people to get into the ballpark of justifying deterrence. In making this point, it is worth reflecting on some figures, noted earlier in this book. With the exception of the years 2011–2014 the number of boat arrivals has been relatively low, with generally less than 5000 people a year arriving. Arrivals peaked in 2012–2013 when 25,173 people arrived on boats. However, these numbers were still relatively low, not just globally but in comparison to Australia's migration programme more generally. For several decades, Australia has resettled about 190,000 skilled migrants through its migration programme, including in the years 2012–2013. Looking at these figures, it seems completely plausible that Australia could easily resettle far more refugees while also granting asylum to boat arrivals.

A similar line of argument advanced by the government is what I will call the "humanitarian argument". Many who have followed these issues will have heard the phrase, "stopping the boats to save lives at sea". Increasingly in recent years, policy shifts related to asylum in Australia have been justified in humanitarian terms and particularly as they save

---

[8] See the above section on important facts, figures and terms about Australia's onshore and offshore humanitarian programmes being linked in 1996.

lives at sea. In 2013, when re-introducing offshore processing, former Prime Minister Julia Gillard largely focused on the vulnerability of those seeking asylum, the risks of travelling to Australia by sea and the exploitative nature of "people smuggling". She went on to conclude that "[t]oday is the day that this House has risen above the politics of this issue and taken the action to save lives" (Gillard, 2012). Shortly after re-taking the Prime Ministership from Julia Gillard and in introducing increasingly harsh policy, which would ensure no boat arrivals would be resettled in Australia, Kevin Rudd stated that "Australians have had enough of seeing people drowning in the waters to our north". After the 2013 election, when the Liberal government took power, former Prime Minister Tony Abbott continued to justify these policies in the face of mounting criticism, after riots, violence and abuse had been widely reported in offshore detention centres. He stated that "[i]n any morality contest, preventing hundreds of deaths at sea surely justifies robust measures to prevent people smuggling" (Abbott, 2015). He even promoted the government's increasingly harsh approach as "[t]he most humanitarian, the most decent, the most compassionate thing you can do" (Cox, 2015). Upon being confronted by allegations of bribing people smugglers to return to Indonesia, he doubled down, stating that stopping the boats was "good for Australia, it's good for Indonesia and it's particularly good for all those who want to see a better world" (Medhora, 2015). The former Minister for Immigration, Peter Dutton has stated, "The Coalition's strong border security arrangements have ended the deaths at sea and enabled the removal of all children from detention" and "[w]ithout OSB [Operation Sovereign Borders] we know there would have been tens of thousands more people continuing to risk their lives on unsafe people smuggling boats and dying at sea" (Dutton, 2016). The humanitarian argument more or less suggests that Australian immigration detention, despite its flaws, is necessary to deter people risking dangerous journeys at sea. These concerns are not unfounded; as discussed earlier in this book, over 1400 people were recorded as dead or missing at sea and a significant number of these deaths occurred between late 2009 and late 2013 after the original Pacific Solution was repealed (The Border Crossing Observatory, n.d.). The humanitarian argument is similar to the argument above; that is, while stopping the boats isn't ideal, it is for the greater good as it saves lives at sea and allows us to resettle others.

There are a few things that can be said about this argument. This narrative often starts with asylum seekers boarding a boat but fails to consider other border controls put in place by the government that have led to dangerous travel (Nethery, Rafferty-Brown, & Taylor, 2013; Weber, 2007, 2013). That is, the increasingly restrictive policies implemented across the Asia-Pacific region championed by Australia have only exacerbated the issue of migration by sea. If processes were in place to assess asylum applications in Indonesia in a fair and timely manner, far fewer people would risk their lives attempting to make the journey to Australia by boat. If visa restrictions did not bar entry, those seeking protection would most likely fly to Australia. Manne (2002, p. 33) provides one disturbing example of how deterrence promotes dangerous journeys by sea. At the time, the Howard government had denied the reunion of refugee families (primarily as a deterrent), which led many to travel to Australia by boat to be reunited with family members:

> The astonishing cruelty of these laws was finally understood recently following the incident where 353 asylum seekers on their way to Australia drowned. Three of these were the daughters of an Iraqi man who had been granted refugee status but who was absolutely refused the right, under the new temporary visa regime, even to apply for reunion with his family. As it happens although his daughters died, the man's wife, after two days in the ocean, survived. The man was informed by the Minister that although he was perfectly at liberty to leave Australia to visit his grieving wife in Indonesia if he did so, because of the conditions attaching to his temporary visa, he would, unfortunately, be unable to return.

Several other points could also be made in response to the government's "humanitarian" argument, suggesting that the government's concern is disingenuous. One only needs to look at the harms of detention itself, boat turn-backs and the government's attacks on those who suggest seemingly reasonable alteratives.[9] Furthermore, the focus on deterrence has cost billions, which could have been used to implement far less

---

[9] I will discuss this in Chap. 5.

costly solutions to process asylum seekers. There are many other ways that dangerous travel could be disincentivized without resorting to immigration detention.[10]

So where does this leave us? As I said above, Australian immigration detention in its current form, along with related policies of denial and deterrence, cannot be justified. Reform is quite clearly needed. Does this mean that future reform should push for the abolition of detention completely? I believe that given current realities, immigration detention is defensible under very limited circumstances. It would, however, have to take on a drastically different form, and genuine attempts would have to be made to seek out alternative arrangements that do not rely on deterrence, particularly throughout the Asia-Pacific region. This also means that any future reform needs to be mindful of its potential regional impact.

The Ethics of Healthcare in Australian Immigration Detention

Discussions about the ethics of healthcare within Australian immigration detention centres have occurred largely in parallel to discussions about the ethics of asylum and migration above. I am not going to attempt to draw these literatures into conversation here, that is a task for another time. Below, I will outline some of the major ethical issues in the delivery of healthcare in detention, how they have been conceptualized and their proposed resolution.

---

[10] I will discuss alternatives in Chap. 5. Also see the literature on the humanitarian border. The humanitarian border has been described as a zone (or zones) of humanitarian government along the territorial edges of nation-states, often the political space separating rights holders and non-rights holders. The humanitarian border is related to other forms of governmentality such as surveillance, securitization, and militarization, and it has expanded largely because of the increasingly punitive response towards asylum seekers and refugees (Walters, 2011). While primarily concerned with alleviating suffering, the humanitarian border does not necessarily work in opposition to securitization and militarization; it may in fact shape and expand restrictive border policies. For example, "there are frequently occasions on which security practices and effects materialize within the institutions and practices of humanitarian government" (Walters, 2011, p. 147). The humanitarian border also gives insight into how humanitarian rhetoric and action may be co-opted for other purposes.

The ethics literature has given substantial consideration to explaining and conceptualizing how healthcare professionals negotiate their roles within detention. To do this, the literature has largely turned to the concept of dual loyalty (Briskman & Zion, 2014; Briskman, Zion, & Loff, 2010; Essex, 2014; Sanggaran, Ferguson, & Haire, 2014; Zion, Briskman, & Loff, 2012). Dual loyalty describes circumstances where healthcare professionals have to manage diverging interests between that of their patient and a third party. These conflicting obligations are not necessarily explicit; they can be implied or perceived, and the tension between loyalties can arise from "legal requirements, threats of professional or personal harm for non-compliance, the culture of the institution or society where the professional practices, or even from the professional's own sense of duty to the state" (Physicians for Human Rights, 2002). In Australian immigration detention, healthcare professionals often find themselves caught between loyalty to those detained and their obligations to the immigration department, security contractors and IHMS, all of whom have differing and conflicting priorities. Drawing on these concepts, the ethics literature has also attempted to provide guidance for healthcare professionals working within detention. For example, in responding to dual loyalty conflicts, the International Dual Loyalty Working Group proposed a comprehensive set of guidelines (Physicians for Human Rights, 2002). While these guidelines outline a range of circumstances where dual loyalty has been particularly problematic, they almost always call for healthcare professionals to place their obligations to the patient above all other interests. If healthcare professionals are to depart from this primary loyalty, it should first be sanctioned by "international standard-setting bodies competent to define the ethical obligations of a health professional" (Physicians for Human Rights, 2002) and that where there is no explicit guidance, healthcare professionals should not attempt to weigh the "interests of society or the state against the human rights of the individual" (Physicians for Human Rights, 2002).

The concept of complicity has also been used to a lesser extent to describe these conflicts (Essex, 2016; Jansen, Tin, & Isaacs, 2018), in particular Lepora and Goodin's (2013) framework of moral complicity. Lepora and Goodin (2013) suggest their model be used as a pragmatic tool to guide thinking, at the very least serving "as a useful heuristic in reminding us what questions we need to ask in assessing acts of complicity morally and comparing them with alternative courses of action" (p. 103). Lepora and Goodin (2013) suggest a minimum threshold for complicity. In short the threshold proposed is one where agents may contribute knowingly in some way to wrongdoing, but not necessarily share the same intentions as the principal wrongdoer. This threshold requires (a) a voluntary contribution (b) knowledge (or culpable ignorance) of the contributory role played by their actions and (c) knowledge (or culpable ignorance) of the primary wrongdoing to which they are contributing. Thus, the degree to which an agent may be complicit is influenced by a number of factors, requiring a number of questions to be asked. Most importantly, how bad the principal wrongdoing was, whether the agent voluntarily and knowingly contributed to it, how much of a contribution was made and to what degree the agent shared in the principal wrongdoer's purposes. Lepora and Goodin's (2013) framework provides a sophisticated way to begin to examine healthcare professional's contribution to wrongdoing, identifying (and in theory) and avoiding the more harmful aspects of the wrongdoing in question. In short, this framework helps healthcare professionals deliberate as to whether they should be involved in certain elements of the system or at all. Take the example of a healthcare professional involved in a deportation. If asked to conduct an assessment for a detainee who is due to be deported, the healthcare professional may opt to take up a position of advocacy, warning of the health and human rights consequences of deportation. They may frame their assessment broadly and make strong recommendations against such action on health and human rights grounds. On the other hand, as suggested by the asylum seeker's testimony cited in Chap. 3, healthcare professionals may become actively involved in a deportation, using chemical restraint and actively facilitating the aims of the immigration department. Quite clearly, one is more problematic than the other. Lepora and Goodin's (2013) framework provides a means to identify such conflicts and, in theory, avoid them or take a more appropriate course of action. I will discuss some broader critiques in the next chapter; however, it is worth noting here that minimizing complicity with wrongdoing may not necessarily lead to better health or healthcare for those detained, and furthermore, the realities found within detention and restrictions placed on healthcare professionals may mean that minimizing complicity is not always possible.

Writing specifically about Australian immigration detention Briskman and Zion (2014) offer pragmatic advice as to how healthcare professionals could respond to conflicts while working within detention. They call for healthcare professionals to engage in both advocacy and subversion, calling on healthcare professionals "to take political action that goes beyond kindness as either mild mannered or outraged dissidents" (p. 283). In this case, they define subversion as "dispensing acts of kindness that may not be valued or even prohibited by the employing or subcontracting authority" (p. 279) and advocacy as "a means for people to take action arising from their witnessing" (p. 279). They thus move beyond calling for absolute loyalty to the patient and begin to outline in more practical terms, how healthcare professionals could respond to the conflicts they face.

While the above concepts provide a foundation for action within detention centres, it has long been recognized that they simply don't offer a resolution to the issues detention creates. That is, for health professionals, even if treading the most ethical path and even if avoiding or subverting the most harmful elements of the system and otherwise acting in their patient's best interest (all things considered), the dilemmas remain. The very fact that healthcare professionals work in detention centres lends the system legitimacy it arguably doesn't deserve. A number of statements can be found hinting that we move away from discussions of health and healthcare purely in terms of clinical ethics, instead focusing on a more activist, political stance. Briskman and Zion (2014, p. 284) suggest that "[f]or the ethical health worker, a focus on maintaining and incrementally improving the system is vexed and the aspiration must be the abolition of the detention system". In aiming to achieve such change, Briskman, Zion, and Loff (2011) call for advocacy. Similarly Koutroulis (2003, p. 384) calls for healthcare professionals to take up "a more active political stance". Mares and Jureidini (2004, p. 526) ask, "At what point is advocacy at a social and political level justified, if not inevitable?". Recognizing that advocacy and reasoned argument had done little to sway a recalcitrant government, Berger (2016, p. 1) makes an impassioned call for protest:

> Advocates of humane treatment for asylum seekers are left once more scratching their heads and wondering how much more evidence is needed before anything will change? As doctors, we are now conditioned to believe that evidence is prime and that progress occurs as a result of refining the evidence base. Even in medicine, however, this is not a smooth process, and in the parallel universe of politics it is even less so. In fact, in our increasingly "post-factual" age, these rules are often reversed … Doctors in Australia must now make a mass public statement of their revulsion at the bipartisan support of our politicians for a policy of cruelty and oppression towards the innocent: "We are your doctors. We live our professional lives by a code of ethics over 2000 years in development. We say that what is happening in Australia is wrong and debases us all. We demand that this ill treatment cease." … I say to all Australian doctors—young, old, the political, and the apolitical—that not just our ethical credibility as a profession but our shared humanity depends on this action. Evidence based argument has failed. Your physical bodies are now needed, in their thousands, to proclaim a message of common decency.

These calls for more radical, political action have been encouraging. There is, however, far more that can be done. In the next chapter, I will bring together the above literatures and my discussions from Chaps. 2 and 3 to consider what reform should look like, the constraints on achieving reform and why current approaches to these issues by the healthcare community are inadequate.

References

Abbott, T. (2015). Australian diary. *The Spectator*. Retrieved from https://www.spectator.co.uk/2015/11/australian-diary-15/

Berger, D. (2016). Australia's torture of asylum seekers. *British Medical Journal*, 354:i4606

Briskman, L., & Zion, D. (2014). Dual loyalties and impossible dilemmas: Health care in immigration detention. *Public Health Ethics, 7*(3), 277–286.

Briskman, L., Zion, D., & Loff, B. (2010). Challenge and collusion: Health professionals and immigration detention in Australia. *The International Journal of Human Rights, 14*(7), 1092–1106. https://doi.org/10.1080/13642980903007649

Briskman, L., Zion, D., & Loff, B. (2011). Care or collusion in asylum seeker detention. *Ethics and Social Welfare, 6*(1), 37–55.

Carens, J. (1996). Realistic and idealistic approaches to the ethics of migration. *International Migration Review, 30*, 156–170.

Carens, J. (2013). *The ethics of immigration.* New York: Oxford University Press.

Cole, P. (2000). *Philosophies of exclusion: Liberal political theory and immigration.* Edinburgh: Edinburgh University Press.

Cox, L. (2015). Tony Abbott: Australians 'sick of being lectured to' by United Nations, after report finds anti-torture breach. *The Sydney Morning Herald.* Retrieved from https://www.smh.com.au/politics/federal/tony-abbott-australians-sick-of-being-lectured-to-by-united-nations-after-report-finds-antitorture-breach-20150309-13z3j0.html

Douglas, B., Higgins, C., Keski-Nummi, A., McAdam, J., & McLeod, T. (2014). *Beyond the boats: Building an asylum and refugee policy for the long term.* Retrieved from http://www.kaldorcentre.unsw.edu.au/publication/beyond-boats-building-asylum-and-refugee-policy-long-term

Dummett, M. (2002). *On immigration and refugees.* London: Routledge.

Dummett, M. (2004). Immigration. *Res Publica, 10*(2), 115–122.

Dutton, P. (2016). *More than 800 days of no illegal boat arrivals to Australia.* Retrieved from http://minister.homeaffairs.gov.au/peterdutton/Pages/More-than-800-days-of-no-illegal-boat-arrivals-to-Australia.aspx

Essex, R. (2014). Human rights, dual loyalties, and clinical Independence. *Journal of Bioethical Inquiry, 11*(1), 75–83.

Essex, R. (2016). Healthcare and Complicity in Australian Immigration Detention. *Monash Bioethics Review, 34*(2), 136–147.

Gibney, M. J. (2004). *The ethics and politics of asylum: Liberal democracy and the response to refugees.* Cambridge: Cambridge University Press.

Gibney, M. J. (2018). The ethics of refugees. *Philosophy Compass, 13*(10), e12521.

Gillard, J. (2012). *House of representatives on 15/08/2012, Questions without notice—People trafficking.* Retrieved from https://www.aph.gov.au/Parliamentary_Business/Hansard/Hansard_Display?bid=chamber/hansardr/e62f1e0d-13c9-446f-9296-82fd78823b75/&sid=0090

Hall, B. (2013). Few asylum seekers charged with crime. *The Sydney Morning Herald.* Retrieved from https://www.smh.com.au/politics/federal/few-asylum-seekers-charged-with-crime-20130228-2f98h.html

Jansen, M., Tin, A. S., & Isaacs, D. (2018). Prolonged immigration detention, complicity and boycotts. *Journal of Medical Ethics, 44*(2), 138–142.

Koutroulis, G. (2003). Detained asylum seekers, health care, and questions of human(e)ness. *Australian and New Zealand Journal of Public Health, 27*(4), 381–384.

Lepora, C., & Goodin, R. E. (2013). *On complicity and compromise*. Oxford: Oxford University Press.

Little, A., & Macdonald, T. (2015). Introduction to special issue: Real-world justice and international migration. *European Journal of Political Theory, 14*(4), 381–390.

Manne, R. (2002). Reflections on the Tampa 'crisis'. *Postcolonial Studies, 5*(1), 29–36.

Mares, S., & Jureidini, J. (2004). Psychiatric assessment of children and families in immigration detention—Clinical, administrative and ethical issues. *Australian and New Zealand Journal of Public Health, 28*(6), 520–526.

Medhora, S. (2015). Tony Abbott sticks to 'stop the boats' in face of claims people smugglers paid. *The Guardian*. Retrieved from https://www.theguardian.com/australia-news/2015/jun/14/tony-abbott-sticks-to-stop-the-boats-in-face-of-claims-people-smugglers-paid

Miller, D. (2005). Immigration: The case for limits. In A. I. Cohen & C. H. Wellman (Eds.), *Contemporary debates in applied ethics* (pp. 193–206). Oxford: Blackwell.

Miller, D. (2007). *National responsibility and global justice*. Oxford: Oxford University Press.

Morrison, S. (2014). *Stopping the boats to help Iraqis and Syrians*. Retrieved from https://trove.nla.gov.au/work/193134573?keyword=Stopping%20the%20boats%20to%20help%20Iraqis%20and%20Syrians

Nethery, A., Rafferty-Brown, B., & Taylor, S. (2013). Exporting detention: Australia-funded immigration detention in Indonesia. *Journal of Refugee Studies, 26*(1), 88–109.

Physicians for Human Rights. (2002). *Dual loyalty and human rights in health professional practice; Proposed guidelines & institutional mechanisms*. Retrieved from http://physiciansforhumanrights.org/library/reports/dual-loyalty-and-human-rights-2003.html

Sampson, R., Chew, V., Mitchell, G., & Bowring, L. (2015). *There are alternatives: A handbook for preventing unnecessary immigration detention*. Retrieved from https://idcoalition.org/wp-content/uploads/2016/01/There-Are-Alternatives-2015.pdf

Sanggaran, J.-P., Ferguson, G. M., & Haire, B. G. (2014). Ethical challenges for doctors working in immigration detention. *Medical Journal of Australia, 201*(7), 1–3.

Saul, B. (2012). Dark justice: Australia's indefinite detention of refugees on security grounds under international human rights law. *Melbourne Journal of International Law, 13*, 685.

Silverman, S. J. (2013). *The normative ethics of immigration detention in liberal states*. Doctoral dissertation, Oxford University, Oxford, UK.

Silverman, S. J. (2014). Detaining immigrants and asylum seekers: A normative introduction. *Critical Review of International Social and Political Philosophy, 17*(5), 600–617.

Sydes, M. (2019). Immigration, ethnicity, and neighborhood violence: considering both concentration and diversity effects. *Race and Justice*.

The Border Crossing Observatory. (n.d.). Australian border deaths database. Retrieved from https://www.monash.edu/arts/border-crossing-observatory/research-agenda/australian-border-deaths-database

Walters, W. (2011). Foucault and frontiers: notes on the birth of the humanitarian border. In U. Bröckling, S. Krasmann, T. Lemke (Eds.), *Governmentality: Current issues and future challenges* (pp. 138–164). New York: Routledge.

Walzer, M. (1983). *Spheres of justice*. New York: Basic Books.

Weber, L. (2007). Policing the virtual border: Punitive preemption in Australian offshore migration control. *Social Justice, 34*(2), 77–93.

Weber, L. (2013). Visible and virtual borders: Saving lives by 'seeing' sovereignty. *Griffith Law Review, 22*(3), 666–682.

Zion, D., Briskman, L., & Loff, B. (2012). Psychiatric ethics and a politics of compassion: The case of detained asylum seekers in Australia. *Journal of Bioethical Inquiry, 9*, 67–75.

5

Reforming Australian Immigration Detention

Overview

In this chapter I will outline how reform should look, the constraints of achieving reform and some fundamental reasons why present approaches to healthcare are not enough to challenge these constraints. First, I will outline an alternate vision for future policy. In doing this I propose what I see to be the minimum reform needed to address and protect the health, wellbeing and rights of asylum seekers in Australia. I draw on human rights to do this, and in outlining my alternative, I call for a major shift, consistent with the human rights instruments to which Australia is signatory. I will then consider the constraints on realizing this change. To do this I will start with Nethery's (2010) thesis which argues that to understand why Australia persists with its policies we need to consider a range of historical, social and political factors. I will also discuss the contemporary political constraints particularly relevant to the question posed by this book. Finally, I want to discuss some fundamental reasons why present approaches to healthcare are not enough to overcome these constraints. This is not to take away from those who have advocated for

© The Author(s) 2020
R. Essex, *The Healthcare Community and Australian Immigration Detention*,
https://doi.org/10.1007/978-981-15-7537-2_5

change for the last three decades; it is simply to say that we can and should do more, a case I will make in Chap. 6.

What Should Reform Look Like?

Australia's current policies of mandatory immigration detention are undoubtedly unjust, but what alternatives are available? In this section, I want to outline an alternate approach to Australian immigration detention and ultimately what we should demand in any future action. Having an idea of alternate policies or in this case the demands we want to make of the Australian government is important, because at least to some degree it will dictate the action we utilize. Like previous sections, I want to be pragmatic in considering these alternatives, but again, striking a balance between what is ideal and what is realistic is no easy task. For this reason, I am proposing what I believe would be the minimum reform needed to see significant improvements in the health and wellbeing of refugees and asylum seekers in Australian immigration detention centres.

Let's start by considering some modest goals, the reform of healthcare without the broader reform of immigration detention policies themselves. This could mean improving oversight of healthcare (such as calls for the re-introduction of independent advisory groups), increasing healthcare staffing, and creating greater accountability and transparency or improvements in healthcare facilities. For those offshore this could mean the introduction of processes around transfer to mainland Australia as was the case with the Medevac legislation. As discussed above, the Medevac legislation resulted in the transfer of more than 135 people from offshore locations to mainland Australia for medical treatment. While the Medevac legislation was undoubtedly a good thing and while it potentially saved a number of lives, change was short-lived and many continued to suffer offshore. Most fundamentally, it did little to address the cause of poor health in offshore detention centres. If we are to see substantial improvements in the health and wellbeing of those detained, more extensive change is needed. That is, regardless of how many improvements are made, while detention remains in its current form, while people are detained potentially indefinitely under the conditions I outlined in previous chapters, and while their suffering is used as a deterrent, we will not see any reasonable improvements in health and wellbeing. While we should welcome small victories like Medevac, if we are to address the health and wellbeing of asylum seekers, we need to demand broader systemic change.

Calling for major reform says little on its own, however, what should this reform look like? There are fortunately a number of reports we can turn to for guidance: the AHRC Human Rights Standards for Immigration Detention (2013) and the AHRC Risk Management in Immigration Detention (2019), the International Detention Coalition Legal Framework and Standards Relating to the Detention of Refugees Asylum Seekers and Migrants (2011) and the There Are Alternatives Report (Sampson, Chew, Mitchell, & Bowring, 2015) and the UNHCR Guidelines on the Applicable Criteria and Standards Relating to the Detention of Asylum-Seekers and Alternatives to Detention (2012). There are also a number of reports that deal with regional issues throughout the Asia-Pacific: the AHRC Pathways to Protection Report (2016), the Beyond the Boats Report (Douglas, Higgins, Keski-Nummi, McAdam, & McLeod, 2014) and the Where to From Here Report (Gleeson, 2016). Using these reports as a foundation, I want to sketch some potential outcomes if we were to pursue major reform consistent with Australia's human rights commitments. The discussion below is far from exhaustive, but I will deal with the major and perhaps more contentious points, starting with explaining some major points contained in the above reports.

The Beyond the Boats (2014) and Where to From Here (2016) reports came from two roundtable discussions focused on policy alternatives for Australian immigration detention, both onshore and throughout the Asia-Pacific region. While there was broad consensus on many points, neither report is a consensus statement, and each notes areas of difference in working towards a sustainable and humane regional framework. The need to balance a humane approach while minimizing deaths at sea weighs heavily in each report. The Beyond the Boats Report recognizes that "Australia cannot accommodate all those in need of protection, but can play a significant role in alleviating the pressure in the system" (p. 32) and goes on to call for an expansion in migration pathways for humanitarian resettlement,[1] swift resolution to unresolved claims,[2] fair and transparent processing of refugees and asylum seekers, and an end to mandatory detention except for initial health, security and identity checks "for the shortest possible time". There was the recognition that offshore detention was likely to remain into the immediate future with the report calling for the government to ensure that those offshore have access to "durable solutions". On this point the report also called for regional dialogue and the development of "a robust regional framework is a long-term goal" (p. 42). The Where to From Here report considered resettlement challenges throughout the Asia-Pacific region. These issues were discussed across four sessions. The first session dealt with offshore processing, again recognizing that it was unsustainable and that a solution was needed as a matter of urgency. The report discusses what an exit strategy from the arrangements in Nauru and Manus Island might look like and whether offshore processing could ever comply with international law. This report also dealt with the issue of how to improve safety at sea, discussing issues such as search and rescue, the targeted use of family reunification programmes, strategic resettlement and multilateral responsibility-sharing arrangements. This report again notes that international law prohibits policies that discriminate against certain groups of asylum seekers by ascribing them different rights based on their method of arrival. Protection throughout the Asia-Pacific region more generally was also considered, with discussions relating to the possible merits and limitations of advancing cooperation on refugee protection through a range of regional structures or models. A number of pragmatic "next steps" were identified, including strengthening existing human rights architecture, promoting practical pilot programmes and improving the region's capacity to protect asylum seekers at sea and respond to situations of mass displacement. Finally, safe pathways to protection were discussed, outlining how to expand and improve access to safe pathways, whether through traditional resettlement programmes or alternative approaches.

There Are Alternatives Report (2015) was written with a global audience in mind. The handbook presents a framework to prevent

---

[1] A particularly pertinent issue for policy as it stood at the time.

[2] At this time, there were tens of thousands of people living in the community on BVEs.

unnecessary detention and to resolve asylum applications in a fair, timely and humane manner from a community setting. It too is a practical guide, providing guidance on community alternatives, outlining minimum standards for these alternatives and providing guidance on decision making about such placements.

Guidance also exists for standards within detention, which, as I said above, could be justified in very limited circumstances. The AHRC Human Rights Standards for Immigration Detention (2013) aims to set "benchmarks for the humane treatment of people held in immigration detention" consistent with "internationally-accepted human rights standards" (p. 6). These guidelines are substantial and cover areas such as food, clothing, healthcare, security and facility management. In summary these guidelines suggest that "[i]mmigration detainees should enjoy the least restrictive environment possible, and the maxim that human rights are a floor, not a ceiling, should be at the forefront of decisions relating to conditions of detention for immigration detainees" (p. 6). Further guidance can be found in the AHRC Risk Management in Immigration Detention report (2019), which makes a range of recommendations related to risk management strategies within immigration detention centres, importantly recommending that the Australian government introduce legislation to place a maximum period of time on detention. Guidance on the length of time people should be detained can be found elsewhere. The UNHCR Guidelines (2012 p. 17) state that "detention must last only as long as reasonable efforts are being made to establish identity or to carry out the security checks, and within strict time limits established in law".

Beyond these reports and while many are based on human rights principles, human rights in themselves provide a powerful platform on which to begin to think about the demands the healthcare community should make.[3] Human rights are also particularly useful as they call for a stan-

---

[3] This is not to say that human rights are without shortcomings; after all, the Australian government has dismissed human rights concerns as they relate to Australian immigration detention, while at the same time remaining signatory to all major human rights instruments. While I will not get into the many critiques of human rights here, on this point it is important to note that human rights are more than just "toothless" international aspirations. Human rights can also be leveraged by those seeking change and those engaging in non-violent resistance. Furthermore, as the Australian government remains committed to almost every major instruments, they retain some power, for

dard to which Australia has already committed. It is worth repeating what I said in Chap. 2 here. Australia was a founding member of the UN and played a prominent role in the negotiation of the UN Charter in 1945. It was one of eight nations involved in drafting the Universal Declaration of Human Rights (UN General Assembly, 1948). Australia is signatory to almost every major human rights instrument, which commit Australia, at a minimum, to respect and cooperate on human rights internationally and, in certain circumstances, protect human rights extra-territorially (OHCHR, 2015).

The above reports and the human rights instruments to which Australia is signatory provide a foundation on which we can begin to think about what reform should look like. Before moving on to what such an approach might look like in practice, it is worthwhile considering some of the advantages of taking a rights-based approach in considering what we should be demanding of the government. I believe the most important contribution of such an approach for the healthcare community is that it shifts the focus of action from that of health and healthcare to that of rights and justice. This is based on the recognition that health is dependent on human rights first being upheld and that human rights cannot be upheld in Australian immigration detention (OHCHR & WHO, 2008).[4] That is, and similar to my argument above, while discussions in relation to health and healthcare within detention remain important, health and wellbeing will not be significantly improved without broader systemic change.

What would be the minimum change needed to protect the health and wellbeing of asylum seekers in Australia? First, onshore detention should only be used as a last resort and only if alternatives have been exhausted. Strict timeframes should be placed on detention. Vulnerable people (such as those who are pregnant or who have a disability), children and families should not be detained. Second, healthcare should be adequately resourced; that is, standards of care should go beyond that in the broader

---

example, criticisms made on human rights grounds have been contentious and often attacked by the government (e.g., the AHRC Forgotten Children report, something I will discuss below). For more, please see Essex (2019).

[4] This comes from the broader recognition that human rights are universal, indivisible, interdependent and interrelated (UN General Assembly, 1993).

Australian community in relation to staffing, timeliness and facilities. Furthermore healthcare services should be transparent and there should be adequate oversight. If the above demands were met, that is, if strict timeframes were placed on detention, such healthcare reforms would be far easier to implement. Finally, an end to offshore detention. While I acknowledge this is a longer-term goal, we should strive for alternatives as a matter of urgency. This includes a more robust regional framework that discourages unsafe journeys while moving away from deterrence. This point however calls for some caution. As noted in previous chapters, there remains the possibility that with any change throughout the Asia-Pacific region people may again decide to risk dangerous journeys at sea. This is not to say we are without direction on this point. In addition to the above reports, guidance can be found in a number of human rights instruments, to which Australia is also signatory. While human rights instruments acknowledge that governments may have a legitimate interest in controlling irregular migration and even an obligation to "prevent and suppress the smuggling of migrants by sea" (UN General Assembly, 2000, art. 7), this does not impact the rights and responsibilities of states in relation to the Convention and Protocol relating to the Status of Refugees (UN General Assembly, 1951, 1967), including the principle of non-refoulement (UN General Assembly, 2000). Furthermore, "detention policies aimed at deterrence are generally unlawful under international human rights law as they are not based on an individual assessment as to the necessity to detain" (UNHCR, 2012, p. 7).[5] Boat turn-backs of asylum seekers and refugees should cease. Furthermore, there is also an obligation to rescue vessels in distress.

There could of course be disagreement with the demands I have outlined above. I hope this discussion serves as a starting point and that within the healthcare community, different demands and ideals can be accommodated. In saying this, the point that major reform is needed shouldn't be too controversial; there is however a greater concern, that regardless of the reform we pursue, the fact that the Australian government has refused to negotiate or collaborate for a number of decades now. In the next section, I will consider the constraints on reform,

---

[5] Also see UNHCR Conclusion on Protection Safeguards in Interception Measures (2003).

explaining why Australia has failed to entertain these seemingly reasonable demands and why Australia continues to persevere with its present
policies.

Constraints on Reform

Fortunately, I don't have to start from scratch when discussing the factors
that constrain Australia in taking a more humane approach. Below I will
first provide some context to this question, by drawing on Nethery (2010)
who sought to explain the closely related question of why Australia continues to persevere with these policies despite longstanding criticism and
their well-established harms. I will then discuss what I see to be the major
constraints on reform today, exploring the steps the Australian government has taken to consolidate power in the implementation and administration of Australian immigration detention.

Why Administrative Detention?

Nethery (2010) argues that to explain why Australian immigration detention persists, we need to consider a number of historical, social and political factors. While she doesn't solely focus on refugees and asylums seekers
and instead looks at administrative detention as a whole, this thesis provides useful context in understanding why Australia does what it does
today, showing that multiple factors explain exclusion and the detention
of outsiders.

While Australian immigration detention is uniquely harmful, these
policies are not completely novel. Present-day policies of immigration
detention can be situated within a broader history of exclusion in relation
to migration. Nethery (2010) and Bashford and Strange (2002) highlight
a number of similarities and continuities with other forms of administrative detention which have been used since European settlement in
Australia. Drawing on the examples of Aboriginal reserves, quarantine
stations and enemy alien internment camps, Nethery (2010) identifies
five distinguishing features of administrative detention. First,

administrative detention has historically been justified, at least in part, in response to a moral panic. Second, administrative detention has historically been an act of executive power, often shutting out decision making by the judiciary. Third, administrative detention highlights the "complex and qualified nature of belonging" (p. 124). In other words, throughout history, administrative detention has communicated to different groups at different times—even those who were Australian citizens or naturalized Australians—that regardless of what they do, they will never fully belong. Fourth, administrative detention maintains boundaries, both social and geographic. That is, it has been used not just to control those external to Australia but also as a means of controlling those already in Australia. Finally, administrative detention has functioned to exclude from society with the permanency of this exclusion often being arbitrary.[6] Nethery (2010, p. 123) concludes that

> the study of administrative detention in Australia is ultimately the study of the classification of people into social groups, the identification of some of these groups as outsiders to Australian society, and the attempt by governments to control and regulate these groups. Implicit in this process is the notion that there is an ideal Australian identity, and the categories of people subject to administrative detention diverge from this identity in some way.

In explaining the social function of administrative detention, Nethery (2010) draws on a number of literatures to highlight three key aspects of Australian immigration detention: incarceration, classification and control, explaining what she calls the "how", "who" and "why" of administrative detention. In explaining how administrative detention achieves its ends, she draws on a range of theorists to argue that detention fulfils certain functions for those on the outside and self-perpetuates by creating and managing delinquent populations (Foucault, 2012; Garland, 2001).

---

[6] Drawing on historical examples, Nethery (2010, p. 126) suggests that "cases of release occurred alongside cases where people were permanently excluded" and that the decision making in relation to who was released appeared arbitrary. However, this was also influenced by a number of factors including "the degree of moral panic or other (including more humanitarian) domestic social pressures, concerns about race, national security, demand for labour, risk of infection, and international pressure" (p. 126).

That is, detention not only controls but also dehumanizes and alienates those detained, reinforcing narratives of illegality and threat. Furthremore detention provides a "spectacle" that shows the government is in control of this threat. Weber (2007) suggests that the spectacle of Australian immigration detention and particularly offshore processing has "nation-binding value". Detention in this sense as a "solution" is "immediate, easy to implement, and can claim to 'work' as a punitive end in [itself] even when [it] fails in all other respects" (Nethery, 2010 p. 139).

Nethery (2010) goes on to explain who is detained. While the majority of asylum seekers who have arrived by boat have been detained, other groups also need to be accounted for, including those who have over-stayed or had their visa cancelled. Nethery (2010) argues that racialization does not fully explain Australia's approach towards administrative detention, nor does it adequately explain why some individuals are detained and others who are seemingly similar are not. She argues that classification provides a complementary approach to racialized explanations, drawing on Durkheim, Solovay, Mueller, and Catlin (1938) to explain the production of social outsiders and M. Douglas (2003) to explain social relations and classification. Together these theories explain why those detained are seen as outsiders, why they are a perceived threat to society and why detention may be understood as a response to this.

Finally, in explaining why, Nethery (2010) argues that the main social and political function of administrative detention is control. The government re-enforces perceived control through a number of means beyond detaining and classifying people. She begins with Cohen's (1972) theory of moral panic to show not only how minor events provoke disproportionate responses but also how these responses may be manipulated to serve greater social and political interests. In the Australian context, control is reflected in the increasing executive power and the extra-legal nature of immigration detention, particularly in offshore centres (Australian Parliamentary Select Committee, 2015). Themes of control have been present in political rhetoric and debates for decades (McKenzie & Hasmath, 2013). As Cronin (1993, p. 87) notes, the government frequently offers "control rhetoric" while the opposition highlights "control failings".[7] Re-enforcing the importance of examining Australian immigration detention historically and as part of a larger administrative detention regime, Nethery (2010, pp. 147–148) concludes:

> The development of administrative detention, like judicial incarceration, is a response to perceived social, economic and political problems, particularly in times of rapid social change or crisis. Like judicial incarceration, administrative detention persists because it fulfils certain functions for those on the outside, and not because of what it achieves for those incarcerated … Administrative detention does not purport to benefit those detained, and functions only for confinement and exclusion … Another key difference is that administrative detention incarcerates groups of people, rather than individuals. [In order to be subject to administrative detention, o]ne is not convicted, put on trial and sentenced for a particular act … Instead, people are incarcerated because they belong to a certain category … Immigration detention in Australia is an attempt to control entry into the population. It is a response to social, economic and political problems attributed to people who are ethnically or racially different.

While the above social and historical factors provide a broader account of immigration detention, they cannot fully account for the treatment of asylum seekers and refugees, particularly those who have arrived by boat. This group is subjected to the most harsh and exclusionary treatment. There are a number of other theories and concepts that provide additional insight into this. Nethery (2010) suggests that racialization, fear of invasion, globalization and economic insecurity are key to understanding this.

Racialization has an ongoing impact on Australia's approach towards refugees. This has a historical basis, in Australia's immigration policies, from white Australia to the rise of the anti-immigration One Nation party in the 1990s and its recent resurgence in 2016 (Perera & Pugliese, 1997). While taking a number of forms, racialization remains present in rhetoric and policy to this day, serving to perpetuate historical exclusion

---

[7] As will be discussed later in this chapter, however, these differences are often marginal, and both major political parties have largely supported the major elements of deterrence.

(Every & Augoustinos, 2007). Nethery (2010) highlights a thought experiment:

> Imagine that in the next few months political conditions in Zimbabwe forced hundreds of white farmers and their families to flee their country without papers or passports. Imagine that the farmers left their wives and children in camps in a contiguous African country and flew to Australia unlawfully. Imagine that on arrival they were detained, despatched at once to the detention centres at Port Hedland and Woomera, kept ignorant of their legal rights and not granted access to a lawyer, and were required to remain in the centres for very many months, uncertain of their fate. Imagine, finally, that they were eventually released, granted a temporary protection visa, refused access to services available to first-class refugees, informed that they had stolen places from people more genuinely in need and forbidden to apply for reunion with the wives and children they had left behind in the squalid setting of an African refugee camp ... [an Australian government] would face overwhelming national outrage. (Manne, 2001, p. 78)

This, however, is no longer a thought experiment. In March 2018, then Immigration Minister, Peter Dutton, suggested that Australia should fast-track white South African farmers' claims for protection because of the "horrific circumstances" they faced. These calls came at a time when South Africa was attempting to pursue legal changes to allow the redistribution of farm land to black South Africans without compensation (Karp, 2018). The persecution which the government claimed existed was blatantly false (Royal Melbourne Institute of Technology, Australian Broadcasting Corporation [RMIT ABC] Fact Check, 2018). Other reasons were given as to why "a civilised country like [Australia]" should help (Karp, 2018). Dutton went on, stating, "[w]e want people who want to come here, abide by our laws, integrate into our society, work hard, not lead a life on welfare. And I think these people deserve special attention and we're certainly applying that special attention now" (Karp, 2018).

Despite this fairly blatant example, racialization alone does not explain Australia's response to asylum seekers and refugees. Nethery (2010, p. 60) explores what she calls a "more complex, deep-seated fear of invasion into the Australian psyche". She contends that this can be attributed to two keys aspects of Australia's history: firstly, Australia's colonial past and the devastating dispossession of Australia's Indigenous peoples.[8] European settlers considered Australia "terra nullius" when settlement began in 1788. Terra nullius refers to "land that is legally deemed to be unoccupied or uninhabited"; in Latin it can be translated as "land belonging to no one" ("Terra Nullius", n.d.). This has meant that territory in Australia has always been contested, creating a latent fear, that it will one day be reclaimed (Burke, 2008). Secondly, Australia's geographical location places it as an "outpost" of Asia leaving it vulnerable to invasion. Both of these factors have led to what Papastergiadis (2006) has termed an "invasion complex". A number of analyses have demonstrated how political rhetoric and the media have both manipulated and perpetuated fear of asylum seekers and refugees, particularly those who arrive by boat (Austin & Fozdar, 2016; Bleiker, Campbell, Hutchison, & Nicholson, 2013; Cooper, Olejniczak, Lenette, & Smedley, 2016; Ellis, Fulton, & Scott, 2016; Leach, 2003; Lueck, Due, & Augoustinos, 2015; Maley, 2003; McKay, Thomas, & Warwick Blood, 2011; McLaren & Patil, 2016; Pickering, 2001). This fear is disproportionate; it has little basis in reality (Burke, 2008), and it has been constructed and used strategically by politicians to achieve policy objectives. Lawrence (2006, p. 40) argues:

> In deliberately portraying asylum seekers as a threat, the Howard government succeeded in gaining traction for the bizarre notion that desperate people in leaky boats were somehow a threat to our national security. It counted on being able to arouse our fear of being overwhelmed by strangers envious of our good fortune. Perhaps our own deep knowledge that we are alien invaders who have stolen the land we occupy allowed them to feed this anxiety.

In addition to racialization and a fear of invasion, McNevin (2007) and Hage (2003) offer a further perspective on Australia's approach towards asylum seekers and refugees. Even though each takes a different

---

[8] This has far broader implications and has shaped many aspects of Australian life today. How it impacts on Australia's approach to migration deserves greater attention.

approach to the issue, they both highlight anxiety arising from economic insecurity due to globalization and the increasing movement of people across borders. A recent example of this came when in 2016 the former Immigration Minister, Peter Dutton, attempted to exploit such fears by claiming that illiterate and innumerate asylum seekers and refugees would be taking Australian jobs (Karp, 2016).

Nethery's (2010) thesis gives context in explaining Australian immigration detention's exceptional status. Its most important contribution, at least for our purposes, is that we should resist seeking simple explanations for these issues. Australia has turned to immigration detention to "manage" outsiders throughout its history and this fear of the other sits deep within the Australian psyche. Today, however, what are the major constraints on achieving the demands outlined earlier in this chapter? I will outline two pervasive issues, which I believe any future response needs to take into account, namely the exceptional status of immigration detention as administrative detention and government's secrecy and hostility towards alternatives.

Structural and Institutional Constraints on Reform Today

The Australian government wields substantial power in relation to Australian immigration detention. The Migration Act (1958) and the Migration Regulations (1994) are the two main pieces of legislation that govern Australia's refugee and immigration policy. This legislation contains little detail about the conditions in which people are detained or how healthcare should be administered. It also makes no distinction between adults, children and other vulnerable people. There are also no limits on the duration of detention. The Migration Act (1958) permits indefinite detention as does Australia's constitution. This was tested in the High Court of Australia in 1994 when a Palestinian man who was born in Kuwait, Ahmed Al-Kateb, was refused a protection visa. Unable to be returned to both Kuwait and Gaza, he was effectively stateless and facing indefinite detention in Australia (Al–Kateb v Godwin, 2004).

Importantly in this ruling, the High Court of Australia re-affirmed that indefinite immigration detention was constitutionally permissible as it was a form of administrative detention. Because of its extra-judicial nature, there are few other checks on the power the Australian government wields. Human rights, at least in a legal sense, have also failed.[9] Despite having agreed to be bound by a number of major international human rights treaties, Australia has no bill of rights and has incorporated very few of its international commitments into domestic law. These issues are only further exacerbated by detention arrangements offshore, which only further dilute accountability and allow the Australian government to divest itself from the consequences of these policies.

A further check on power could come from political opposition. While some minor parties in Australia have long opposed immigration detention and other policies of deterrence, both major political parties have supported the core elements of these policies, as discussed by Grewcock (2013, p. 11):

> Both the [then] ruling Labor party and the opposition Liberal-National party coalition share a mutual disdain for the arrival of any new boat bringing refugees into Australian waters, distinguishing themselves only by a willingness to blame the other for allowing such breaches of Australia's forward defences or indulging in squabbles over the impact of government policy on refugee movements in the region. While this occasionally throws up superficial differences in emphasis about how best to 'stop the boats', there is, fundamentally, a high level of bipartisan agreement that unauthorised refugees should be deterred through measures such as the mandatory and indefinite detention of all unauthorised non-citizens; the use of offshore processing; extensive naval interdiction programmes; and a punitive anti-people-smuggling regime.

---

[9] See my comments earlier regarding the shortcomings of human rights.

Secrecy and Government Hostility

While the Australian government wields extensive power in relation to Australian immigration detention and while there has been little political opposition, successive governments have only further sought to consolidate this power by limiting oversight, attacking critics and rejecting cooperative action. Nethery and Holman (2016) suggest there are at least five ways the Australian government has restricted transparency. First, by framing the issue of refugee and asylum seeker boat arrivals as one of national security. The securitization of immigration issues has allowed the government to restrict and control the information provided to the public. For example, the government has for many years declined to report on "on water matters" (O'Brien, 2013). Second, there has been little accountability for contractors working within centres and contractor performance has been largely unregulated. Third, for centres offshore, the Australian government has capitalized on the deficits in democratic processes in Nauru and Papua New Guinea. That is, the Australian government has long disputed whether it has any responsibility for offshore centres and has capitalized on the control both the Nauruan and Papua New Guinean governments exercise over institutions like the judiciary and the media. Fourth, the government has restricted access to journalists and even referred a number to the Australian Federal Police for investigation. For example, the Federal Police accessed the phone records of the former Medical Director of IHMS, Dr. Peter Young, who spoke out against these policies (Farrell, 2016). Finally, the denial of access to independent observers. For decades the government has denied access to multiple international and domestic human rights organizations; in relation to health, in late 2013, the government disbanded the Immigration Health Advisory Group, an independent group of experts who provided oversight and advice on healthcare within detention centres (Laughland, 2013).[10] The government has also attempted to block the release of data related to the mental health of detainees (Young & Gordon, 2016) and long blocked research within centres (Steel & Silove, 2004).

---

[10] While there has arguably been some ongoing medical oversight, this has not been independent or transparent (e.g., Farrell, 2018).

There are a few further examples worth noting about the secrecy promoted by the government, its hostility towards criticism and its dismissal of cooperative efforts aimed at reform.

In 2015, Save the Children staff, who were contracted to deliver services on Nauru, were removed from the island. The government accused them of encouraging asylum seekers to self-harm and of fabricating stories of abuse. Furthermore, Save the Children offices were raided by Nauruan police and equipment was seized in an attempt to hunt down journalists' sources (Farrell, 2015a, 2015b). The Australian government later apologized and paid compensation to these staff members, admitting that there was no legal basis for the raids and their expulsion (Davidson, 2016). Attacks have also extended to the Australian Human Rights Commission. After the release of the AHRC (2014) Forgotten Children Report, the government called for the resignation of the Commission's President, Gillian Triggs in a series of vitriolic attacks (Borrello & Glenday, 2015). The government has also attacked a number of other contractors and individuals. As was noted in Chap. 3, in 2018, MSF was removed from Nauru. In the same year two of IHMS chief medical officers were also removed from Nauru. Dr. Christopher Jones' visa was reportedly cancelled after disagreements with the Nauruan government about medical transfers while Dr. Nicole Montana was removed from Nauru with IHMS citing a "breach of regional processing centre rules" (Koziol, 2018).

As a whole, Australian immigration detention is not just harmful; the measures taken by the Australian government strike at a range of democratic norms (Reilly, Appleby, & Laforgia, 2014). Evidence and reason, particularly in more recent years, have seemingly become increasingly irrelevant, with the government seemingly immune to the suffering it has created. It is no understatement to say that anybody seeking reform has their work cut out for them. Before outlining my case in the next chapter, I will outline what I see to be some of the shortcomings of how the healthcare community have approached these issues.

Why Current Approaches to Healthcare Are Inadequate

In this chapter I have outlined what reform should entail if we are to address the health and wellbeing of asylum seekers and refugees. I then outlined some of the major constraints on achieving these demands. I will now discuss some of the most common pitfalls in the healthcare communities' present approach to Australian immigration detention and reasons why this approach inadequate to overcome the above constraints. First, current responses tend to individualize health and healthcare, including the resolution of clinical and ethical dilemmas faced in detention, distracting from the broader systemic injustice of these policies. Second, and following this point, there has been no clear strategy outlined that demands broader social and political change.

Before moving on, however, it is worth clarifying that my critique below is not to say that the need for major systemic reform has gone unrecognized or that we should dismiss present approaches completely. It is also not to take away from those who have advocated for change for the last three decades. It is worth reflecting on some of contributions of these efforts. First, the existing efforts have thoroughly documented the issues facing healthcare professionals and how government policy deliberately undermines healthcare. Testimony has been gathered from numerous sources and given insight as to why healthcare professionals engaged and persevered working in immigration detention centres (Briskman, Zion, & Loff, 2011). Dual loyalty (and its related concepts) has provided a straightforward way to conceptualize the issues and conflicts that undermine almost every aspect of healthcare within detention. This research has informed multiple inquiries and has provided a platform for advocacy outside of immigration detention. The restrictions placed on healthcare and detentions' impact on health and wellbeing have been central to calls for reform for over two decades. Testimony from healthcare professionals has also formed a central part of a number of legal challenges. For the same period of time, this research has continued to help keep these issues in the spotlight, both within and outside of academic circles, domestically and internationally. Outside of detention, healthcare professionals and professional bodies have led and bolstered the impact of protest, which has, at different times, been relatively influential.

Despite all of this, however, I believe there is room to critically reflect. Returning to my first criticism, the concepts and guidance found throughout the literature and discussed in professional statements in Chaps. 3 and 4 too often frame issues as being the responsibility of the individual healthcare professional. While this criticism is somewhat new in relation to Australian immigration detention, it fits within a larger literature that has critically examined professional codes of ethics (Sutrop, 2011). One major criticism is that codes of ethics tend to isolate health and healthcare from the broader systemic and political forces that shape them, often reducing issues of justice and rights to clinical dilemmas and resulting in healthcare professionals being individually responsible for their resolution. Furthermore, this focus often obscures the source of these problems and how they could be addressed, failing to inform strategy for broader social and political change.

For example, looking again at the bioethics literature discussed in Chap. 4, both dual loyalty and Lepora and Goodin's (2013) framework of complicity start with the assumption of conflict or wrongdoing. Both also focus on the healthcare professionals' response in either mediating or resolving this conflict. While it is possible to have relatively benign dual loyalty conflicts, this is not the case in Australian immigration detention. What should be issues of rights and justice are framed as clinical dilemmas, for which individual healthcare professionals are responsible. While discussions about healthcare and ethical conduct within detention centres should continue, we should be under no illusions about the limitations of such action. These concepts say little about how to truly address the sources of these conflicts or the initial wrongdoing that creates them.

Professional bodies have fallen into a similar trap. The AMA (2015) position statement, for example, recognizes that reform is needed, and calls for a solution to "prolonged, indeterminate detention … as a matter of urgency". It recognizes that "immigration detention centres violates basic human rights and contributes adversely to their [i.e. detainees'] health" while at the same time calling for healthcare professionals to "at all times insist that the rights of their patients be respected and not allow lower standards of care to be provided".[11] This puts healthcare professionals in an impossible position. Human rights cannot be protected within Australian immigration detention centres. The RANZCP (2016) guidance raises similar issues. The limitations facing healthcare professionals, however, are more squarely acknowledged, with the RANZCP (2016) stating that they are "concerned that the capacity of psychiatrists to provide high quality mental healthcare and to practice ethically and effectively in detention centres and alternative places of detention is currently limited".

This approach has other shortcomings. It also leaves a number of questions unanswered regarding clinical and ethical decision making for healthcare professionals working within detention. There remains a stark contrast between the concepts and guidance discussed in Chap. 4 and the testimony of healthcare professionals discussed in Chap. 3. Sanggaran and Zion (2015, p. 561) have described this as "the chasm between acceptable standards of medical care and what we know is being practiced in immigration detention". I have written elsewhere that not only does healthcare within detention fail to be provided to a standard found in the broader Australian community, but that such a standard makes little sense as long as detention remains in its current form, that while "Australian immigration detention is geared to promote suffering as a means of deterrence, there looks to be few ways to address these issues in any capacity, let alone achieve health and healthcare that are equivalent to that found in the broader Australian community" (Essex, 2016, p. 979). This does not mean that standards in relation to healthcare should be abandoned,[12] however, defining them is far more difficult than simply falling back on the fiction of a standard equivalent to the broader Australian community. Other questions remain. If healthcare professionals are acting in their patient's best interests, as they would in the broader

---

[11] The AMA (2015, para. 13) position statement also calls for "professional medical organisations should develop a set of ethical guidelines to support medical practitioners working with asylum seekers and refugees in whatever context". This has yet to happen and again seems to be passing responsibility to engage with the very difficult issues healthcare within Australian immigration detention raises.

[12] As was discussed above, the RACP (2015) is the only professional body to acknowledge the difficulties in defining a standard of care and refrains from providing advice.

Australian community, does this mean they should advocate for their release or simply pursue care as usual? What does upholding a patient's dignity mean when their rights are being intentionally violated? What is autonomy for those locked up indefinitely? Dignity could mean resistance. Autonomy could mean insisting on healthcare outside of detention. Over 80% of paediatricians consider immigration detention to be a form of child abuse (Corbett, Gunasekera, Maycock, & Isaacs, 2014). Clearly providing well-resourced paediatric care is not enough. There is substantial scope for further discussion about these issues, but there also is a need to look beyond them, as without significant reform, many of these dilemmas will remain.

In summary, while existing concepts and guidance may be used to highlight the need for systemic, social and political change, their framing of issues as being the responsibility of the individual healthcare professional have ensured they say little about how such change could be achieved. This is not to say that the literature and professional bodies haven't recognized the need for reform or the need to take more assertive social and political action, which leads to my next issue.

Throughout the literature and as noted in Chap. 4, a number of statements can be found hinting that we move away from discussions of health and healthcare purely in terms of clinical ethics, instead focusing on a more activist, political stance. Briskman and Zion (2014, p. 284) suggest that "[f]or the ethical health worker, a focus on maintaining and incrementally improving the system is vexed and the aspiration must be the abolition of the detention system". Beyond this and other calls for action, however, little has been said about strategy or how healthcare professionals should contribute to such change. This has resulted in at least two major issues as it relates to broader social and political change. First, action has been led from the "bottom-up"; that is, healthcare professionals have often taken it upon themselves to protest, with the majority of action being improvised and reactive.[13] This is not a problem in itself and such action has at times been relatively impactful; however, without an overarching strategy, past action has likely failed to recognize and capitalize on many opportunities. Second, action has often fallen back on

---

[13] Many examples of this were outlined in Chap. 3.

familiar repertoires such as advocacy, research and strongly worded statements, the majority of which assumes that the government is open to evidence and change. This clearly isn't the case. Some have expressed their frustrations with this. Sanggaran and Zion (2015, p. 561) ask, "[W]hat more could be done to make us pay attention to the need to move beyond the multiple peak body position statements?". Berger (2016, p. 1) recognizes that "evidence of ill treatment alone is not going to change things and that in this topsy-turvy world it may even make things worse". Despite these more recent frustrations, however, the discussion about what to do and what action could be effective has evolved little beyond McNeill's (2003, p. 501) recognition of these difficulties over 15 years earlier:

> The acceptable public health strategies of disseminating information and advocacy may not be enough. Something more is needed. Not violence—although the Australian Government has resorted to it—for the obvious reason that in resorting to violence we become the perpetrators of harm ourselves. Reasoned advocacy may not be sufficient. It is time for a more passionate response … These actions may go beyond dissemination of information and reasoned advocacy, and could include any number of political activities including: participating in demonstrations, direct lobbying of government members and political parties, and withdrawal of services.

References

Australian Human Rights Commission. (2013). *Human rights standards for immigration detention*. Retrieved from https://www.humanrights.gov.au/our-work/asylum-seekers-and-refugees/publications/human-rights-standards-immigration-detention

Australian Human Rights Commission. (2014). *The forgotten children: National inquiry into children in immigration detention*. Retrieved from https://www.humanrights.gov.au/our-work/asylum-seekers-and-refugees/publications/forgotten-children-national-inquiry-children

Australian Human Rights Commission. (2016). *Pathways to protection: A human rights-based response to the flight of asylum seekers by sea*. Retrieved from https://www.humanrights.gov.au/our-work/asylum-seekers-and-refugees/publications/pathways-protection-human-rights-based-response

Australian Human Rights Commission. (2019). *Risk management in immigration detention*. Retrieved from https://humanrights.gov.au/our-work/asylum-seekers-and-refugees/publications/risk-management-immigration-detention-2019

Al–Kateb v Godwin. (2004). High court of Australia 37.

Australian Medical Association. (2015). *Position statement on health care of asylum seekers and refugees - 2011. Revised 2015*. Retrieved from https://ama.com.au/position-statement/health-care-asylum-seekers-and-refugees-2011

Austin, C., & Fozdar, F. (2016). Framing asylum seekers: The uses of national and cosmopolitan identity frames in arguments about asylum seekers. *Identities, 25*(3), 1–21.

Australian Parliamentary Select Committee. (2015). *Select Committee on the recent allegations relating to conditions and circumstances at the Regional Processing Centre in Nauru*. Retrieved from https://www.aph.gov.au/Parliamentary_Business/Committees/Senate/Regional_processing_Nauru/Regional_processing_Nauru/Final_Report

Bashford, A., & Strange, C. (2002). Asylum–seekers and National Histories of detention. *Australian Journal of Politics & History, 48*(4), 509–527.

Berger, D. (2016). Australia's torture of asylum seekers. *British Medical Journal, 354*:i4606

Bleiker, R., Campbell, D., Hutchison, E., & Nicholson, X. (2013). The visual dehumanisation of refugees. *Australian Journal of Political Science, 48*(4), 398–416.

Borrello, E., & Glenday, J. (2015). Gillian Triggs: Tony Abbott says Government has lost confidence in Human Rights Commission president. *Australian Broadcasting Corporation News*. Retrieved from http://www.abc.net.au/news/2015-02-24/gillian-triggs-says-brandis-wants-her-to-quit-rights-commission/6247520

Briskman, L., & Zion, D. (2014). Dual loyalties and impossible dilemmas: Health care in immigration detention. *Public Health Ethics, 7*(3), 277–286.

Briskman, L., Zion, D., & Loff, B. (2011). Care or collusion in asylum seeker detention. *Ethics and Social Welfare, 6*(1), 37–55.

Burke, A. (2008). *Fear of security: Australia's invasion anxiety*. Cambridge: Cambridge University Press.

Cohen, S. (1972). *Folk devils and moral panics: The creation of the mods and rockers*. London: MacGibbon & Kee.

Cooper, S., Olejniczak, E., Lenette, C., & Smedley, C. (2016). Media coverage of refugees and asylum seekers in regional Australia: A critical discourse analysis. *Media International Australia, 162*(1), 78–89.

Corbett, E., Gunasekera, H., Maycock, A., & Isaacs, D. (2014). Australia's treatment of refugee and asylum seeker children: The views of Australian paediatricians. *The Medical Journal of Australia, 201*(7), 393–398.

Cronin, K. 1993. A culture of control: An overview of immigration policy-making. In J. Jupp and M. Kabala (eds), *The Politics of Australian Immigration*. Canberra: Australian Government Publishing Service.

Davidson, H. (2016). Immigration department compensates save the children over sacked Nauru workers. *The Guardian*. Retrieved from https://www.theguardian.com/australia-news/2016/may/06/immigration-department-pays-compensation-sacked-nauru-save-the-children-workers

Douglas, B., Higgins, C., Keski-Nummi, A., McAdam, J., & McLeod, T. (2014). *Beyond the boats: Building an asylum and refugee policy for the long term*. Retrieved from http://www.kaldorcentre.unsw.edu.au/publication/beyond-boats-building-asylum-and-refugee-policy-long-term

Douglas, M. (2003). *Purity and danger: An analysis of concepts of pollution and taboo*. London: Routledge.

Durkheim, E. (1938). The Rules of Sociological Method (S. A. Solovay & J. H. Mueller, Trans). G. E. G. Catlin (Ed.). Chicago: The University of Chicago Press.

Ellis, K., Fulton, J., & Scott, P. (2016). Detention attention: Framing a Manus Island riot. *Pacific Journalism Review, 22*(1), 74.

Essex, R. (2016). A community standard: Equivalency of healthcare in Australian immigration detention. *Journal of Immigrant and Minority Health, 19*(4), 974–981.

Essex, R. (2019). Contentious politics, human rights and Australian immigration detention. *Australian Journal of Human Rights, 25*(3), 376–390.

Every, D., & Augoustinos, M. (2007). Constructions of racism in the Australian parliamentary debates on asylum seekers. *Discourse & Society, 18*(4), 411–436.

Farrell, P. (2015a). Nauru police take phones and laptops from save the children staff and others. *The Guardian*. Retrieved from https://www.theguardian.com/world/2015/oct/13/nauru-police-take-phones-and-laptops-from-save-the-children-staff-and-others

Farrell, P. (2015b). Police carry out more raids on Save the children staff at Nauru detention centre. *The Guardian*. Retrieved from https://www.theguardian.com/world/2015/oct/22/police-carry-out-more-raids-on-save-the-children-staff-at-nauru-detention-centre

Farrell, P. (2016). Australian police accessed phone records of asylum whistle-blower. *The Guardian*. Retrieved from https://www.theguardian.com/australia-news/2016/may/24/australian-police-accessed-phone-records-of-asylum-whistleblower

Farrell, P. (2018). The secret committee determining medical transfers from Nauru and Manus Island. *Australian Broadcasting Corporation News*. Retrieved from https://www.abc.net.au/news/2018-12-04/secret-immigration-committee-medical-transfers-from-nauru-manus/10579072

Foucault, M. (2012). *Discipline & punish: The birth of the prison*. New York: Vintage.

Garland, D. (2001). *The culture of control: Crime and social order in contemporary society*. Oxford: Oxford University Press.

Gleeson, M. (2016). *Where to from here? Report from the expert roundtable on regional cooperation and refugee protection in the Asia-Pacific*. Retrieved from https://www.kaldorcentre.unsw.edu.au/publication/where-to-from-here

Grewcock, M. (2013). Australia's ongoing border wars. *Race & Class, 54*(3), 10–32.

Hage, G. (2003). *Against paranoid nationalism*. Annandale: Pluto Press.

International Detention Coalition. (2011). *Legal framework and standards relating to the detention of refugees, asylum seekers and migrants*. Retrieved from https://idcoalition.org/publication/legal-framework/

Karp, P. (2016). Peter Dutton says 'illiterate' refugees would be 'taking Australian jobs'. *The Guardian*. Retrieved from https://www.theguardian.com/australia-news/2016/may/18/peter-dutton-says-illiterate-refugees-would-be-taking-australian-jobs

Karp, P. (2018). Australia considers fast-track visas for white South African farmers. *The Guardian*. Retrieved from https://www.theguardian.com/australia-news/2018/mar/14/dutton-considers-fast-track-visas-for-white-south-african-farmers

Koziol, M. (2018). Australia's chief medical officer on Nauru deported amid health policy crisis. *The Sydney Morning Herald*. Retrieved from https://www.smh.com.au/politics/federal/australia-s-chief-medical-officer-on-nauru-deported-amid-health-policy-crisis-20181017-p50a3r.html

Laughland, O. (2013). Coalition disbands advisory group on asylum seeker healthcare. *The Guardian*. Retrieved from http://www.theguardian.com/world/2013/dec/16/tony-abbott-disbands-advisory-group-on-asylum-seeker-healthcare

Lawrence, C. (2006). *Fear and politics*. Carlton North: Scribe.

Leach, M. (2003). "Disturbing practices": Dehumanizing asylum seekers in the refugee "crisis" in Australia, 2001–2002. *Refuge, 21*(3), 25–33.

Lepora, C., & Goodin, R. E. (2013). *On complicity and compromise.* Oxford: Oxford University Press.

Lueck, K., Due, C., & Augoustinos, M. (2015). Neoliberalism and nationalism: Representations of asylum seekers in the Australian mainstream news media. *Discourse & Society, 26*(5), 608–629.

Maley, W. (2003). Asylum-seekers in Australia's international relations. *Australian Journal of International Affairs, 57*(1), 187–202.

Manne, R. (2001). *The barren years: John Howard and Australian political culture.* Melbourne: Text Publishing.

McKay, F. H., Thomas, S. L., & Warwick Blood, R. (2011). 'Any one of these boat people could be a terrorist for all we know!' media representations and public perceptions of 'boat people' arrivals in Australia. *Journalism, 12*(5), 607–626.

McKenzie, J., & Hasmath, R. (2013). Deterring the 'boat people': Explaining the Australian government's people swap response to asylum seekers. *Australian Journal of Political Science, 48*(4), 417–430.

McLaren, H. J., & Patil, T. V. (2016). Manipulative silences and the politics of representation of boat children in Australian print media. *Continuum, 30*(6), 602–612.

McNeill, P. M. (2003). Public health ethics: Asylum seekers and the case for political action. *Bioethics, 17*(5–6), 487–502.

McNevin, A. (2007). The Liberal paradox and the politics of asylum in Australia. *Australian Journal of Political Science, 42*(4), 611–630.

Migration Act. (1958). *Migration Act 1958* (Cth) (Austl.).

Migration Regulations. (1994).

Nethery, A. (2010). *Immigration detention in Australia.* (Doctoral dissertation, Deakin University, Victoria, Australia). Retrieved from http://dro.deakin.edu.au/view/DU:30032385

Nethery, A., & Holman, R. (2016). Secrecy and human rights abuse in Australia's offshore immigration detention centres. *The International Journal of Human Rights, 20*(7), 1018–1038.

O'Brien, N. (2013). No comment: Government silent over fate of asylum seekers. *Sydney Morning Herald.* Retrieved from https://www.smh.com.au/national/no-comment-government-silent-over-fate-of-asylum-seekers-20131109-2x8a1.html

Office of the United Nations High Commissioner for Human Rights, & World Health Organisation. (2008). *The right to health: Fact sheet no. 31*. Retrieved from https://www.refworld.org/docid/48625a742.html

Papastergiadis, N. (2006). The invasion complex: The abject other and spaces of violence. *Geografiska Annaler. Series B, Human Geography, 88*(4), 429–442.

Perera, S., & Pugliese, J. (1997). 'Racial suicide': The re-licensing of racism in Australia. *Race & Class, 39*(2), 1–19.

Pickering, S. (2001). Common sense and original deviancy: News discourses and asylum seekers in Australia. *Journal of Refugee Studies, 14*(2), 169–186.

Royal Australian College of Physicians. (2015). *Policy on refugee and asylum seeker health*. Retrieved from https://www.racp.edu.au/advocacy/policy-and-advocacy-priorities/refugee-and-asylum-seeker-health

Royal Australian and New Zealand College of Psychiatrists. (2016). *Professional practice guideline 12: Guidance for psychiatrists working in Australian immigration detention centres*. Retrieved from https://www.ranzcp.org/Files/Resources/College_Statements/Practice_Guidelines/PPG-12-Guidance-for-psychiatrists-working-in-Austr.aspx

Reilly, A., Appleby, G., & Laforgia, R. (2014). 'To watch, to never look away': The public's responsibility for Australia's offshore processing of asylum seekers. *Alternative Law Journal, 39*(3), 163–166.

Royal Melbourne Institute of Technology, Australian Broadcasting Corporation Fact Check (2018). Fact check: Were 400 white South African farmers murdered last year? *Australian Broadcasting Corporation News*. Retrieved from http://www.abc.net.au/news/2018-04-05/fact-check-were-400-white-south-african-farmers-murdered-year/9591724

Sampson, R., Chew, V., Mitchell, G., & Bowring, L. (2015). *There Are Alternatives: A Handbook for Preventing Unnecessary Immigration Detention*. Retrieved from https://idcoalition.org/wp-content/uploads/2016/01/There-Are-Alternatives-2015.pdf

Sanggaran, J.-P., & Zion, D. (2015). Call for Australia's ratification of the optional protocol to the convention against torture. *The Medical Journal of Australia, 202*(11), 561–562.

Steel, Z., & Silove, D. (2004). Science and the common good; indefinite, non-reviewable mandatory detention of asylum seekers and the research imperative. *Monash Bioethics Review, 23*, S93–S103.

Sutrop, M. (2011). Changing ethical frameworks: From individual rights to the common good? *Cambridge Quarterly of Healthcare Ethics, 20*(04), 533–545.

Terra Nullius. (n.d.). In Oxford dictionaries. Retrieved from https://en.oxford-dictionaries.com/definition/terra_nullius

UN General Assembly. (1948). *Universal declaration of human rights.*

UN General Assembly. (1951). *Convention relating to the Status of Refugees.*

UN General Assembly. (1967). *Protocol relating to the status of refugees.*

UN General Assembly. (1993). *Vienna declaration and programme of action.* A/CONF.157/23.

UN General Assembly. (2000). *Protocol against the smuggling of migrants by land, sea and air, supplementing the United Nations convention against transnational organized crime.*

UN Office of the High Commissioner for Human Rights. (2015). *Who will be accountable? Human rights and the post-2015 development agenda.* Retrieved from http://www.ohchr.org/Documents/Publications/WhoWillBeAccountable_summary_en.pdf

UNHCR. (2003). *Conclusion on protection safeguards in interception.* Retrieved from https://www.unhcr.org/uk/excom/exconc/3f93b2894/conclusion-protection-safeguards-interception-measures.html

UNHCR. (2012). *Guidelines on the applicable criteria and standards relating to the detention of asylum-seekers and alternatives to detention.* Retrieved from https://www.unhcr.org/uk/publications/legal/505b10ee9/unhcr-detention-guidelines.html

Weber, L. (2007). Policing the virtual border: Punitive preemption in Australian offshore migration control. *Social Justice, 34*(2), 77–93.

Young, P., & Gordon, M. S. (2016). Mental health screening in immigration detention: A fresh look at Australian government data. *Australasian Psychiatry, 24*(1), 19–22.

6

The Case for Non-violent Resistance

Overview

In previous chapters I argued that Australian immigration detention violates almost all major human rights norms and is devastating to the health and wellbeing of asylum seekers. The need for reform has long been recognized within the healthcare community; however, little progress has been made and healthcare remains hopelessly compromised within centres. In thinking about the reform of detention, a number of reasonable alternatives appear to be open to the government which take into account the need to disincentivize dangerous travel by sea while acting consistently with international human rights instruments. The government however has failed to consider these, rejecting cooperative efforts, acting to consolidate its power, stifling debate and attacking opponents.

Despite this, there remain a number of avenues for possible action. On the one hand, we could of course, do nothing, settle for the status quo. Another option would be to continue to chart the same course. On the other hand, however, we could look elsewhere for answers. In this chapter, I will make the case for a different way of thinking and acting in

© The Author(s) 2020
R. Essex, *The Healthcare Community and Australian Immigration Detention*,
https://doi.org/10.1007/978-981-15-7537-2_6

response to Australian immigration detention. As the title of this book has already given away, this approach incorporates non-violent resistance. I will first situate my discussion amongst the broader literature that discusses the role of healthcare professionals and their involvement in social and political change. While there are many forms of action that are generally accepted, such as research, advocacy and lobbying, there is far less consensus on more confrontational, disruptive and less orthodox forms of action. I will then define what I mean by non-violent resistance, outlining some key terms and concepts. While this book is also primarily concerned with how we should respond, in this chapter, I will also deal with the question of why the healthcare community should incorporate non-violent resistance into any future response. Finally, I will discuss what embracing such action would mean for the healthcare communities' response and strategy more generally. It should go without saying that turning to non-violent resistance involves more than the three forms of action I discuss in subsequent chapters, it also involves a range of strategic considerations; some of which I will touch upon below.

The Healthcare Community and Involvement in Political Action

What role should the healthcare community have in social and political change? Before moving on to the question of whether the healthcare community should engage in non-violent resistance in response to Australian immigration detention, it is worthwhile considering the discussions on the role of healthcare professionals in social and political change more generally. Some forms of action and some issues have been more widely accepted than others. Anti-tobacco programmes, harm minimization programmes, lobbying of governments to act on poverty and inequality and research have been largely uncontroversial within the healthcare community. Much less has been said about the type of action I am calling for in this book: contentious and adversarial action, protest, sit-ins and other forms of disruption.

While traditionally advocacy has been defined as "seeking access to health and social care resources on behalf of individual patients" (Gallagher & Little, 2017, p. 371), in recent years it has also come to involve addressing the social determinants of health and the promotion of health amongst communities and populations. In making this point, it is worthwhile introducing a simple but important distinction proposed by Dobson, Voyer, and Regehr (2012). In parsing the role of healthcare professionals in relation to advocacy, they draw a distinction between what they call agency and activism. They suggest that "[a]gency involves advancing the health of individual patients ('working the system'), and activism involves advancing the health of communities and populations ('changing the system')" (p. 1161). While not always clear cut, for most part, this distinction should be fairly straightforward; however, there are potentially many ways we could go about "changing the system". Gruen, Pearson, and Brennan (2004) attempt to define what such action could entail. They outline four domains where healthcare professionals could act to address patient health beyond that of individual patient care: first, access to healthcare; second, the direct socioeconomic influences on health or areas where the link between policy and health is well established, such as tobacco control; third, broad socioeconomic influences on health, such as income disparities, housing or education; and finally, global influences on health, such as the distribution of resources, knowledge and opportunity.

Another helpful conceptualization of these issues, beyond the agency-activism distinction and beyond thinking about the domains in which healthcare professionals could act, comes from Carlisle (2000) who outlines a framework for advocacy. This framework provides a useful starting point for considering the role of healthcare professionals in advocacy. In this framework, health advocacy is located on two intersecting axes. On one axis, advocacy can take place at the level of cases or causes while its two main goals are the protection of the vulnerable (representational advocacy) and empowerment of the disadvantaged (facilitated advocacy). The other axis represents "cases" (individuals and groups) and "causes" (policy and structure). Both the type of advocacy and its goals will determine where action sits on both of these axes. This is in fact one of a number of frameworks that can be found in the public health literature; I use it as an example here to begin to show that broader social and political change could be approached in a number of ways; that is, we could aim to protect refugees and asylum seekers in Australia or empower them, and we could advocate for individual or for broader structural change. Each has a place in the type of strategy I will outline below. A final distinction worth highlighting has been outlined by Raphael (2009), who suggests two possible avenues for action: "professionally-oriented rational or knowledge-based approaches" and "social and political movement-based materialist or political economy-oriented approaches" (p. 145). Professionally oriented approaches entail "research, knowledge dissemination, and public policy advocacy with the aim of convincing policymakers to enact health-supporting public policy" (p. 160) and assumes that governments will be receptive to ideas and evidence. A movement-based approach recognizes powerful interests that may be resistant to such ideas and "suggests the need for developing strong social and political movements with the aim of forcing policymakers to enact health-supporting public policy" (p. 160). Raphael (2009) argues that a movement-based approach is more effective when attempting to shift "liberal political economies" (p. 161).

While all of this helps us clarify thinking about what we could possibly do, these frameworks are largely descriptive; that is, they give little insight into what we should do. In beginning to outline this let's start with a position that is not widely held, that is, that healthcare professionals have little or no responsibility to advocate beyond that of their traditional clinical roles. Huddle (2011, 2013), for example, argues that healthcare professionals do not have a responsibility to advocate on behalf of social goals, even those directly aimed at improving health and wellbeing and similarly that social justice does not belong among professional norms. He argues that healthcare professionals should provide the best care possible, but under the conditions that society has determined and that social and political issues, along with how these should be addressed, should be decided by everybody. Furthermore, while healthcare professionals should participate in discussions about social and political issues, their opinions should not necessarily be given any extra weight and such action should not be considered professional work (Huddle, 2014). Many years earlier Jonsen and Jameton (1977) similarly argued that the social and political roles of healthcare professionals should arise at the limits of their primary responsibility towards patients and that "they should be considered symbolic responsibilities, fulfilled largely by symbolic acts and bearing witness to the promise and finitude of medicine" (p. 397). There are several issues related to these positions. Such positions appear to view health as purely biomedical; that is, they ignore or dismiss its broader determinants of health. They overlook widely accepted ethical norms, namely justice, which is referenced in almost every medical code. Furthermore, in assuming that healthcare professionals have little role to play in social and political change, these positions overlook entrenched inequalities and the influence of powerful vested interests in shaping what "society has determined". If the conditions that society has determined are unjust, then there is still work to be done. For refugees and asylum seekers who have no say in political issues, such a position appears to be completely inadequate. Furthermore, such a position appears to have little to say about healthcare professionals' complicity in wrongdoing in apartheid South Africa, rules out important work on public health such as tobacco control (unless sanctioned by society), and also appears to rule out any industrial action by healthcare professionals, even in protesting for better conditions or pay.

Most, however, have accepted that the healthcare community has at least some role to play in social and political change; the difficulty is, however, in determining what issues should be taken up and what action is justified. Gruen et al. (2004), who proposed one of the frameworks above, argue that healthcare professionals have a responsibility to engage in social and political action. They go on to argue that healthcare professionals have a professional responsibility to provide individual patient care, address issues in accessing care and issues which have a direct socioeconomic influence on health (such as tobacco policy) but not to address indirect socioeconomic or global influences on health. These arguments are made on the basis of feasibility and efficacy; that is, the authors argue that it is far more feasible for healthcare professionals to pursue change in these domains and action is more likely to influence change (recall above, the four domains, access to healthcare, direct socioeconomic influences on health, broad socioeconomic influences on health, and global influences on health). Gruen et al. (2004) acknowledges that healthcare professionals could be effective in working in the broader areas of their model; however, they argue that there is often little evidence pointing to a direct causation between health and indirect socioeconomic factors, and therefore, the involvement of health professionals may be no different from the involvement of regular citizens. In considering the type of action which could be acceptable, Gruen et al. (2004) do briefly outline how healthcare professionals could act in their "public roles" discussing action such as raising public awareness, letter writing, encouraging a medical society to act on an issue, voting or "[a]ttending a rally or protest or participating in a boycott" (p. 97). Importantly, they also recognize the importance of collective action in each of these domains. While I agree with aspects of Gruen et al.'s (2004) argument, I believe there is a much stronger case to engage with broad socioeconomic and global influences on health than what is made out. A major premise in Gruen et al.'s (2004) argument is that broad socioeconomic influences such as income disparities, housing or education are not adequately linked to health. This simply isn't the case. There is ample evidence that links these factors to health and wellbeing (e.g., Assari, 2018). There is also substantial evidence that links global influences on health and wellbeing, for example, climate change (e.g., Hayes, Blashki, Wiseman, Burke, & Reifels, 2018). Failing to act on broader socioeconomic influences means watching on passively in the face of climate change, mass displacement and other injustices. Furthermore, just because the healthcare community may not be as effective (a premise which is questionable in itself) in advocating for change in these areas doesn't mean that action should not be taken.

The literature that discusses the roles of healthcare professionals' involvement in social and political change leaves a lot unanswered; it has failed to comprehensively outline and justify the involvement (or not) of healthcare professionals in social action, and in particular, it has failed to discuss what action might be justified. That is, the literature has generally failed to deal with specific injustices and how the healthcare community should respond to these. Furthermore, little consideration has been given to the many historical and now generally celebrated examples of healthcare professionals who have resisted injustice or who have taken risks to challenge unjust policy. I will discuss a number of examples in upcoming chapters. As could be expected, I believe there is a case for healthcare community to play an active role in most social and political issues, but particularly when faced with egregious injustices. None of the arguments against such action are convincing and all overlook the consequences of failing to act. In the next section, I will make the case as to why we should consider non-violent resistance in response to Australian immigration detention; however, I will first outline what I mean by non-violent resistance.

What Is Non-violent Resistance?

One of the major arguments I hope to make throughout this book is that the healthcare community should expand its repertoire of action that is utilized in opposition to Australian immigration detention; that is, we need to adopt strategies and action beyond what is conventional and incorporate adversarial and contentious action in our response. But how could we describe actions such as strikes, boycotts, whistleblowing, sit-ins, marches, subversion, civil disobedience and other provocative, disruptive action? There is of course not a complete consensus in the literature on what each of these concepts or forms of action is, so in the following paragraphs I will draw on existing definitions to clarify what I mean by non-violent resistance.

Non-violent resistance is a strategy that seeks social and political change. It stands alongside but is different to principled non-violence. On the one hand, non-violence could refer to the rejection of all violence, essentially an actively pacifist lifestyle, on the other, it may apply specifically to prosecuting an acute conflict without resorting to violence or coercion (Schock, 2013). Resistance is usually used as a "diffuse catch-all concept" (Scheuerman, 2018, p. 5), but can be described as "a broad range of dissident activities, of varying scope and impact, which express opposition, and perhaps refusal to conform, to a dominant system of values, norms, rules, and practices" (Delmas, 2018, p. 40). Most fundamentally, resistance "involves refusing to cooperate with, and trying to undermine, the mechanisms that produce and sustain" injustice (Delmas, 2018, p. 41). Similarly, and in bringing these two terms together, non-violent resistance has been described as "the application of unarmed civilian power using nonviolent methods such as protests, strikes, boycotts, and demonstrations, without using or threatening physical harm against the opponent". Non-violent resistance generally employs unconventional tactics that work "outside the defined and accepted channels for political participation defined by the state" (Chenoweth & Cunningham, 2013, p. 271) and is thus distinguishable form more orthodox forms of action that aim to bring about some type of change.

There are a number of forms of action that could be considered non-violent resistance. Sharp (1973), for example, identified 198 separate methods ranging from mass petitions to distributing pamphlets, vigils, strikes and boycotts. For this reason, the action employed by those engaging in non-violent resistance is often seen as existing within a repertoire. While it would be impossible to examine each form of action, there are some important distinctions we can make here. Action could be undertaken in view of the public or secretively; those engaging in the action could be anonymous or identifiable. Action could be collective or individual; it could also be legal or illegal. Action could also be direct or indirect; that is, it could directly target the institutions, people or practice where change is being sought or have other indirect targets. Action could also be civil, polite and uncontroversial, or it could be deliberately controversial, contentious or uncivil. The action I discuss in upcoming chapters provides an example of each of these things.

Action could also potentially be violent. While non-violent resistance precludes violence by definition, it is worth outlining why I think this should be the case. My two main objections to the use of violence relate to its instrumentality and potential consequences; that is, it is less likely to be effective than non-violent alternatives and it carries far too many risks, both in its consequences and for those who pursue violent action. In saying this, however, this doesn't mean that acts of violence are never justified in seeking change for egregious injustices or that the healthcare community shouldn't show solidarity with those who engage in such acts. An example of this as it relates to Australian immigration detention can be seen in any of the numerous riots within centres.[1] Riots within detention centres have been short-lived and shut down aggressively, with those who

---

[1] For more on this, see Fiske (2016).

engage in this action punished harshly. Furthermore, riots within centres have failed to shift policy and, if anything, have fed into the government narrative, of why immigration detention is needed in the first place. For healthcare professionals, in addition to possibly being arrested and charged, a further issue relates to professional regulations and registration. While I can only speculate, I am fairly certain that violent action would be, at the very least, frowned upon by regulatory bodies. A range of further issues exist. In practice, the line between violence and non-violence in practice is further blurred; for example, some parts of a movement could practice non-violence while other parts slip into violence. Violence also comes in a number of forms; it could be directed towards property or towards people. Obviously, each has different implications. And finally, it is completely possible that violent action is actually less harmful than non-violent action (Raz, 2009). In this sense, we can never completely remove all risk, and for this reason, and as I will show in upcoming chapters, we should be somewhat cautious in any action we take. Needless to say, there is substantial scope for further discussion on the intersection of violence and non-violence as it relates to social and political change, both more generally and as it relates to Australian immigration detention.

It is worth clarifying a few related concepts here. A term that exists in close proximity to non-violent resistance is activism. Activism can be defined as action that goes beyond the routine or conventional, "involving actors beyond the formal political sphere" (Kenyon & Garcia, 2016, p. 199) which aims to influence opinion, policy or practice (Martin, 2007). Another similar term is contentious politics. Contentious politics has been defined as "episodic, public, collective interaction among makers of claims and their objects when: (a) at least one government is a claimant, an object of claims, or a party to the claims, and (b) the claims would, if realized, affect the interests of at least one of the claimants or objects of claims" (Tarrow, 2013, p. 1). In short and put another way, similar to non-violent resistance, contentious politics utilizes controversial, adversarial, confrontational or disruptive action (or a combination of these) to achieve a political end. While I could have labelled the action I discuss as activism or contentious politics, I have opted not to use non-violent resistance to describe the approach I outline here. I prefer this term as I feel it is more encompassing. That is, it can account for day-to-day acts of resistance, those which often go unnoticed as well as organized and public action.

In summary, for our purposes here, non-violent resistance is a strategy in seeking the reform of Australia's policies related to mandatory immigration detention. It seeks to oppose, subvert and undermine Australian immigration detention (and related policies) through action that is generally unorthodox, adversarial or disruptive. This approach recognizes that change will not come through consensus or collaboration alone and instead leverages the power of the healthcare community to demand change. Non-violent resistance utilizes a range of action including strikes, boycotts, sit-ins and principled disobedience. While the discussions in this book will largely be about the type of action that is justified, the methods or tactics of non-violent resistance also deserve consideration. In upcoming chapters I will focus on three forms of action that fall under the umbrella of non-violent resistance: strike action, whistleblowing and civil disobedience. Before this, however, I will say a few things below about why such action is justified and about broader strategic considerations as they relate to non-violent resistance.

Why Non-violent Resistance Is Justified

While the majority of this book to this point has been making a case about *how* the healthcare community should respond to immigration detention, now that I have clarified what I mean by non-violent resistance I will deal with a further important question, namely, *why* the healthcare community should engage in such action. For many I understand that this could be a particular sticking point, even if sympathetic to the healthcare community having a role in political change and the reform of immigration detention, many might believe that such action is not justified. While others, who might be sympathetic to non-violent resistance may not think it is the responsibility of healthcare communities to take such action. I argued above that there is a more general role for the healthcare community to play in the pursuit of social and political change, and in the discussion below, I want to establish that there is a prima facie justification for non-violent resistance. That is, while non-violent resistance is justified on face value, non-violent resistance could involve a range of actions, the justification for which will need to be considered in greater detail. I will deal with these more specific questions when I discuss strike action, whistleblowing and principled disobedience in upcoming chapters. Finally, while this has been written with the healthcare community in mind, many of the reasons why we should engage in non-violent resistance apply to the general public, anyone more generally who wishes to see the reform of these policies.

How might we justify the healthcare community engaging in action that seeks the reform of Australian immigration detention more generally? First, I believe few would argue with the statement that those working in detention (and the healthcare community more generally) have a responsibility to protect human rights and promote justice and furthermore that these values are widely held professional norms. This responsibility to protect human rights and promote justice could be grounded in a number of ways. These duties are clear in all major professional codes, with almost all referring to concepts such as dignity, justice and rights either implicitly or explicitly (AMA, 2016; APS, 2011; RACP, 2015). This responsibility could also come from various human rights instruments or from the close relationship between health and human rights. That is, health, wellbeing and human rights cannot be separated in this context; that is, health can only be realized through human rights, and human rights through health, and vice versa (World Health Organization, 2017). Finally, we could also look towards "role obligations", that is, by making the decision to work as a health professional, one "acquires a special set of normative powers—rights and duties—that people do not normally have in other capacities" (Ceva & Bocchiola, 2020, p. 7). If we could uphold these values or fulfil these responsibilities while working within immigration detention, then there may not be a case for broader systemic reform, which brings me to my second point: that health professionals simply cannot act consistently with a range of professional commitments, values and norms, such as justice, while working within Australian immigration detention centres. This should be clear from previous chapters, where I not only outlined the harm created and perpetuated by these policies but demonstrated that healthcare delivery within immigration detention centres is almost futile.

Given these two points and if the healthcare community is to rectify this, there is a need to look elsewhere, to seek systemic change. This point too should be largely uncontroversial for those who wish to see change. This recognition that broader change is needed is also not new. McNeill (2003, p. 500) outlined a case for such action over 15 years ago:

> The case for political action is well established. What is not clear is the kind of political action that might be both justified and effective. The commentators are agreed that disseminating information and advocacy are legitimate activities in public health. The difficulty is when neither seems sufficient. In Australia, the Prime Minister and Minister of Immigration have been unresponsive to information that revealed the harmful effects of their policies. They appeared to be immune even to extreme accounts of human suffering. Advocacy may not be sufficient to influence a Government that is willing to resort to the harshest of measures in dealing with the most vulnerable of people.

While many will accept that political action is the answer, some may still not be convinced that we should turn to more disruptive forms of action, so why should we turn to non-violent resistance? I believe there are at least four major reasons that justify such a response; again, looking at the evidence presented in previous chapters, these should be uncontroversial.

First, and I have made this point previously, these policies have a devastating impact on those detained. They are callous and engineered to dehumanize. That is, this harm is deliberate, with the Australian government using this group of particularly vulnerable people to deter others. On this point, those detained are vulnerable not just in regard to their health status, but because they often cannot seek to redress themselves. They are lacking what Arendt (1958, p. 296) recognized as the precursor to all other human rights, that is, "a place in the world which makes opinions significant and actions effective". Further to this point, Hall et al. (2018, p. 49) introduced the concept of "belonging by proxy", that is, "citizens protesting in their own name but also on behalf of those not given the right to settle in Australia". Recognizing that it may not always be in the best interests of asylum seekers and refugees to participate in protest, belonging by proxy "demonstrates solidarity between those privileged with the safety of residency and citizenship who can express their concerns and dissent, and those absent from the rallies precisely because they are denied those rights". The need for action from others and particularly those who have worked in close proximity to the system is not only important but necessary.

Second, beyond being harmful and targeting a particularly vulnerable group, these policies are exceptionally unjust and strike at a number of democratic norms. Again, I hope I have made this case throughout previous chapters, what I haven't done however is attempt to quantify this. Most would agree Australian immigration detention is unjust, but just how unjust? We can find some guidance here. Building on Smith (2013), Delmas (2018) outlines a typology of injustice, which provides a foundation for us to begin to think about the extent of these issues. First, deliberative disrespect occurs when a group of citizens are denied free and equal status by a democratic majority or where there are "democratically sanctioned violations of the basic rights and dignity of noncitizens at home and abroad" (Delmas, 2018, p. 84). Australia's policies are inarguably discriminatory, violate multiple human rights instruments and, not only this, have denied many the right to even seek "free and equal status". Second, deliberative inertia occurs when certain issues or discourses are blocked from the public sphere. Recall the discussion in Chap. 5, the government has undeniably taken a number of steps to reduce transparency and ensured issues are blocked from the public sphere. Third, official misconduct occurs when "authorities routinely violate the duties associated with their office" (Delmas, 2018). This perhaps one issue I haven't discussed; however, needless to say, this has also occurred. Over the years, the government has attempted to increasingly shut out the judiciary in migration-related decisions making, and there have been multiple scandals and clear cases involving abuse of power (Cave & Kwai, 2018). Finally, public ignorance occurs when the authorities conceal information from the public or try and cover up misconduct. As noted previously, the Australian government has actively attempted to cover up the circumstance in detention, attacking critics, denying access to centres and as was the case with the Border Force Act for a time, outlawing disclosures from staff who had worked in centres. Reilly, Appleby, and

Laforgia (2014) argue this secrecy is not only unjust but also potentially unconstitutional.

In this environment and given these circumstances, it is not so much that our options to pursue reform are limited; we can still after all, research, report and lobby politicians; it is that these forms of action are likely to have limited impact. This leads to my fourth point that out of the options available, non-violent resistance has a greatest chance of having an impact. On this point, we can learn from history that non-violent resistance has been key in bringing about a range of positive social change, from civil rights movements, feminist movements and environment movements, all of which have utilized, to varying degrees, non-violent resistance.

Finally, there is also a precedent for such action. In engaging in non-violent resistance, I am not asking the healthcare community to do something completely new. The examples I outlined in previous chapters, the case of Baby Asha and the response to the Border Force Act all included examples of non-violent resistance. Furthermore, healthcare bodies have all at least tacitly supported such action; they have supported healthcare professionals advocating and reporting on the health and well-being of those detained, even when this became illegal under the Australian Border Force Act. They have supported whistleblowers (Laughland & Davey, 2014; Owler, 2016) and joined health professionals in protest (Berger, 2016; Safi & Farrell, 2015). Beyond the discussions above, there is a rich literature that deals with the ethics of disobeying unjust laws and, more recently, unjust immigration laws. I will introduce some of this literature in upcoming chapters and when exploring principled disobedience in response to these policies.

Stepping back for a minute and repeating an important point from earlier, non-violent resistance is one strategy in seeking political change. It is one strategy amongst many; it is a strategy which we should employ because of a range of factors which have limited other avenues for change. This approach alone cannot account for the complexities of working within Australian immigration detention or the complexities associated with social and political change. In this respect, non-violent resistance should be seen amongst a repertoire of different actions and theory that could be used to not only explain these issues but respond to them. It needn't come at the cost of existing efforts. Quiet, conscientious, non-public action is valuable and should continue. Solidarity with those in the community and detention should continue. Debates about the role of healthcare professionals working within centres remain important. Where possible, these issues should continue to be challenged in court. All of these actions could also be seen as acts of resistance.

The Healthcare Communities' Role in Challenging Australian Immigration Detention

Leaving the conversation here, I could leave you with the impression that I am only concerned about the type of action that is justified in response to Australian immigration detention. While I will dedicate the next three chapters to exploring different forms of action, it would be an oversight to limit the discussion in such a way. Calling for non-violent resistance in response to Australian immigration detention opens up a range of possibilities and questions beyond the type of action we undertake: how the action is framed, the political environment in which it occurs and the range of other external factors which shape the impact of such action. Campaigns, movements and even individual acts of resistance are often dynamic and relational; that is, their impact and consequences change with time and the actors involved. In beginning to understand these issues, we can draw from the many historical examples of non-violent campaigns and a growing empirical literature. So while I am only dedicating a small section of this book to these issues, for those who are concerned or interested, there is substantial scope for further investigation.

Non-violent resistance is not just about what we do. Each form of action comes with its own relative strengths and trade-offs. Action could be disruptive. There are many examples of this as they relate to Australian immigration detention; blocking deportations (Australian Associated Press, 2016a, 2016b) and interrupting parliament (Hutchens, 2016; Karp, 2016) are just two. A strike by healthcare staff, which will be discussed in the next chapter, is another example. Action could also be more contained, civil and uncontroversial, think about the numerous marches, vigils and open letters calling for change. Each form of action serves a different purpose; for example, while disruptive action may more easily grab headlines and be used for greater leverage, it is also shut down more easily and generally carries more risks. Occasionally, action that is routine and that should be largely uncontroversial is also attacked; the AHRC Forgotten Children Report (2014) is one example.

Another important consideration relates to how we organize in response to these issues. Hundreds of organizations in Australia have called for reform. Some of these organizations deal with a range of issues; others solely focus on Australia's policies towards refugees and asylum seekers. Some focus on lobbying and other less controversial action (e.g., the Refugee Council of Australia[2]). Some are smaller and more activist and at times involved in disruption (Hutchens, 2016; Karp, 2016; Mums4Refugees). This of course for the most part hasn't been problematic; however, it has at times created tension. Tazreiter (2010), for example, discusses how during 2001 amongst a climate of increasing hostility towards boat arrivals and the introduction of offshore processing, there was criticism of larger organizations who had closer ties with government and who had refrained from criticizing this increasingly punitive approach. Today, while many organizations have worked together, priorities have differed, as have views on what action may be most appropriate to achieve change. While consensus is unlikely and while there is no right or wrong way to organize (however, some may dispute this), what is clear is that there is strength in numbers; both within and outside of the healthcare community, solidarity is important. The case of Baby Asha is testament to this; it showed how impactful a united front could be and how the healthcare communities' actions could be effectively amplified by the media and other protesters.

How the healthcare community frames these issues also matters. Take the response to the Border Force Act, for example. After the Border Force Act was introduced, those protesting its introductions could have done so on a number of grounds, for undermining free speech or even violating core democratic norms. It was however mainly challenged on the basis

---

[2] https://www.refugeecouncil.org.au.

that it would simply stop healthcare professionals from being able to do their job and report problems such as child abuse.[3] In this respect, this argument depoliticized healthcare within detention as the government has also often claimed to do (i.e., holding that healthcare was provided to an equivalent standard found in the Australian community). While the government had attacked critics alleging political partisanship after the AHRC Forgotten Children Report (2014) in the case of the Border Force Act, the government failed to take action despite multiple healthcare professionals breaking the law.[4] How this issue was framed aguably played a role in pacifying potential attacks from the government about partisanship or playing politics.

A further important feature of non-violent resistance relates to how individuals respond to threats and opportunities. Opportunities and threats refer to (mostly) external forces that shape action and strategy. Tarrow (2011, p. 32) defines opportunities as "consistent—but not necessarily formal, permanent, or national—sets of clues that encourage people to engage in contentious politics". How doctors responded to the Baby Asha, calling national attention to the case through the media, could be seen as the exploitation of an opportunity—as could the pressure placed on the government to introduce the Medevac legislation. While each of these cases were impactful, they were both short-lived; opportunities are often fickle and shut down quickly.

Beyond these considerations there is a rich literature that deals with other elements of non-violent resistance, such as how movements mobilize and demobilize, how governments respond to movements[5] and how non-violent resistance shifts across borders, something which is particularly relevant for anyone concerned with issues facing refugees and

---

[3] This is not necessarily at odds with the shift I call for in taking more adversarial and political action. Future action needs to be strategic in a political sense; this does not mean employing political rhetoric if it is going to be less effective or even harmful. It is also not to say that protest was apolitical or failed to recognize the broader implications of this law. Examples of this can be seen throughout the "Open Letter on the Border Force Act" (The Guardian Australia, 2015) where the Border Force Act (2015) was largely framed as impeding healthcare professionals in being able to report child abuse or other child protection issues.

[4] Not only broke the law but publicized and promoted their breaking of the law through the media; more on this in Chap. 9.

[5] For more on this and an overview of many of these issues, see Tarrow (2011).

asylum seekers more generally. A further consideration is how we build partnerships and collaborate, not just within the healthcare community but beyond it. Partnerships between lawyers and healthcare professionals have already served to be powerful in challenging the government.[6] One example comes from the Medevac legislation, discussed in Chap. 3. Talbot and Newhouse (2019, p. 89) give an example of how such a collaborative approach worked prior to its introduction:

> The Medevac Bill negotiation saw doctors, lawyers, caseworkers and others in the sector collaborating in previously unseen ways. While the lawyers continued to fight the Minister in court, doctors and other organisations worked with MPs and the media to explain the nature of the health crisis, the urgency of the situation and to correct circulating misinformation.

In addition to informing action, a deeper engagement with the literature related to non-violent resistance allows for an exploration of issues across time and place, identifying commonalities, differences, successes and failures. While non-violent resistance has been central to many positive social gains, such as the civil rights movement, feminist movements, the anti-apartheid struggle in South Africa, the path to change is often rocky. Consider Australia's ratification of the OPCAT.[7] Healthcare professionals, healthcare bodies and human rights organizations long called for increased surveillance within immigration detention, particularly since the re-opening of offshore centres and the ongoing reports of harm from within centres. In late 2015, 18 professional bodies called for ratification of the OPCAT in news and journal articles (Anderson, 2015; Sanggaran, 2015; Sanggaran & Zion, 2015). Little more was heard about this for about 6 months. In July 2016, ABC News aired a report on the Don Dale Youth Detention Centre, revealing abusive and violent conditions that were likened to torture (Meldrum-Hanna & Elise, 2016). This report caused public outrage, and the government announced a Royal Commission into the Protection and Detention of Children in the

---

[6] See my discussion in Chap. 3 regarding the Medevac legislation.

[7] Also see my discussion in Chap. 2, after signing the OPCAT and in July 2019, the UN subcommittee on the prevention of torture announced it would visit Australia and Nauru to inspect detention facilities.

Northern Territory[8] shortly afterwards. In February 2017, the government announced that it would ratify the OPCAT (Beech, 2017). What contribution, if any, did those advocating for greater transparency within immigration detention make? While this question may seem beside the point and it is undoubtedly a good thing that Australia is now ratifying the OPCAT, this example shows how social and political action may have a range of unintended and indirect impacts (or no impact at all) that are often difficult to measure.

A final area that has often been overlooked relates to facilitating and promoting international pressure—in other words, creating and placing pressure on the Australian government externally, rather than from within Australia. While the government has responded with hostility to a number of international human rights organizations, there are a number of other potential courses of action that deserve consideration. Furthermore, there is a growing literature on what has been labelled transnational contention, which has increasing potential to guide action in Australia (Bell, Clay, & Murdie, 2017; Pianta & Marchetti, 2012; Tarrow, 2012). One avenue for action would involve bringing to light Australia's approach through international media (Laney, Lenette, Kellett, Smedley, & Karan, 2016). More modestly, anyone who travels internationally could expose Australia's policies, whether on business or as a tourist. To maximize the impact of such action, opportunities that put Australia in the spotlight could be seized, international business, political or sporting events, capitalizing on existing publicity and world attention. Australian healthcare professionals and professional bodies should also call on their international peers to condemn Australia's policies. Finally, the possibility of a boycott, divestment and sanctions campaign aimed at Australia more generally should be debated (Loewenstein, 2017). This, of course, could involve any of Australia's exports or even those thinking of travelling to Australia. While a total boycott of Australia is unlikely, such calls would be a provocative way of gaining further support and highlighting the harm Australia is doing globally, serving to place further pressure on the Australian government.

---

[8] A Royal Commission is a major public investigation generally into issues that are controversial or have significant public importance.

References

Australian Medical Association. (2016). *Code of ethics 2004. Editorially revised 2006. Revised 2016.* Retrieved from https://ama.com.au/position-statement/code-ethics-2004-editorially-revised-2006-revised-2016

Anderson, S. (2015). Leading health agencies call for Australian detention centres to be independently monitored. *Australian Broadcasting Corporation News.* Retrieved from http://www.abc.net.au/news/2015-10-16/call-for-independent-monitoring-of-detention-centres/6859642

Australian Human Rights Commission. (2014). *The forgotten children: National inquiry into children in immigration detention.* Retrieved from https://www.humanrights.gov.au/our-work/asylum-seekers-and-refugees/publications/forgotten-children-national-inquiry-children

Australian Psychological Society. (2011). *Psychological wellbeing of refugees and asylum seekers in Australia: A Position Statement prepared for The Australian Psychological Society.* Retrieved from https://www.psychology.org.au/About-Us/What-we-do/advocacy/Position-Statements/Psychological-wellbeing-refugees-and-asylum-seeker

Arendt, H. (1958). *The origins of totalitarianism.* Cleveland: The World Publishing Company.

Assari, S. (2018). Life expectancy gain due to employment status depends on race, gender, education, and their intersections. *Journal of Racial and Ethnic Health Disparities, 5*(2), 375–386.

Australian Associated Press. (2016a). Protesters at Melbourne airport fail to stop transfer of asylum seeker. *Australian Broadcasting Corporation News.* Retrieved from http://www.abc.net.au/news/2016-07-26/protesters-try-to-deportation-of-asylum-seeker-to-manus-island/7660140

Australian Associated Press. (2016b). Student who protested against asylum seeker's deportation on flight found guilty. *The Guardian.* Retrieved from https://www.theguardian.com/australia-news/2016/sep/02/student-who-protested-against-asylum-seekers-deportation-on-flight-found-guilty

Beech, A. (2017). OPCAT: Australia makes long-awaited pledge to ratify international torture treaty. *Australian Broadcasting Corporation News.* Retrieved from http://www.abc.net.au/news/2017-02-09/australia-pledges-to-ratify-opcat-torture-treaty/8255782

Bell, S. R., Clay, K. C., & Murdie, A. (2017). Join the chorus, avoid the spotlight: The effect of neighborhood and social dynamics on human rights organization shaming. *Journal of Conflict Resolution 63*(1) 167–193.

Berger, D. (2016). Australia's torture of asylum seekers. *British Medical Journal,* 354:i4606

Border Force Act 2015 (Cth) (Austl.).

Carlisle, S. (2000). Health promotion, advocacy and health inequalities: A conceptual framework. *Health Promotion International, 15*(4), 369–376.

Cave, D., & Kwai, I. (2018). In Australia, one man can decide a migrant's fate. Did he abuse that power? *The New York Times.* Retrieved from https://www.nytimes.com/2018/09/06/world/australia/peter-dutton-au-pair.html

Ceva, E., & Bocchiola, M. (2020). Theories of whistleblowing. *Philosophy Compass, 15*(1), e12642.

Chenoweth, E., & Cunningham, K. G. (2013). Understanding nonviolent resistance: An introduction. *Journal of Peace Research, 50*(3), 271–276.

Delmas, C. (2018). *A duty to resist: When disobedience should be uncivil.* Oxford: Oxford University Press.

Dobson, S., Voyer, S., & Regehr, G. (2012). Perspective: Agency and activism: Rethinking health advocacy in the medical profession. *Academic Medicine, 87*(9), 1161–1164.

Fiske, L. (2016). *Human rights, refugee protest and immigration detention.* London: Palgrave Macmillan

Gallagher, S., & Little, M. (2017). Doctors on values and advocacy: A qualitative and evaluative study. *Health Care Analysis, 25*(4), 370–385.

Gruen, R. L., Pearson, S. D., & Brennan, T. A. (2004). Physician-citizens— Public roles and professional obligations. *JAMA, 291*(1), 94–98.

Hall, S., Lenette, C., Murray, S., Chan, C., Flannery, A., & Vickery, K. (2018). # LetThemStay: Visual representations of protests and community mobilization for asylum seekers in Australia. *Journal of Critical Thought and Praxis, 7*(1), 4.

Hayes, K., Blashki, G., Wiseman, J., Burke, S., & Reifels, L. (2018). Climate change and mental health: Risks, impacts and priority actions. *International Journal of Mental Health Systems, 12*(1), 1–12.

Huddle, T. S. (2011). Perspective: Medical professionalism and medical education should not involve commitments to political advocacy. *Academic Medicine, 86*(3), 378–383.

Huddle, T. S. (2013). The limits of social justice as an aspect of medical professionalism. *Journal of Medicine and Philosophy, 38*(4), 369–387.

Huddle, T. S. (2014). Political activism is not mandated by medical professionalism. *The American Journal of Bioethics, 14*(9), 51–53.

Hutchens, G. (2016). Pro-refugee protesters disrupt parliament and shut down question time. *The Guardian.* Retrieved from https://www.theguardian.com/

australia-news/2016/nov/30/pro-refugee-protesters-disrupt-parliament-and-shut-down-question-time

Jonsen, A. R., & Jameton, A. L. (1977). Social and political responsibilities of physicians. *The Journal of Medicine and Philosophy, 2*(4), 376.

Karp, P. (2016). Refugee protesters abseil down Parliament House and dye fountain red. *The Guardian*. Retrieved from https://www.theguardian.com/australia-news/2016/dec/01/refugee-protesters-abseil-down-parliament-house-and-dye-fountain-red

Kenyon, K. H., & Garcia, R. A. (2016). Exploring human rights-based activism as a social determinant of health: Insights from Brazil and South Africa. *Journal of Human Rights Practice, 8*(2), 198–218.

Laney, H. M., Lenette, C., Kellett, A. N., Smedley, C., & Karan, P. (2016). "The most brutal immigration regime in the developed world": International media responses to Australia's asylum-seeker policy. *Refuge: Canada's Journal on Refugees, 32*(3), 135–149.

Laughland, O., & Davey, M. (2014). Peter Young praised for revealing detention's toll on asylum seekers. *The Guardian*. Retrieved May 8, 2014, from http://www.theguardian.com/world/2014/aug/05/peter-young-praised-revealing-detentions-toll-asylum-seekers

Loewenstein, A. (2017). *Manus protest is failing, so let's talk about a boycott of Australia*. Retrieved from https://www.crikey.com.au/2017/11/13/loewenstein-protest-is-failing-lets-talk-about-a-boycott-of-australia/

Martin, B. (2007). Activism, social and political. In G. L. Anderson, K. G. Herr (Eds.), *Encyclopedia of Activism and Social Justice* (pp. 19–27). California: Sage.

McNeill, P. M. (2003). Public health ethics: Asylum seekers and the case for political action. *Bioethics, 17*, 487–503.

Meldrum-Hanna, C., & Elise, W. (2016). Evidence of 'torture' of children held in Don Dale detention centre uncovered by Four Corners. *Austrlian Broadcasting Corporation News*. Retrieved from http://www.abc.net.au/news/2016-07-25/four-corners-evidence-of-kids-tear-gas-in-don-dale-prison/7656128

Owler, B. (2016). *Speech to AMA forum on health of asylum seekers*. Retrieved from https://ama.com.au/media/ama-speech-prof-owler-ama-asylum-seeker-health-forum

Pianta, M., & Marchetti, R. (2012). *Global social movement networks and the politics of change*. Retrieved from http://works.bepress.com/mario_pianta/94/

Royal Australian College of Physicians. (2015). *Policy on refugee and asylum seeker health*. Retrieved from https://www.racp.edu.au/advocacy/policy-and-advocacy-priorities/refugee-and-asylum-seeker-health

Raphael, D. (2009). Reducing social and health inequalities requires building social and political movements. *Humanity and Society, 33*(1–2), 145–165.

Raz, J. (2009). *The authority of law: Essays on law and morality.* New York: Oxford University Press.

Reilly, A., Appleby, G., & Laforgia, R. (2014). 'To watch, to never look away': The public's responsibility for Australia's offshore processing of asylum seekers. *Alternative Law Journal, 39*(3), 163–166.

Safi, M., & Farrell, P. (2015). AMA joins protest against asylum law that can jail detention centre staff. *The Guardian.* Retrieved from https://www.theguardian.com/australia-news/2015/jul/01/ama-joins-protest-against-asylum-law-that-can-jail-detention-centre-staff

Sanggaran, J.-P. (2015). Asylum seekers are being abused on our watch. It's time to put detention under surveillance. *The Guardian.* Retrieved from https://www.theguardian.com/commentisfree/2015/sep/12/asylum-seekers-are-being-abused-on-our-watch-its-time-to-put-detention-under-surveillance

Sanggaran, J.-P., & Zion, D. (2015). Call for Australia's ratification of the optional protocol to the convention against torture. *The Medical Journal of Australia, 202*(11), 561–562.

Scheuerman, W. E. (2018). *Civil disobedience.* London: John Wiley & Sons.

Schock, K. (2013). Nonviolence/nonviolent action. In D. A. Snow, D. della Porta, B. Klandermans, D. McAdam (Eds.), *The Wiley-Blackwell Encyclopedia of Social and Political Movements.* Malden: Blackwell Publishing.

Sharp, G. (1973). *The politics of nonviolent action.* Boston: Porter Sargent.

Smith, W. (2013). *Civil disobedience and deliberative democracy.* London: Routledge.

Talbot, A., & Newhouse, G. (2019). Strategic litigation, offshore detention and the medevac bill. *Court of Conscience Issue, 13*, 85.

Tarrow, S. (2011). *Power in movement: Social movements and contentious politics.* Cambridge: Cambridge University Press.

Tarrow, S. (2012). *Strangers at the gates: Movements and states in contentious politics.* New York: Cambridge University Press.

Tarrow, S. (2013). Contentious politics. In D. A. Snow, D. della Porta, B. Klandermans, D. McAdam (Eds.), *The Wiley-Blackwell Encyclopedia of Social and Political Movements.* Malden: Blackwell Publishing.

The Guardian Australia. (2015). Open letter on the Border Force Act: 'We challenge the department to prosecute'. Retrieved from https://www.theguardian.com/australia-news/2015/jul/01/open-letter-on-the-border-force-act-we-challenge-the-department-to-prosecute

Tazreiter, C. (2010). Local to global activism: The movement to protect the rights of refugees and asylum seekers. *Social Movement Studies, 9*(2), 201–214.

World Health Organization. (2017). *Leading the realization of human rights to health and through health: Report of the high-level working group on the health and human rights of women, children and adolescents.* Retrieved from https://www.who.int/life-course/publications/hhr-of-women-children-adolescents-report/en/

7

Strike Action

Overview

Above, I have outlined the case for non-violent resistance. This opens a
range of avenues for action. In the next three chapters I will consider
three forms of action, and in this chapter I will consider whether strike
action is justified. A strike is important to consider for two reasons. First,
given the nature of the system and the almost futile nature of healthcare
within in, for the individual healthcare professional it would not be
unreasonable to resign or decline to participate, so it is worthwhile considering the implications if such action were to be pursued collectively.
Second, unlike the other forms of action in upcoming chapters, a strike
has already been debated amongst the healthcare community—I hope to
expand on these discussions here. I will start by outlining what I mean by
a strike and provide a brief overview of this action more generally. I will
then outline the discussions that have been had in relation to strike action
in response to Australian immigration detention. Using a framework proposed by Selemogo (2013), I will then discuss the most important
points when considering the justification for strike action. This is not a
simple check box exercise; the type of strike undertaken, the demands

© The Author(s) 2020
R. Essex, *The Healthcare Community and Australian Immigration Detention*,
https://doi.org/10.1007/978-981-15-7537-2_7

made and a range of other factors will impact on the decision as to whether a strike can be justified. In any action I argue that the health and wellbeing of detainees should weigh heavily and for this reason I don't believe a strike can be justified, nor would it be feasible. This of course does not mean we should accept the status quo or should dismiss a strike completely; it should be seen amongst a repertoire of other action, both within and external to detention centres and whether a strike could be justified will change with shifts in policy or conditions within centres. I will conclude by discussing some other avenues for action for those working within detention centres.

What Is a Strike?

A strike has been one of the most common disruptive forms of action the healthcare community has turned to when calling for change. Strikes have been common since the industrial revolution, and even a brief scan of the literature reveals that strikes carried out by the healthcare community are remarkably common. From Israel (Siegel-Itzkovich, 2000) to South Korea (Watts, 2000) to Zimbabwe (Sidley, 1996), healthcare workers have taken strike action. While many have been successful in having their demands at least partially met (Butt & Duffin, 2018), others have not been as fortunate (Nursing Standard, 2007). Many have faced more punitive action. In Pakistan, for example, in response to a strike by junior doctors, the police raided several hospitals in an attempt to break it up, "arresting, attacking, and humiliating" (Riaz & Bhaumik, 2012, p. 97) hundreds in the process. In Syria, over 90 health professionals were detained for over a decade after participating in a general strike to protest human rights violations (Kirschner, Hannibal, & Elahi, 1991). While the majority of strike action has been undertaken for seemingly just ends, like improvements in working conditions or concerns related to patient safety, not all strike action deserves veneration; in India, for example, doctors undertook strike action in response to an affirmative action plan to open more places in medical schools for "low-caste" students (Chatterjee, 2006).

While common and while there is a substantial literature reporting on strike action undertaken by the healthcare community, these articles are almost always descriptive and often relatively brief. There is a small literature that has attempted to investigate these issues empirically and to offer some normative analysis. I will discuss these articles; first, however, it is necessary to outline just what a strike is. A strike has been defined as a "temporary stoppage of work by a group of employees in order to express a grievance or enforce a demand" (Hyman, 1989, p. 17). That is, a strike is collective, temporary and calculated. Thus, strike action can be distinguished from other forms of action undertaken in the workplace such as a go-slow or "work to rule strike".[1] Beyond this, however, strikes vary significantly. Strikes vary in their duration, and can range from a few days to a few months (or even indefinitely), the circumstances under which they are carried out, and the demands or grievances that are attached to them. In terms of strike action carried out by healthcare professionals, on the one hand, some have argued that no distinction can be made between the healthcare community and other workers in pursuing such action (Park & Murray, 2014), however others have argued that strike action undertaken by the healthcare community is distinct. I agree with Roberts (2016) that healthcare strikes are distinct for at least two reasons. The first relates to the risks in striking; that is, "there may be far more serious consequences to suspending medical care than, say, public transport or postal services", (p. 698) and the second relates to the need to safeguard trust in the professions more generally, as Roberts (2016) notes, "[b]esides the stakes involved, that relationship is precisely what makes the medical profession different from many others: maintaining trust and respect is important in medicine in a way that is simply not the case elsewhere".

In one of the earliest debates of strike action undertaken by healthcare professionals, Veatch & Bleich (1975) discussed its justification. Veatch made the case that strike action could be justified, arguing that while healthcare professionals have a more immediate obligation to their

---

[1] Generally, a go-slow refers to action where employees deliberately slow their work, while a work to rule strike refers to action where employees work strictly to the rules, policies or procedures in their workplace to reduce their efficiency.

patients, they also had the duty to balance the longer-term interests of society more generally. Veatch concludes that justifying strike action "would require showing substantial benefits to others who are or will be particularly less well-off" (p. 8). Bleich on the other hand was more sceptical about such action, proposing the following analogy:

> May a person on the way to a class on first-aid instruction ignore the plight of a dying man, on the plea that he must perfect skills which may enable him to rescue a greater number of persons at some future time? ... No person may plead that an activity designed to advance future societal benefits is justification for ignoring an immediate responsibility ... The "here and now" test is a general rule of thumb which may be applied to most situations requiring an ordering of priorities. (p. 9)

Muyskens (1982) argued that healthcare professionals not only have responsibilities for their individual patients but a collective responsibility to maintain high standards of practice. He takes on Bleich's point above, essentially arguing that the dying man on the street scenario is disanalogous to what most strikes resemble, arguing that a strike is permissible; however, that the most important consideration in weighing up whether it is justified relates to "how one balances the collective responsibility to maintain and improve the quality of nursing care with an individual nurse's responsibility to her/his own patients" (p. 101). He goes on to argue that in beginning to think about how this could be balanced, we should think about a Rawlsian original position "in which members of the public cannot know when or what nursing care they may need (they are under a veil of ignorance) and nurses also do not know in what situation they will find themselves" (p. 110).

There is a common theme throughout the literature: regardless of whether you are for or against a strike, the welfare of the patient weighs heavily. Discussions about this have persisted to this day. While some have outright dismissed strikes, concluding that there can "be little justification for a physicians' strike, no matter what the provocation" (Glick, 1985, p. 197), many have been far more open to such action. Toynbee, Al-Diwani, Clacey, and Broome (2016), for example, discussing junior doctor strikes in the UK, concluded that a strike could be justified if all patients had access to emergency care, that the maintenance of patient wellbeing was a goal and if a strike was a last resort.

A Strike in Response to Australian Immigration Detention

Before moving on to the discussions about a strike in relation to Australian immigration detention, some clarification on terminology is needed. Some of the literature below refers to a strike, that is the temporary stoppage of work within centres, as a boycott. While somewhat similar, they are distinct. While a boycott could be used as a means to stop people working in detention, a boycott stands in contrast to a strike as it also generally encourages others "to refrain from purchasing certain goods or using certain public services" while utilizing "marketplace means to achieve what may or may not be marketplace ends" (Forno, 2013, p. 1).

Strike action was initially raised in the literature by Sanggaran, Ferguson, and Haire (2014, p. 378), who called for the discussion of "the potential role of a professional boycott to motivate change". Against a backdrop of increasingly alarming reports from within detention centres and an increasingly secretive and combative approach taken by the government, including the introduction of the Border Force Act, Isaacs (2015, p. 2) called a boycott "the only ethical option available". The only major healthcare body to publicly discuss a strike was the AMA. During its forum on the health of asylum seekers, the AMA acknowledged that Australian immigration detention amounted to a "state-sanctioned form of child abuse"[2] and called for the immediate release of all children along with a moratorium on asylum seeker children being returned to immigration detention. The AMA also called for the re-establishment of an independent body of experts to report on the welfare of asylum seekers and refugees, and furthermore, if the satisfactory healthcare could not be provided, the government's "policies should be revisited". The AMA

---

[2] The AMA (2015) position statement on the Health Care of Asylum Seekers and Refugees does not call for an end to the detention of children, which also seems in conflict with this point.

called for no further action. The reasons against a boycott were specifically addressed. The AMA asserted that by working in immigration detention healthcare professionals were not complicit in wrongdoing, rather they were simply placing patients first, and that if any change should come, it should be through the weight of public opinion (Owler, 2016). This statement was somewhat perplexing, calling detention state-sanctioned child abuse, while also complacently calling for public opinion to first change. It also oversimplifies and denies the realities of delivering healthcare in immigration detention and is at odds with the testimony of healthcare professionals and well-documented issues with healthcare discussed in previous chapters.

Others engaged with these issues in more depth. In an article published shortly after the AMA forum, Sanggaran (2016), a doctor who formerly worked in detention, called for a boycott. He cites the contradictions of working within immigration detention and the AMA Code of Ethics (2016) and discusses both the compromised nature of healthcare and how healthcare professionals have enabled human rights abuses. He also directly addresses a number of arguments against a strike including the impact a strike would have on detainees, that public opinion must shift first, that Australian staff would be replaced by staff from overseas and the need for consensus amongst professionals to strike.

A number of weeks later, Berger and Miles (2016) debated this issue. Berger, arguing for a strike, outlined the harm that immigration detention does and the restrictions on providing healthcare in these environments, including healthcare professionals being co-opted by the system. He went on to say that healthcare professionals should continue to offer their services, but only if "the conditions for torture ... end" (p. 1). Miles, argued that "these egregious circumstances do not justify a boycott that would further isolate internees from adequate care ... The AMA should buttress its commendable reports and ethics codes with more aggressive action. It should help frontline healthcare professionals to transmit reports, pictures, and data through encrypted and anonymous web channels to international human rights organisations" (p. 2). Miles goes on and calls for a legal defence fund to be set up for any healthcare professionals prosecuted under the Border Force Act and that if a boycott were to be considered, "they should target the government rather than the detainees. Action could include withdrawing from working in staff clinics within government ministries (such patients can go to the regular healthcare system). It could include pausing consultative roles with government ministries, suspending the submission of government forms (birth and death certificates or medical clearance for military service), and so on" (p. 2). The only further article to discuss a strike in any length was an article written by myself (Essex, 2019). This chapter is an updated and expanded version of this article. For those who have read my previous work, my conclusions do not differ substantially here.

There are a few things worth saying about the discussions about a strike before moving on and beyond what has already been said. Many of the discussions above have either implicitly or explicitly assumed that a strike would mean a total, temporary stoppage of work. That is, all healthcare staff would cease working in detention centres. However, a strike could take a number of forms. Should a strike involve all healthcare workers within immigration detention centres? Or should emergency (or essential) staff remain? Should there be rolling strikes? Or would another form of workplace action be more effective? Furthermore, there has also been little distinction made between detention centres, onshore, offshore, APODs, and so on. Those in onshore APODs face very different circumstances to those detained offshore. While generalizations across centres can still be made, it is important that these differences are not overlooked if a strike is to be justified, even in part on the conditions in which people are detained. Finally and looking ahead, detention centres have changed and are likely to change into the future. The calculus in justifying a strike would shift if all people were removed from offshore centres, for example. While there is substantial scope for further discussion in relation to these issues and while I will touch upon some of them below, I will move forward under the assumption that a strike is a complete and temporary stoppage of healthcare work in detention centres.

The Ethics of Strike Action

The most comprehensive framework to examine strike action by health-care workers comes from Selemogo (2013), who draws on just war theory to highlight a number of key issues that should be considered before withdrawing services in a healthcare context. These criteria include almost all normative considerations discussed above by other authors and act to some degree as a safeguard, asking those who are contemplating a strike to consider a series of important questions. These include (1) whether the cause for strike action is just; (2) whether a strike is a last resort and other non-disruptive alternatives have been considered; (3) whether the declaration of the strike action projects the view of the majority of the peers in the profession; (4) whether in the current circumstances, the strike is likely to achieve its objectives and (5) whether the strike will disproportionately harm patients. Finally, he also calls on those who intend on striking to (6) make a formal public declaration about the intended action, outlining the reasons for striking. This framework, while useful, is not faultless; Selemogo (2013) suggests that each of the above criteria need to be met before a strike could be justified. I will outline why I don't believe this is necessary below. I also believe there is a need to greater explore the weight given to each criteria and their relational nature. As I noted above, the proportionality of a strike and the chances of it harming patients (detainees) should weigh heavily. I will discuss why below.

Would strike action in response to Australian immigration detention meet any of these criteria? First, there should be little doubt that the cause for a strike is just; for Selemogo (2013, p. 36), this relates to intent, namely that a strike is motivated by a desire to "defend (or stop grave violations of) the right to the health of individuals or communities". Muyskens (1982) similarly argued that a strike couldn't be justified if it were solely for higher wages. For those who have called for strike action in response to Australian immigration detention, there should be little doubt about their motivation, with little to gain personally and often exposing themselves to significant risk by calling for such action. Furthermore, the impact of detention is devastating and many who remain detained are at risk of imminent harm. If the amount of pro-bono work that is already done is anything to go by, it is almost certain that many healthcare professionals would take a pay cut to work in centres, if not volunteer their time, if there were major reform.

More doubt hangs over other questions, however. Have all alternatives to a strike been exhausted? Most simply, if the government was willing to negotiate and somewhat open to reform, then yes, we needn't to consider a strike; however, this is obviously not the case. The government has been set in its position for many years now insisting that these policies need to be maintained, and if anything made increasingly punitive. Over this time, the healthcare community has engaged in a range of action, advocacy, research, lobbying, whistleblowing and civil disobedience, which has seemingly had little impact. As will be seen in upcoming chapters, when considering principled disobedience, many philosophers have also called for such action to be used as a last resort. This is usually qualified however noting that this needn't literally be the case; instead, all other less disruptive forms of action should be seen as being ineffective before turning to action such as a strike or principled disobedience.

A further question relates to whether healthcare professionals have the support of the majority in the profession or a central body such as a professional body or union. Selemogo (2013) argues that the support of professional bodies creates an added "safeguard and legitimacy" and guards against "militant" healthcare professionals. While there is no shortage of Australian healthcare professionals who would like see reform (*The Guardian Australia*, 2018), we have little indication that a majority would support a strike. Furthermore, such action has not yet received support from any professional bodies or agencies that represent healthcare professionals. As noted above, the AMA is the only professional body to have discussed this issue and state their position publicly (Owler, 2016). Practically, a strike would only be effective if all agreed to participate, so this question raises a further concern, one of feasibility and whether such action should or could be enforced. If a strike was not enforced it would risk being ineffective, as it is unlikely all healthcare professionals would participate. If a strike were enforced a range of further questions would be raised. Who could enforce it and how might this be done? We would at least need a degree of consensus outside Australia as well. In the event of a strike, the Australian government could employ foreign staff, which would be relatively easy to do in offshore centres. On the other hand, however, replacing Australian staff with foreign staff may also lend further support to taking strike action; that is, foreign staff may provide some level of care, providing a degree of assurance that this action will not disproportionality harm detainees. A similar argument could be made if emergency staff were left in place during a strike. These possibilities raise the issue of proportionality, something which will be discussed below.

Would a strike achieve its objectives? It depends on the objectives we set. Would it make the Australian government act consistently with its human rights obligations? Probably not. Would it achieve something more modest, like improvements in healthcare within detention centres? Possibly. If ambitious demands were made we would need to be prepared to strike for a protracted period, and we would also need to consider what compromises we might be willing to accept. A protracted strike would also raise a range of further practical issues, such as how to support strikers and their families over such a period. If more modest demands were made and they were met, there would be far more work to be done. Finally, and related to this point, a strike may not directly advance its originally planned objectives. For example, what if the greatest achievement of a strike were to raise awareness and galvanize further support in the medical community?

Whether a strike is proportional and would harm detainees should weigh heavily in any decision making, particularly because of the nature of detention, the lack of access to healthcare outside what is provided in centres (particularly offshore) and the vulnerability of those detained. More generally, proportionality is one of the greatest concerns and apprehensions discussed in the literature. Let me start with a counterargument to this point, namely that healthcare is largely futile anyway. I have referred and continue to refer to healthcare as largely futile myself, so I think it's a reasonable point to make. Sanggaran (2016) makes this argument, stating that "[o]ne must consider the patients' best interests. Does it in fact serve a patient's best interests to provide the documented substandard care? Or is the patient better served by the withdrawal of medical services so that the pretence of care is not maintained?" While I think that little can be done within detention, this does not mean that nothing can be done. If nothing else, healthcare professionals have witnessed and reported on the suffering in centres and a great deal of what we know today has come from those who worked in centres. Not only this, one only needs to imagine detention centres without healthcare professionals. In looking at this point in more detail and in attempting to strike a balance, some have turned to Lepora and Goodin's (2013) framework of complicity.[3] Weighing the costs and benefits of current engagement, while also identifying a number of ways healthcare professionals may be able to reduce their contribution to wrongdoing while working within immigration detention, Jansen, Tin, and Isaacs (2017, p. 141) conclude that, on balance, healthcare professionals should continue to work in detention, stating "it is right for doctors to continue to provide medical care to people seeking asylum … doctors must practise in an uncompromisingly humanistic way, should publicly speak out about the harms being perpetrated and should be constantly mindful of the potential for corruption".

Finally, we need to consider how a strike is communicated, not only this, but how it is framed and how to counter the government's response. I agree that there should be a declaration; a strike is a public facing action and it should be made clear what is being demanded, but this is only the first consideration. Many in Australia will not support a strike, I assume that support or opposition for a strike would be as polarized as the public's views on detention more generally. Recall above, that the AMA argued that if any change should come, it should be through the weight of public opinion (Owler, 2016). Sanggaran (2016) challenged this point, arguing that rather than wait for public opinion, a strike had "the potential to be moved by such an action". While I agree with Sanggaran on this point, that is, history has shown that many just causes have not had the support of the general public, maintaining trust is something we need to be mindful of if pursuing strike action. In saying this, however, I still don't believe that it should weigh as heavily as the welfare of those who remain detained.

---

[3] Discussed in Chap. 4.

Should the Healthcare Community Strike?

A strike is appealing when weighing the present costs and benefits of continuing to work within immigration detention centres. Little can be done working within centres to mitigate the devastating harm that is created and perpetuated; furthermore, the government has been unwilling to entertain alternatives for over two decades. However, when considering the potential costs and benefits of a strike, that is, the impact a strike could have, the same cannot be said. The potential harm of a strike provides reason to be, at a minimum, cautious. Some assumptions can be made with more certainty than others. Swift and significant policy change is unlikely. In fact, conditions would likely worsen without the involvement of the Australian healthcare professionals. Furthermore, the Australian government could employ healthcare professionals from other countries to address staffing shortages while continuing to pursue its present policy. The well-documented vulnerabilities of those detained only provide further reason for caution. Taking all of this into account, a strike becomes difficult to justify. Beyond its justification, a strike also seems unlikely from a practical point of view. If it were to go ahead, we would need to overcome a range of practical barriers. A strike is a collective action. No professional bodies have voiced their support and only one has publicly engaged with these issue. Even without professional bodies, any such action would require near consensus among the healthcare community.

Could we better balance concerns about proportionality and feasibility by pursuing a different form of strike action, that is, what if emergency staff were left in place or what if a strike were time limited? Perhaps we could, but while such action might have less of an impact on detainees, it would also likely be far less disruptive and thus effective. Furthermore, if history is anything to go by, it is likely that staff who participate in the strike would be dismissed and replaced with people who are less likely to question these policies. What if our goals were less demanding? Again, this could change the above calculus, but such an approach risks achieving little while still having a disproportionate impact on detainees. Finally, what about a general strike? That is, strike action in which all healthcare professionals in Australia participated to protest these policies. This would overcome a number of the concerns above; however, it would also require near consensus among the entire Australian healthcare community. Quite clearly, there are a number of options regarding how a strike is organized, so while I don't think a strike is the best form of action for the ethical and practical reasons outlined above, it shouldn't be dismissed completely. A strike may become more or less appealing if circumstances within immigration detention centres changed. For example, while on face value it may be appealing to strike if conditions in detention were made worse, these conditions could also leave detainees more vulnerable and give weight to continuing to work in centres. Similarly, increasingly secretive policy could also make a strike more appealing; on the other hand, it may compel healthcare professionals to stay to witness and report on subsequent abuse.

A strike is not the only type of action that could occur within detention centres that would protest or disrupt these policies. While the focus of this book is not on how healthcare professionals should deal with the irresolvable conflicts while working in detention centres, some discussion is warranted here. What might other forms of resistance look like within detention centres? Like a strike, such action could be collective, public facing, make explicit demands or be disruptive; however, the trade-offs for such action would also be quite high. It would involve substantial risk to the healthcare professionals involved, and as I said above, it would likely be shut down quite quickly. Briskman and Zion (2014, p. 279) have discussed what they call subversion, that is, "dispensing acts of kindness that may not be valued or even prohibited by the employing or subcontracting authority". Beyond this, there are a number of clandestine forms of resistance that healthcare professionals could chose to engage in over and above their regular roles. It is useful here to introduce the term "infrapolitics". Infrapolitical action occurs "outside the visible spectrum of what usually passes for political activity" and includes examples of actions such as "foot-dragging, poaching, pilfering, dissimulation, sabotage, desertion, absenteeism, squatting, and flight" (Scott, 2014, p. xx). Infrapolitical action occurs when there isn't the luxury for open political opposition. It also overcomes the need for consensus and often comes with fewer risks for those engaging in it. As noted by Scott (2014, p. xx), "[w]hy risk getting shot for a failed mutiny when desertion will do just as well? Why risk an open land invasion when squatting will secure de facto land rights? Why openly petition for rights to wood, fish, and game when poaching will accomplish the same purpose quietly?"

Another way to work within the system is to facilitate refugees and asylum seekers speaking out or standing in solidarity with those engaging in acts of resistance. While not as widely spoken about as the devastating impact of detention, resistance within detention has been common:

> It would be wrong to present a picture of detainees solely as victims, deteriorating into serious mental illness and self-harm. The detention regime was also consistently a place of organised and sustained collective resistance. In some instances the resistance was spontaneous, an incident of violence by a guard triggering an angry response which prompts other detainees to join in support. In others it was highly organised with tools stolen and stashed in advance, mass meetings to plan actions and communication networks distributing information through various groups of detainees. (Bailey, 2009, p. 119)

There are numerous examples of refugees and asylum seekers speaking out, both from detention and after their release, for example, projects and organizations such as Behind the Wire,[4] RISE: Refugees, Survivors and Ex-detainees[5] and the Refugee Art Project.[6] Since Manus Island was re-opened, those detained have had a growing presence in the media, both in Australia and internationally. Behrouz Boochani, an asylum seeker and journalist who was detained, has gained increasing attention and provided a powerful account of the experience of detention, writing and leading peaceful protests (Boochani, 2016). There is a greater role for healthcare professionals and professional bodies to play (particularly because they work in such close proximity) to facilitate greater communication between those detained and the Australian public.

Again, it is impossible to go into the pros and cons of each type of action; needless to say, there is substantial scope for further research in this area. One thing, however, should be said about more orthodox

---

[4] http://behindthewire.org.au.
[5] http://riserefugee.org/.
[6] https://facebook.com/TheRefugeeArtProject.

clinical practice before moving on. Regardless of whether one decides to resist or not, at a minimum, healthcare professionals should attempt to provide the highest standard of care possible given the circumstances. Furthermore, they should act to minimize their involvement with the particularly harmful elements of the system and avoid creating additional dilemmas in the longer term. Thus, in some cases, it may be appropriate to abide by the restrictions put forth by centre management. In other cases it might be more appropriate to advocate for those detained or act subversively when it presents minimal risk and there is likely to be few repercussions. While healthcare professionals cannot necessarily influence decisions on the release of refugees and asylum seekers, they may be able to take steps to alleviate some of the stressors associated with detention. This could include addressing issues related to accommodation or administrative restrictions within centres. In many cases, more orthodox clinical intervention may not be warranted or even desirable.

Finally, one final reflection on strike act is worth making. A strike is a collective, coordinated action. Importantly, as a collective act, strike action can be distinguished from an individual making the choice not to work or cease working in immigration detention centres. Put another way, my argument above is largely consequentialist; that is, a strike is treated as a means of achieving a desired end. If a deontological approach was taken, however, different conclusions could be reached. For example, what if the motivation to strike was instead to ensure that healthcare professionals were not complicit in wrongdoing. This individualistic and broadly deontological motive does not necessarily change the consequentialist reasons for striking. In this sense, from a deontological perspective, for healthcare professionals who do not want to be complicit in wrongdoing their own (personal) strike could still be justified.

References

Australia Border Force Act (2015). *Border Force Act 2015* (Cth) (Austl.).
Australian Medical Association. (2015). *Position statement on health care of asylum seekers and refugees - 2011. Revised 2015.* Retrieved from https://ama. com.au/position-statement/health-care-asylum-seekers-and-refugees-2011

Australian Medical Association. (2016). *Code of ethics 2004. Editorially revised 2006. Revised 2016.* Retrieved from https://ama.com.au/position-statement/code-ethics-2004-editorially-revised-2006-revised-2016

Bailey, R. (2009). Up against the wall: Bare life and resistance in Australian immigration detention. *Law and Critique, 20*(2), 113–132.

Berger, D., & Miles, S. H. (2016). Should doctors boycott working in Australia's immigration detention centres? *British Medical Journal,* 352:i1600

Boochani, B. (2016). This is Manus Island. My prison. My torture. My humiliation. *The Guardian.* Retrieved from https://www.theguardian.com/commentisfree/2016/feb/19/this-is-manus-island-my-prison-my-torture-my-humiliation

Briskman, L., & Zion, D. (2014). Dual loyalties and impossible dilemmas: Health care in immigration detention. *Public Health Ethics, 7*(3), 277–286.

Butt, H., & Duffin, J. (2018). Educating future physicians for Ontario and the physicians' strike of 1986: The roots of Canadian competency-based medical education. *CMAJ: Canadian Medical Association Journal, 190*(7), E196–E198.

Chatterjee, P. (2006). India's doctors protest over caste quota plans. *Lancet, 367*(9526), 1892–1892.

Essex, R. (2019). Should clinicians boycott Australian immigration detention? *Journal of Medical Ethics, 45*(2), 79–83.

Forno, F. (2013). Boycotts. In D. A. Snow, D. della Porta, B. Klandermans, D. McAdam (Eds.), *The Wiley-Blackwell Encyclopedia of Social and Political Movements.* Malden: Blackwell Publishing.

Glick, S. M. (1985). Physicians' strikes—A rejoinder. *Journal of Medical Ethics, 11*(4), 196–197.

Hyman, R. (1989). *Strikes.* London: Macmillan.

Isaacs, D. (2015b). Doctors should boycott working in Australia's immigration centres and must continue to speak out on mistreatment of detainees-despite the law. *British Medical Journal, 350*, h3269.

Jansen, M., Tin, A. S., & Isaacs, D. (2017). Prolonged immigration detention, complicity and boycotts. *Journal of Medical Ethics, 44*(2), 138–142.

Kirschner, R. H., Hannibal, K., & Elahi, M. (1991). Health professionals held as political prisoners in Syria. *New England Journal of Medicine, 324*(8), 567.

Lepora, C., & Goodin, R. E. (2013). *On complicity and compromise.* Oxford: Oxford University Press.

Muyskens, J. L. (1982). Nurses' collective responsibility and the strike weapon. *The Journal of Medicine and Philosophy, 7*(1), 101–112.

Nursing Standard. (2007). Pay protests in Poland fail to win better offer from prime minister. *Nursing Standard, 21*(44), 7–7.

Owler, B. (2016). *Speech to AMA forum on health of asylum seekers.* Retrieved from https://ama.com.au/media/ama-speech-prof-owler-ama-asylum-seeker-health-forum

Park, J. J., & Murray, S. A. (2014). Should doctors strike? *Journal of Medical Ethics, 40*(5), 341–342.

Riaz, M., & Bhaumik, S. (2012). Police target doctors over strike action in Pakistan. *Lancet, 380*(9837), 97–97.

Roberts, A. J. (2016). A framework for assessing the ethics of doctors' strikes. *Journal of Medical Ethics, 42*(11), 698–700.

Sanggaran, J.-P. (2016). First, do no harm. Why doctors should boycott working in Australian detention centres. *The Guardian.* Retrieved from https://www.theguardian.com/commentisfree/2016/mar/05/first-do-no-harm-why-doctors-should-boycott-working-in-australian-detention-centres

Sanggaran, J.-P., Ferguson, G. M., & Haire, B. G. (2014). Ethical challenges for doctors working in immigration detention. *Medical Journal of Australia, 201*(7), 1–3.

Scott, J. C. (2014). *Two cheers for anarchism: Six easy pieces on autonomy, dignity, and meaningful work and play.* Princeton, NJ: Princeton University Press.

Selemogo, M. (2013). Criteria for a just strike action by medical doctors. *Indian Journal of Medical Ethics, 11*(1), 35–38.

Sidley, P. (1996). Health workers strike in Zimbabwe. *British Medical Journal: International Edition, 313*(7066), 1165.

Siegel-Itzkovich, J. (2000). Doctors' strike in Israel may be good for health. *British Medical Journal, 320*(7249), 1561.

The Guardian Australia. (2018). Almost 6,000 doctors sign letter to PM demanding children be taken off Nauru. *The Guardian.* Retrieved from https://www.theguardian.com/australia-news/2018/oct/15/almost-6000-doctors-sign-letter-to-pm-demanding-children-be-taken-off-nauru

Toynbee, M., Al-Diwani, A. A., Clacey, J., & Broome, M. R. (2016). Should junior doctors strike? *Journal of Medical Ethics, 42*(3), 167–170.

Veatch, R. M., & Bleich, D. (1975). Interns and residents on strike. *The Hastings Center Report, 5*(6), 8–9.

Watts, J. (2000). Seoul strikes continue in South Korea as doctors fight drug reform. *The Lancet, 356*(9241), 1583.

8

Whistleblowing

Overview

Unlike a strike, whistleblowing in response to Australian immigration detention hasn't just been debated; there have been numerous whistleblowers from the healthcare community who have come forth after working in detention centres. In this chapter, I will consider whether whistleblowing by healthcare professionals can be justified in response to Australian immigration detention. To do this I will first outline what I mean by whistleblowing, discussing its key features and significance. I will then consider some examples of whistleblowing from healthcare professionals who formerly worked in Australian immigration detention centres, outlining their disclosures, the impact they had and the repercussions that came as a result of their whistleblowing. I will then consider some major justificatory theories of whistleblowing. Using Ceva and Bocchiola (2020) as a starting point, I will provide an overview of two major theories of whistleblowing, extra ratio and deontic approaches. I will show how each theory can be used to provide a complementary explanation and justification of whistleblowing, which is particularly important as neither view on its own can fully explain or justify

© The Author(s) 2020   **167**
R. Essex, *The Healthcare Community and Australian Immigration Detention*,
https://doi.org/10.1007/978-981-15-7537-2_8

whistleblowing as it relates to Australian immigration detention. I will then consider how this applies to Australian immigration detention, arguing that with some constraints on how whistleblowing is carried out along with careful consideration about the risks in taking such action, whistleblowing can be justified.

What Is Whistleblowing?

Over the last two decades, whistleblowers have dominated the headlines. In 2013, after leaking over 700,000 classified military and diplomatic documents, Chelsea Manning was sentenced to 35 years in prison. Julian Assange, while now imprisoned in the UK, has been attempting to avoid extradition to the US for over a decade for his role in publishing these documents along with many others through WikiLeaks. Edward Snowden discovered a mass surveillance network run by the National Security Agency (NSA) and close allies, which monitored telephone and communications networks across the globe. In 2013 Snowden disclosed thousands of classified NSA documents. He sought asylum in Russia soon after, where he remains to this day. More recently in 2019 a whistleblower prompted the impeachment of Donald Trump after raising concerns about Trump's conduct on a phone call to the Ukrainian President Volodymyr Zelensky. In addition to these high-profile cases, whistleblowing has also been common in the healthcare community.

By 1985, apartheid policies in South Africa had already inflicted over three decades of institutional violence on the black population. This year also saw increasing resistance to these policies, resulting in an upsurge in violent and non-violent action, with the government declaring a number of states of emergency. The same year, while working in the medical examiner's office in Port Elizabeth, Dr. Wendy Orr became the first and only doctor employed by the government to reveal the torture and abuse of political detainees. After protests to her superiors had failed, Orr began gathering data to document the violence and torture perpetrated by the state, including assault, suffocation and electric shock (Dowdall, 1991). With the support of human rights lawyers, Orr made an urgent application to the Supreme Court detailing a pattern of extensive torture and abuse of detainees, requesting a restraining order against the police. While this application was successful, the ramifications of this case were wider reaching than a legal victory, exposing this maltreatment and torture to the South African public and the international community.

Speaking out in healthcare also carries substantial risks. For almost four decades, Dr. Binayak Sen, an Indian paediatrician, provided healthcare to some of the most marginalized in Indian society, in the central Indian state of Chhattisgarh. Sen remains a human rights activist and spent the last four decades documenting and speaking out against the inequities and failures of government. In 2005, Sen documented the brutality of a counterinsurgent militia that was supported by the state. He was charged with sedition in 2007 and sentenced to life imprisonment. He spent several years in jail before being released without comment from the Supreme Court of India in 2011. Sen's work continues to be celebrated, and today, however 13 years later, his appeal is still pending.

More recently, in December 2019, Dr. Li Wenliang, an ophthalmologist, practising in Wuhan, China, noticed a series of patients with upper respiratory infections. After sharing his concerns, he was detained by police who accused him of "spreading false rumours". He was one of eight people who were targeted. Almost two months later he had died from COVID-19, a virus that by then had spread around the world, killing hundreds of thousands. It was only after his death and the public outrage that followed that the Chinese government exonerated him.

Whistleblowing has been defined as "the disclosure by organization members (former or current) of illegal, immoral or illegitimate practices under the control of their employers to persons or organizations that may be able to effect action" (Near & Miceli, 1985, p. 4). While a useful starting point, this definition has been criticized as it sets the bar too low for disclosures to be considered whistleblowing. That is, this definition suggests that any report of wrongdoing or misconduct to a manager (or anyone else in an organization for that matter) is an act of whistleblowing. For this reason, Skivenes and Trygstad (2010) draw a distinction between what they call "weak" and "strong" whistleblowing. While the above definition is an example of "weak" whistleblowing, strong whistleblowing "focuses on process and on cases where there is no improvement in, explanation for, or clarification of the reported misconduct from those who can do something about it. In such cases, an employee must report the misconduct again and is thus engaging in strong whistle-blowing" (p. 1077). For example, a healthcare professional reporting a colleague to a manager for some kind of wrongdoing would be an example of weak whistleblowing. If this then went unaddressed or if there were systemic issues that were going unaddressed, the healthcare professional may then take this matter further, disclosing to external parties. These differences aside, there are generally three defining features of whistleblowing: first, an intentional disclosure by a member of an organization or institution. Second, this disclosure is generally about some kind of wrongdoing or malpractice. Third, the intent of the disclosure is to address this wrong-doing (Ash, 2016). It is worthwhile to break this down a little further; Ceva and Bocchiola (2020) suggest that whistleblowing has at least six elements. Thinking through each is particularly important when think-ing about whether whistleblowing is justified. The first element is the act of whistleblowing itself. Whistleblowing could occur within an organiza-tion, or it could be public. It could also be authorized or unauthorized, legal or illegal. The second element relates the misconduct or wrongdoing itself. Wrongdoing could take the form of corruption, nepotism, systemic failings, abuse or a cover-up of any of these things. The third element relates to the whistleblower. By definition a whistleblower has to come from within the organization in question; however, organizational mem-bership could vary. The whistleblower could be permanent or a contrac-tor, senior or newly employed. The fourth element relates to the organization or institution. Organizations could be public, private, gov-ernmental or non-governmental. As can be imagined, organizational functions, their structures, cultures and values vary greatly. The fifth ele-ment relates to audience or addressee of the whistleblowing. As noted above, most fundamentally, disclosures could be aimed at those within or outside of the organisation in question. The sixth and final element relates to the aims of the whistleblowing. Whistleblowing is intentional and aimed at addressing some type of wrongdoing. Wrongdoing is subjective and the motivations for such action could vary; however, generally, a whistleblower's actions seek positive change or to challenge the status quo.

Beyond the vast differences between whistleblowers, the wrongdoing they bring to light, the organizations and institutions they belong to, and the reception they receive, whistleblowing is dynamic and relational. That is, how whistleblowing is received and the repercussions or changes that it prompts are dependent on a range of contextual and relational factors. For example, the acceptance of whistleblowing has been found to differ substantially between countries (Skivenes & Trygstad, 2010).

Regardless of how widely accepted or protected whistleblowing is, one commonality is that whistleblowing almost always involves some degree of risk. The cases discussed at the beginning of this chapter are testament to this. Whistleblowing sets the individual against powerful collectives and even where legal protections are available and often under the best circumstances, many lose their job while having their credibility and integrity attacked (Ahern & McDonald, 2002). This is one of the most notable differences between whistleblowing and a strike, discussed in the previous chapter. Whistleblowing is largely an individual act, with the individual shouldering almost all of the burden. For Ash (2016, p. 16), whistleblowing "is an act of loyalty, a commitment to doing right, to doing no more harm" which "touches some of the very deep recesses of what it is to be human, to bear witness to wrongdoing, or to turn away" (p. 12). To become a whistleblower takes a great deal of thought about the numerous risks that come with such action, along with the potential consequences of failing to act. Before considering this in more detail, it is worthwhile considering some examples of whistleblowing as they relate to Australian immigration detention.

Whistleblowing and Australian Immigration Detention

Whistleblowing in response to Australian immigration detention has been common. As was outlined in previous chapters, the government has also frequently pursued or attacked those critical of these policies, as was the case with the AHRC Forgotten Children Report (2014). While every act of whistleblowing has been slightly different, there are some generalizations that can be made. With the exceptions of whistleblowing done under the Border Force Act, it has almost always been legal. While other staff have spoken out, healthcare professionals have been the overwhelming majority of whistleblowers. The nature of these disclosures has varied: some have gone to the media, while others have simply written for academic audiences or lent their support to existing causes. Finally, majority of whistleblowers have not revealed anything revelatory about immigration detention. Most have simply given further weight to the well-established view that immigration detention has devastating consequences for those detained. This is not to say that this type of disclosure is not important, after a disclosure controversy ensues, the debate is somewhat refreshed, and immigration detention remains in the headlines for at least another few days. Below I will discuss a number of whistleblowers who have come forward to speak of their experiences in immigration detention. There are a number of notable examples I don't speak about below that deserve to be mentioned here, like those who testified during the People's Inquiry (ACHSSW, 2006) and Glenda Koutroulis, a nurse who formerly worked in Woomera immigration detention centre (Koutroulis, 2003, 2009). There are also many more who have decided to remain anonymous; over the years, media outlets have published a range of documents, many of which are likely to have been leaked by employees within detention centres.

In late 2013, shortly after the government had re-introduced offshore processing, an open letter was written by 15 doctors who worked on Christmas Island (Christmas Island Medical Officer's Letter of Concern, 2013), which was subsequently published by *The Guardian* (Marr, 2013). At the time, it was the most widely publicized example of whistleblowing since the re-introduction of offshore processing. The letter outlined a range of concerns, underpinning almost all of these complaints was the fact that patient care was compromised by IHMS' relationship with the Australian government (Laughland & Marr, 2013). The letter stated:

> A conflict of interest exists, as a result of IHMS' relationship with the Department of Immigration and Border Protection that can influence decisions regarding patient care. Decisions made by IHMS do not appear to have always been made in the best interest of patients. The shifting of responsibility between the DIBP and IHMS is likely to result in neither party acting appropriately in regards to patients ... Even when mitigating factors, such as the remote location and the practical limitations imposed by the DIBP, are considered, many aspects of the IHMS health service fall

well below accepted standards for clinical practice and are unnecessarily dangerous. (p. 5)

Importantly throughout the letter and in response to each of the identified complaints, recommendations were made, with the authors demanding a response from IHMS. A number of authors went on to write about healthcare in immigration detention in academic journals (Sanggaran, Ferguson, & Haire, 2014), with Sanggaran and Zion (2015) leading calls for Australia's ratification of the OPCAT and sparking debate amongst the healthcare community about potential strike action (Sanggaran, 2016).

In 2014, Peter Young, a Psychiatrist and former Medical Director of IHMS, spoke out. At the time, and perhaps still, he was the most senior figure to speak out about immigration detention, testifying at the AHRC Forgotten Children Inquiry (2014). In evidence to the inquiry, Young alleged figures showing the extent of mental health issues among child asylum seekers that had been covered up by the immigration department. He testified that while data had been collected by IHMS, the immigration department asked to remove these figures from reports. This was in fact only a symptom of a larger problem, with Young going on to expand upon this in a wide-ranging interview and with *The Guardian* (Marr & Laughland, 2014). Young likened Australian immigration detention to torture, stating that "if we take the definition of torture to be the deliberate harming of people in order to coerce them into a desired outcome, I think it does fulfil that definition" (Laughland & Davey, 2014). He went on to outline the harms of the system more generally, importantly highlighting the fact that almost all issues related to healthcare were systemic and not only this but engineered to act against good health and the provision of healthcare.[1]

Shortly after, a number of professional healthcare bodies threw their support behind Young. The RANZCP stated that it "would like to commend its member Dr Peter Young for speaking out about the shocking treatment of asylum seekers on Nauru, Christmas and Manus Islands ... The college appreciates that Dr Young has taken this public stand at some

---

[1] Also see Dr. Peter Young's testimony in Chap. 3.

personal cost". The RACP stated that "the RACP strongly supports physicians and other medical professionals who place their duty of care to patients first and foremost. The oath taken by all doctors, 'to first, do no harm' guides their conduct. This oath and a doctors' ability to act in their patient's best interests, must be respected in all circumstances, including in Australia's immigration detention facilities" (Laughland & Davey, 2014). Young went on to publish the data (Young & Gordon, 2016) and do a number of subsequent interviews. This action didn't come without costs, however; while there were no public reprisals, Young was investigated by the Australian Federal Police (AFP). In 2016 it was revealed that the AFP compiled hundreds of pages of investigative file notes and reports on him (Farrell, 2016). While heavily redacted, the files state that Young was a suspect in an investigation related to leaked medical information because of "comments attributed to him being highly critical of [the immigration department] and IHMS in their handling of asylum seeker medical care". The notes went on to state that "Dr Young's phone did not identify contact with any media outlets or journalists during the period surrounding the publication of the media articles". This investigation was eventually discontinued due to a lack of evidence.

In mid-2016, *The Guardian* published an interview with Psychologist Paul Stevenson (Doherty & Marr, 2016). Stevenson worked for contractors Wilson Security providing support for security staff. In a bold act of whistleblowing,[2] Stevenson went on the record to outline the "atrocity" of offshore detention. Furthermore, he was connected with the leak of over 2000 pages of "incident reports" from within the centres. In the following months, more details were provided to *The Guardian*, and these reports became known as the "Nauru files" (*The Guardian*, 2016). This collection of documents contained over 8000 pages and 2000 incident reports and outlined the despair and desperation of those offshore detention. Stevenson's contract was cancelled shortly after this interview was published (Doherty, 2016).

In 2018, an article written by Nick Martin, a General Practitioner who had formerly worked on Nauru, was published by *The Guardian* (Martin, 2018a). In it he questioned whether he was part of the solution or part of

---

[2] These articles were published while the Border Force Act was still in effect, making these disclosures illegal.

the problem and discussed the incompatibility of immigration detention and medical ethics. This was followed up by an article in Meanjin (Martin, 2018b), which provides one of the most powerful accounts of what it is like to work as a healthcare professional in Australia's offshore detention centres. He also wrote about his decision to go public; it is worth quoting at length:

I had thrown so much of myself into the job, had tried my best to get these poor buggers the help they desperately needed. And now I was outside the tent and felt completely impotent. I had a couple of days to chew it over. Was it time to speak out? I had tried to bring about change from within the system. Now that I saw it from an outsider's perspective, I realised it was insane. I spoke to my family, to some trusted friends. I was amazed at how much I had normalised, how much that had seemed almost acceptable at the time was clearly inhumane. I just couldn't walk past it. I made some calls, my indignation rising. I spoke with some people who had blown the whistle before. I spoke with lawyers who were very reassuring. With each call I felt my resolve growing. This crazy, dreadful, inhumane episode had to end one day, and I did not want to have to explain to those who knew me why I had done nothing.

I contacted a journalist who I knew had been involved with the Nauru files leak: the thousands of documents that showed the banality of detention, the depressing collision of bureaucracy and humanity, people's existence reduced to ticked boxes, documenting the extent of their self-harm, the seriousness of their suicide attempts, the myriad indignities suffered daily. I thought he'd be a good place to start. One final talk with family and friends before I jumped in. Any more delays and I would get cold feet. Was this the right thing to do? It was the only thing to do. How could I look my kids in the eye in years to come otherwise?

Things happened quickly. Television crews, interviews and hours answering questions as honestly as I could, trying to keep it solely medical when of course it would all boil down to politics. I hoped that the ex-military aspect would work in my favour. I'm not your average social justice warrior.

When the story came out, I was away from home doing a locum. My phone started to ring, and then messages started arriving. The media had done a great job as far as I could see. I felt I'd had a chance to get my message across: that medically what was happening was unacceptable, that no matter what your stance on boats, borders and refugees, it was a basic obligation, having locked people up, to look after them.

Unsurprisingly, Martin didn't return to work on Nauru. Since this time, Martin has continued his advocacy, speaking out against these policies. Furthermore, his evidence formed key evidence presented to several successful federal court challenges that brought seriously unwell children to Australia. In 2019 he was awarded the Blueprint for Free Speech prize, an award previously won by Chelsea Manning (Doherty, 2019).

The Ethics of Whistleblowing

There have been two major normative approaches to whistleblowing. Ceva and Bocchiola (2020) label these the "extrema ratio" and "deontic" views of whistleblowing. Drawing on their work, I will outline each below consider what they mean for each other and importantly, consider what they mean for whistleblowing as it relates to Australian immigration detention. For simplicity, I will work on the assumption that whistleblowing is legal. While there have been examples of whistleblowing that have broken the law, and while I still believe such action is still justified, I will consider the ethics of breaking the law in the next chapter on principled disobedience.

The extrema ratio view frames whistleblowing as an "exceptional individual response to some serious organizational wrongdoing" (Ceva & Bocchiola, 2020, p. 4). That is, it is a response to or an attempt to remedy exceptional circumstances where other "organizational reporting mechanisms have proved unviable, unavailable, or inefficient" (Ceva & Bocchiola, 2020, p. 4). Those who endorse this view generally see whistleblowing as presumptively wrong. That is, whistleblowing is wrong unless there are some fairly stringent reasons to override these concerns. Boot (2017), for example, argues that whistleblowing is wrong for three reasons. First, it violates promissory obligations; for example, many employees may sign a confidentiality agreement or in some way agree not to disclose internal information. Second, because of "role obligations". That is, the employee in question is obligated to act in a certain way which stems from their role in the organization. Finally, whistleblowing fails to "respect the democratic allocation of power" (p. 541). This is not to say that whistleblowing is impermissible, with Boot (2017) suggesting that whistleblowing can be justified if it meets three conditions. First, disclosures should be of grave wrongdoing. Second, all alternative channels to report this wrongdoing should be exhausted. Third, the whistleblower should take steps to minimize harm that may result from the disclosure, whether this be harm to themselves, other individuals or things like national security.

Arguments from the extrema ratio position generally employ two strategies, harm-based or complicity-based justifications (Ceva & Bocchiola, 2020). Harm-based justifications hold that individuals ought to blow the whistle if not doing so would allow some kind of grave harm and as long as this comes at a reasonable cost to the individual (Kumar & Santoro, 2017). The obvious limitation from the harm perspective relates to how high the bar is set in defining harm, failing to account for wrongdoing such as "misconduct or minor professional malpractice" (Ceva & Bocchiola, 2020, p. 5). Complicity-based justifications suggest that one "ought to blow the whistle when she believes that doing so could avoid her complicity with the occurrence of some wrongful individual behavior" (Ceva & Bocchiola, 2020, p. 5). There are two major responses to this position: first, complicity decouples the decision to whistleblow from the wrongdoing that has occurred. Second, there are several issues with complicity itself, mainly related to its definitional and conceptual clarity.

As can start to be seen, the extrema ratio view of whistleblowing only helps us to think about the justification of whistleblowing in exceptional situations and when "the normative status of either the object of the report (the actual or expected harm generated by an organizational practice or individual behavior) or its agent (the degree of implication in the alleged occurrence of an organizational wrongdoing) is clear" (Ceva & Bocchiola, 2020, p. 6). It fails to appreciate day-to-day acts of whistleblowing as a normalized practice.

The deontic view of whistleblowing begins to address these shortcomings. From the deontic perspective, whistleblowing is dutiful, "pertaining to the ordinary set of answerability measures that any legitimate organization should implement to monitor its overall performance and the contribution that its members give towards—or against—it" (Ceva & Bocchiola, 2019). The deontic view essentially argues that organizational roles are structurally interrelated and rely on every "role-occupant" performing their role. In a perfect world, however, people often fail to comply with the expectations of their roles, which can lead to a range of wrongdoing, some serious, some minor. Given this, if one person fails to undertake their role or engages in some kind on wrongdoing, others in the organization owe it to one another to hold this person to account. From the deontic perspective it is not the harm which may result, it is the "alteration of the normative order" which is wrong (Ceva & Bocchiola, 2020, p. 7). That is, those working within an organization have an obligation not only to carry out tasks directly relevant to their role but to also "prevent their joint work to go off track or take corrective action against it when a failure nevertheless occurs" (Ceva & Bocchiola, 2020, p. 8). The deontic perspective is thus far more permissive in justifying whistleblowing and unlike extrema ratio positions, whistleblowing can generally be justified regardless of the consequences it brings about. To view whistleblowing from this perspective means to justify it first and foremost as a fundamental organizational duty.

While both of the above positions could be seen as being in conflict, they can also be used to complement one another, offering a justification for whistleblowing both as an extraordinary individual act and as part of an organizational duty. Each of these positions, when applied to Australian immigration detention, has its potential strengths and drawbacks; however, both together paint a more complete picture in explaining and justifying whistleblowing. I will discuss this below along with considering whether healthcare professionals should whistleblow and what limits should be placed on disclosures.

Should Healthcare Professionals Whistleblow?

Whistleblowing in response to Australian immigration detention has been relatively common, it has also brought to light some very important information. Without it we would know far less about the conditions within detention centres, the impact of detention and other important issues related to these policies. But should we whistleblow? Below I will consider this question from both the extrema ratio and deontic perspectives, along with considering a number of constraints on disclosures.

First, the most permissive of the two justifications, the deontic view of whistleblowing. As was discussed above, the deontic view of whistleblowing holds that in addition to the duties that attach to their regular role, individuals also have a duty to "hold the failing fellow members answerable for their conduct" (Ceva & Bocchiola, 2020, p. 8). While this position is useful when applied to Australian immigration detention, for many of the same reasons above (i.e., it sees whistleblowing as a duty, and it can account for day-to-day wrongdoing), it doesn't paint the whole picture. As the deontic view is primarily about holding individuals within organizations to account, in Australian immigration detention it may not necessarily be an individual who is responsible for the wrongdoing in question. The wrongdoing may relate to the system itself. It is completely possible that everybody could undertake their role as normal and follow procedure, and the system would still be just as harmful. There are, of course, some people who are more responsible than others, and misconduct by individual employees is common, however, and as was outlined earlier, the majority of the whistleblowing that has occurred in relation to Australian immigration detention has mainly focused on systemic harm rather than individual acts of wrongdoing. In short, while whistleblowing could be justified from this perspective, it doesn't tell the whole story in relation to the harm that is engineered as part of the system.

The extrema ratio view holds that whistleblowing is wrong unless a number of fairly stringent criteria are all met. Unlike the deontic view, it is primarily concerned with the harms in question that are being reported as an exceptional response to serious wrongdoing. Before discussing whether whistleblowing in relation to Australian immigration detention meets this criteria, I want to first deal with some of the major arguments above, which are used to justify the view that whistleblowing is pro tanto wrong as I feel a number of them do not hold in this case. The first issue has to do with promissory obligations and "role obligations". As noted in previous chapters, I used "role obligations" as one of the reasons to why the healthcare community should consider non-violent resistance; this is may seem to be in conflict with this point. While healthcare professionals may have obligations to their employer and while they may have signed a contract that either prohibits or limits disclosures, healthcare professionals also have clear obligations to their patients. As I have already outlined, almost every major code and piece of guidance calls for healthcare professionals to put the interests of their patient first. If the presumption not to whistleblow is based on the idea of promissory or role obligations of healthcare professionals, we are already on shaky ground. Boot (2017, p. 541) suggests the other reason that whistleblowing is wrong is that it fails to "respect the democratic allocation of power". Australia is a democracy and immigration detention has been maintained by successive, elected governments. From this perspective, Australian immigration detention appears to be democratically justified. However, as I argued earlier in this book, these policies strike at democratic norms of accountability and transparency, and there is good reason to believe that Australian immigration detention is an abuse power. The steps the government has taken to cover up the harm created by these policies, shut out the judiciary and limit dissent have ensured these policies operate with little accountability and oversight. Reilly, Appleby, and Laforgia (2014, p. 166) argue that the Australian constitution "creates a system whereby power is ultimately held and exercised on behalf of the people", so while the government in Australia is empowered to make decisions, they are also required to be held accountable to the people through the parliament and judiciary. Given these clear and egregious failings, I don't believe we should view whistleblowing as presumptively wrong as it relates to Australian immigration detention.

This aside, it is worth considering the other points put forward in favour of whistleblowing. As noted above, Boot (2017) suggests that whistleblowing could be justified if it meets three conditions. First, disclosures should be of grave wrongdoing. Second, all alternative channels to report this wrongdoing should be exhausted. Third, the whistleblower should take steps to minimize harm that may result from the disclosure, whether this be harm to individuals or things like national security. Together these set a threshold condition (grave wrongdoing) and two procedural conditions (exhausting all other channels and minimizing harm), that say more about the manner in which whistleblowing is carried out. I hope it goes without saying that Australian immigration detention more generally meets the first criteria of wrongdoing. For Boot (2017, p. 557), however, it is not just about wrongdoing itself, but covering up the wrongdoing, that is, "secretly carrying out policies and programs on the justness and desirability of which reasonable people may disagree, thus rendering public debate on matters of public concern impossible". Two further conditions exist before whistleblowing can be justified from the extrema ratio position. First, all alternative channels of complaint should be exhausted. There is good reason to believe that the above whistleblowing met this criterion. Evidence, advice and complaints have been raised within the system for years; however, the government has almost always failed to act. Both Peter Young and the Christmas Island doctors raised concerns within the system before going public. After the release of the Nauru files, a government investigation was conducted which noted that the lack of accountability surrounding Australian immigration detention was "disturbing" (The Australian Senate Legal and Constitutional Affairs References Committee, 2017).

In minimizing harm, Boot (2017) is fundamentally talking about harm to individuals and harm to national security, furthermore he goes on to note any information made public should not be faulty or misleading. Kumar and Santoro (2017) expand on this point suggesting a number of "communicative constraints"; that is, for a disclosure to be justified, it should be as informative as possible, as truthful as possible and based on evidence. These are important points and are worth reflecting on as they relate to Australian immigration detention. Healthcare professionals should be careful in the information they disclose. For example, information could bring harm to individuals, particularly detained asylum seekers and refugees. Furthermore, the disclosure of such information may violate well-established principles of confidentiality. Healthcare professionals should also be careful if divulging information about staff; they too could be put at risk. It should go without saying that the information disclosed should be as accurate as possible. Individual whistleblowers must also consider the risk to themselves. That is, even if the disclosure is legal, retribution, repercussions and possible referral to the police are likely.

So where does all of this leave us regarding whistleblowing? First, given the clear and egregious failings of Australian immigration detention, we shouldn't make an assumption against whistleblowing. The harms of the system and their cover-up are clear and have been longstanding. Second, whistleblowing can generally be justified from either the extrema ratio or deontic perspectives. Some constraints on this, however, relate to how disclosures are carried out, whether the disclosure is truthful, communicated clearly and based on a degree of evidence. Furthermore, healthcare professionals will need to carefully weigh up the risks associated with whistleblowing, particularly to those detained, but also to themselves. Finally and referring back to previous chapters, ongoing whistleblowing is another good reason to continue support healthcare professionals working in detention centres and against taking strike action. There is a need for further discussions about how such action could be facilitated and those making these disclosures given greater protection.

References

Ahern, K., & McDonald, S. (2002). The beliefs of nurses who were involved in a whistleblowing event. *Journal of Advanced Nursing, 38*(3), 303–309.

Ash, A. (2016). *Whistleblowing and ethics in health and social care.* London: Jessica Kingsley Publishers.

Australian Council of Heads of Schools of Social Work. (2006). We've boundless plains to share: The first report of the People's Inquiry into detention. *Australian Council of Heads of Schools of Social Work.*

Australian Human Rights Commission. (2014). *The forgotten children: National inquiry into children in immigration detention.* Retrieved from https://www.humanrights.gov.au/our-work/asylum-seekers-and-refugees/publications/forgotten-children-national-inquiry-children

Boot, E. R. (2017). Classified public whistleblowing: How to justify a pro tanto wrong. *Social Theory and Practice, 43*(3), 541–567.

Ceva, E., & Bocchiola, M. (2019). *Is whistleblowing a duty?* Cambridge: Polity.

Ceva, E., & Bocchiola, M. (2020). Theories of whistleblowing. *Philosophy Compass, 15*(1), e12642.

Christmas Island Medical Officer's Letter of Concern. (2013). *The Guardian.* Retrieved from https://www.theguardian.com/world/interactive/2014/jan/13/christmas-island-doctors-letter-of-concern-in-full

Doherty, B. (2016). Offshore detention whistleblower loses job after condemning 'atrocity' of camps. *The Guardian.* Retrieved from https://www.theguardian.com/australia-news/2016/jun/21/offshore-detention-whistleblower-loses-job-after-condemning-atrocity-of-camps

Doherty, B. (2019). Nauru doctor wins global free speech award for speaking out on offshore immigration. *The Guardian*. Retrieved from https://www. theguardian.com/australia-news/2019/jan/17/nauru-doctor-wins-global-free-speech-award-for-speaking-out-on-offshore-immigration

Doherty, B., & Marr, D. (2016). The worst I've seen—Trauma expert lifts lid on 'atrocity' of Australia's detention regime. *The Guardian*. Retrieved from https://www.theguardian.com/australia-news/2016/jun/20/the-worst-ive-seen-trauma-expert-lifts-lid-on-atrocity-of-australias-detention-regime

Dowdall, T. (1991). Repression, health care and ethics under apartheid. *Journal of Medical Ethics, 17*, 51–54.

Farrell, P. (2016). Australian police accessed phone records of asylum whistle-blower. *The Guardian*. Retrieved from https://www.theguardian.com/australia-news/2016/may/24/australian-police-accessed-phone-records-of-asylum-whistleblower

Koutroulis, G. (2003). Detained asylum seekers, health care, and questions of human(e)ness. *Australian and New Zealand Journal of Public Health, 27*(4), 381–384.

Koutroulis, G. (2009). Public health metaphors in Australian policy on asylum seekers. *Australian and New Zealand Journal of Public Health, 33*(1), 47–50.

Kumar, M., & Santoro, D. (2017). A justification of whistleblowing. *Philosophy & Social Criticism, 43*(7), 669–684.

Laughland, O., & Davey, M. (2014). Peter Young praised for revealing detention's toll on asylum seekers. *The Guardian*. Retrieved from http://www.theguardian.com/world/2014/aug/05/peter-young-praised-revealing-detentions-toll-asylum-seekers

Laughland, O., & Marr, D. (2013). Rush to send asylum seekers offshore may risk lives, doctors warn. *The Guardian*. Retrieved from http://www.theguardian.com/world/2013/dec/20/rush-to-send-asylum-seekers-offshore-may-risk-lives-doctors-warn

Marr, D. (2013). Doctors reveal 'harmful' standards of medical care for asylum seekers. *The Guardian*. Retrieved from https://www.theguardian.com/world/2013/dec/19/revealed-doctors-outrage-over-unsafe-refugee-patients

Marr, D., & Laughland, O. (2014). Australia's detention regime sets out to make asylum seekers suffer, says chief immigration psychiatrist. *The Guardian*. Retrieved from http://www.theguardian.com/world/2014/aug/05/-sp-australias-detention-regime-sets-out-to-make-asylum-seekers-suffer-says-chief-immigration-psychiatrist

Martin, N. (2018a). As doctors working on Nauru, we thought we were help-ing. Now I know we were not. *The Guardian*. Retrieved from https://www.theguardian.com/commentisfree/2018/oct/12/as-doctors-working-on-nauru-we-thought-we-were-helping-now-i-know-we-were-not

Martin, N. (2018b). The Nauru diaries. *Meanjin*. Retrieved from https://meanjin.com.au/essays/the-nauru-diaries/

Near, J. P., & Miceli, M. P. (1985). Organizational dissidence: The case of whistle-blowing. *Journal of Business Ethics, 4*(1), 1–16.

Reilly, A., Appleby, G., & Laforgia, R. (2014). 'To watch, to never look away': The public's responsibility for Australia's offshore processing of asylum seek-ers. *Alternative Law Journal, 39*(3), 163–166.

Sanggaran, J.-P. (2016). First, do no harm. Why doctors should boycott work-ing in Australian detention centres *The Guardian*. Retrieved from https://www.theguardian.com/commentisfree/2016/mar/05/first-do-no-harm-why-doctors-should-boycott-working-in-australian-detention-centres

Sanggaran, J.-P., & Zion, D. (2015). Call for Australia's ratification of the optional protocol to the convention against torture. *Medical Journal of Australian, 202*(11), 561–562.

Sanggaran, J.-P., Ferguson, G. M., & Haire, B. G. (2014). Ethical challenges for doctors working in immigration detention. *Medical Journal of Australia, 201*(7), 1–3.

Senate Legal and Constitutional Affairs References Committee. (2017). *Serious allegations of abuse, self-harm and neglect of asylum seekers in relation to the Nauru Regional Processing Centre, and any like allegations in relation to the Manus Regional Processing Centre*. Retrieved from https://www.aph.gov.au/parliamentary_business/committees/senate/legal_and_constitutional_affairs/nauruandmanusrpcs/report

Skivenes, M., & Trygstad, S. C. (2010). When whistle-blowing works: The Norwegian case. *Human Relations, 63*(7), 1071–1097.

The Guardian Australia. (2016). The Nauru files. Retrieved from https://www.theguardian.com/news/series/nauru-files

Young, P., & Gordon, M. S. (2016). Mental health screening in immigration detention: A fresh look at Australian government data. *Australasian Psychiatry, 24*(1), 19–22.

9

Principled Disobedience

Overview

In this chapter I will consider whether principled disobedience can be justified in response to Australian immigration detention. While there is a degree of overlap, one of the major differences between principled disobedience and the action discussed in previous chapters is that principled disobedience deliberately seeks to break the law. I will start by defining principled disobedience. I will first discuss more traditional approaches to civil disobedience and their shortcomings, namely that they are too restrictive and fail to take into account a range of principled law breaking, such as action that is deliberately offensive, covert and anonymous. I introduce the concept of uncivil disobedience, as outlined by Delmas (2018), as a means to remedy this. Uncivil and civil disobedience sit alongside one another, providing a more robust foundation to explain principled law breaking or, as it will be labelled here, principled disobedience. I go on to consider principled disobedience in Australian immigration detention, discussing examples of action that could be considered principled disobedience. I will then consider justifications that have been offered for principled disobedience and apply these to Australian

© The Author(s) 2020
R. Essex, *The Healthcare Community and Australian Immigration Detention*,
https://doi.org/10.1007/978-981-15-7537-2_9

immigration detention. Unlike strike action and whistleblowing, it is somewhat difficult to be as specific with principled disobedience as it could take a number of forms. In saying this, however, I conclude that there is a prima facie justification for both civil and uncivil disobedience.

What Is Principled Disobedience?

Civil disobedience has a long history and we don't need to look far for to find many well-known instances and figures who have employed civil disobedience. In 1846, Henry Thoreau spent a night in jail after refusing to pay poll taxes for seven consecutive years in protest of the war in Mexico, slavery and the treatment of Native Americans. Inspired by Thoreau and after returning to India in 1915, Mohandas Karamchand Gandhi began what was to be decades of non-cooperation and civil disobedience. In 1930, Gandhi organized what was arguably his most successful campaign, the Salt March. The march was organized in protest of a law which prohibited Indians from collecting or selling salt and against British colonial rule more generally. Thousands joined the 388 km, 25-day march. In 1955, in Montgomery, Alabama, Claudette Colvin, a black nurse aid, refused to give up her seat to a white man, violating Jim Crow laws that enforced racial segregation. Later that year and perhaps more famously, Rosa Parks followed suit, refusing to give up her seat. In response and drawing inspiration from Thoreau and Gandhi, Martin Luther King organized a boycott of buses in Montgomery that lasted a little over a year. King's home was bombed, and he was arrested during the boycott until racial segregation on all public transport was ruled unconstitutional in 1956.

While far less common relative to whistleblowing and strike action, civil disobedience has also been pursued by the healthcare community. In 1978 the Billboard Utilising Graffitists Against Unhealthy Promotions (BUGA UP) were formed (Chapman, 1996). BUGA UP were an Australian collective who took direct action against tobacco advertising. Over a decade from the late 1970s onwards, BUGA UP "re-faced" tens of thousands of billboards across Australia. This usually involved carefully altering the lettering on billboards, into often humorous alternate slo-gans. A number of other subversive and occasionally illegal activities were also pursued; an alternative advertising awards evening and busking as "The Royal Carcinogenic Orchestra" outside tobacco-sponsored events of the Royal Philharmonic Orchestra were just two examples. A number of healthcare professionals were involved in BUGA UP's activities and many were arrested. BUGA UP inspired several movements globally.[1] At around the same time, Australia was facing a growing number of cases of AIDS. In 1986, Dr. Alex Wodak, the director of drug and alcohol services at St Vincent's Hospital in Sydney, began a needle-exchange programme. This came after writing to the government seeking permission to do so, how-ever failing to gain support. A number of years later, he stated, "I knew it was illegal but I also knew the law was wrong and the only way to change that law was through civil disobedience … I knew I was taking a hell of a risk—for myself, my family and my [medical] registration, but I was cer-tain I was right. I just didn't realize at the time how right I was" (Benson, 2010). Today, health professionals continue to engage in civil disobedi-ence, perhaps most notably in response to climate change. Writing in the *Lancet*, Dr. Robin Stott, a retired doctor, not only called for healthcare professionals to do more in response to climate change but also provided a first-hand account of his arrest:

> I am blocking the road in Whitehall, London, with fellow Extinction Rebellion activists. I have just heard the Prime Minister, Boris Johnson, make demeaning and derogatory remarks about Extinction Rebellion activists, whose actions, together with those of schoolchildren, have done more to alert the world to its crisis than have any other group. I am angry and determined. I have an interaction with the police, who are courteous throughout, and I respond to them in kind. Although the police appear to be a little confused about how and why they were arresting me, neverthe-less, arrested I was … (Stott, 2019, p. 309)

Since the 1960s there has been considerable discussion about the nature of civil disobedience and its justification. One of the most revisited accounts of civil disobedience was proposed by Rawls (2009). Civil disobedience from this perspective is a conscientious, politically motivated and public, non-violent breach of the law, which is aimed to influence the majority to address some kind of injustice or inequity in a nearly just society. Furthermore, most of those who support this position suggest those engaging in such action should accept or even seek out consequences to demonstrate their respect of the law more generally.

This account of civil disobedience however is not without its shortcomings. I won't go into the history of these debates here,[2] however, today, there is contention related to three major points (Delmas, 2016). First, whether civil disobedience needs to be carried out publicly, not secretively or anonymously. Second, whether civil disobedience needs to be non-violent and non-coercive. Third, whether those who engage in civil disobedience should accept the consequences of their actions. In recent years, meeting the traditional criteria of civil disobedience has been seen to be overly restrictive, failing to capture a range of action that also conscientiously breaks the law; however, it is these elements of civil disobedience, as Delmas (2016) points out, that are also seen to make civil disobedience "civil". Let's consider some of the actions above. BUGA UP, while meeting the criteria for being conscientious and non-violent, whether it was public is questionable. While many activists were arrested and while many accepted their punishment (and used their trials as an opportunity to further promote their cause), many seemingly acted anonymously. This may seem like semantics, but this distinction is clearer in other action. In the case of Dr. Alex Wodak, for example, while a conscientious breach of the law, its publicity was also questionable as was the degree to which it was trying to influence broader society in changing their attitude towards harm minimization strategies. Returning to the previous chapter, whistleblowing can also break the law. Edward Snowden was one example discussed earlier; while his actions arguably met a number of the above criteria, he evaded its consequences, fleeing to Russia

---

[2] There are a number of schools of thought in relation of civil disobedience: what it is, how it should be justified and what action qualifies as civil disobedience. There isn't the scope to go into these here, nor is it necessary as this has already been done (Scheuerman, 2018). One of Scheuerman's (2018) criticisms (of which I am also guilty) is that too much focus has been placed on Rawls' view of civil disobedience.

(Scheuerman, 2014). Delmas (2018) provides a number of other examples that begin to challenge civil disobedience as it has been traditionally defined, particularly the notion of "civility". She argues that the traditional definition of civil disobedience also often excludes harmless but offensive protests like Pussy Riot's "Punk Prayer" in Moscow's Cathedral of Christ the Savior. The Hong Kong protests throughout 2019 were not civil, nor did they seek to be (Delmas, 2020). Beyond the examples of BUGA UP and Dr. Alex Wodak above, other secretive, anonymous action also falls outside the traditional definition of civil disobedience; providing aid or assistance to undocumented migrants is one example. Not only this, Delmas (2018) argues that the action carried out by Thoreau, Gandhi and King didn't fit the traditional account of civil disobedience. She also takes issue with civility itself, arguing that historically, the outward submission of many notable figures to the law does not mean that its legitimacy was accepted or that this was attached to some deep moral commitment; this was as much a tactical decision as anything else. The idea of what is civil can also be contested, pointing out that harmless and legal acts have been labelled uncivil and that those in power often use such accusations to silence protesters. A striking example that I have already discussed in previous chapters was the AHRC Forgotten Children Report (2014). This report was rigorous and well researched. It reached reasonable conclusions and made sensible recommendations; that is, if Australia was to act consistently with its human rights obligations, it would have to stop detaining children. Few could have predicted the vitriol from the government in response to these findings.

While a number of authors have attempted to expand the concept of civil disobedience, Delmas (2018) draws a simple conclusion, namely that the reasons why the above action fits so poorly with traditional accounts of civil disobedience is because this action actually isn't civil disobedience. She argues that there is a need to expand accepted forms of unlawful resistance, and to do this she introduces the concept of uncivil disobedience which sits alongside civil disobedience, both of which fall under the umbrella term of principled disobedience. Uncivil disobedience is a cluster concept; that is, it entails a range of actions and activities. Uncivil disobedience can be defined as "disobedient acts that are principled yet also deliberately offensive, covert, anonymous, more than minimally destructive, not respectful of their targets, or which do not aim to communicate to an audience the need to reform laws, policies, or institutions" (Delmas, 2016, p. 685). That is, generally if, while breaking the law, action is either covert, evasive, anonymous, destructive or offensive, it could be considered uncivil. It includes actions such as clandestine and uncivil law breaking such as riots and vigilantism. While principled disobedience can explain violent action, this doesn't necessarily mean violence is justified. Principled disobedience simply provides a broader foundation to explain the action I have outlined above and importantly, clandestine, anonymous law breaking which I strongly suspect is most commonly carried out by healthcare professionals working in Australian immigration detention centres.

There are a few more things worth saying before moving on. A major distinction between action discussed in previous chapters and principled disobedience is that principled disobedience attempts to achieve its goals by resorting to unlawful action; there is however substantial overlap, particularly with whistleblowing when it is illegal. When talking about the justification of principled disobedience, this could also apply to illegal whistleblowing.

Principled Disobedience and Australian Immigration Detention

Could any of the actions spoken about throughout this book be considered principled disobedience? If we restrict our discussion to action carried out by the healthcare community, there are only a few examples. Perhaps the most obvious was the action taken before the Border Force Act was amended in 2016. As I already discussed in previous chapters, this legislation outlawed any current or former staff speaking about their role in detention with a potential prison sentence of two years. This wide-reaching law was protested and the day before it came into effect, *The Guardian* published an open letter, signed by over 40 professionals who had worked in detention centres (*The Guardian Australia*, 2015). I was signatory to this letter and wrote a further article for *The Guardian* (Essex,

2015b). It was no accident these were published the day before the legislation came into effect on 30th June 2015. While provocative, these were
not illegal; they were, however, used to point out that the next day, such
communications would be. After the act came into force and before it
was amended, a number of former healthcare professionals published in
academic journals (Essex, 2015a, 2016a, 2016b, 2016c; Isaacs, 2015a,
2015b, 2015c; Sanggaran, 2015, 2016; Sanggaran, Haire, & Zion, 2016;
Sanggaran & Zion, 2016; Young & Gordon, 2016). While these articles
didn't interview healthcare professionals, almost all relied on each author's
knowledge of working in detention. Professor David Isaacs, who was signatory to the open letter and who authored a number of the articles I am
referring to above, continued to speak to the media (Aubusson, 2015)
and wrote to the then Prime Minister Malcolm Turnbull, Immigration
Minister Peter Dutton and then opposition leader Bill Shorten requesting they prosecute him or repeal the legislation (Scott & Robinson,
2016). Given the broad reach of the Border Force Act and its scope to
include almost any type of disclosure, these disclosures were almost
certainly illegal.

While the above action could arguably be called both civil disobedience and whistleblowing, are there any examples of uncivil disobedience that has been carried out by healthcare professionals, that is, action
that has broken the law that has been offensive, covert or anonymous? I
believe it's safe to assume such action is relatively common; however this
of course is difficult to quantify as it would defeat the purpose of being
covert and anonymous, furthermore, it may be that (particularly for
those working within detention) covertly breaking the law or subverting
the rules (as I discussed in Chap. 7) is equally as effective as publicly
breaking the law, while also carrying far fewer risks.

Before moving on, it is worthwhile reflecting on some examples of
principled disobedience from outside the healthcare community. The
Whistleblowers, Activists and Citizens Alliance[3] are one group who has
been fairly active, organizing a series of actions protesting immigration
detention. In late 2016, they attended parliament house and superglued
their hands to railings in the public gallery, shouting down the

---

[3] https://www.waca.net.au/.

government's policies and disrupting parliament. The next day they returned, abseiling down the front of parliament house to unfurl a banner which called for the closure of detention centres. These two actions gained national and international media attention. Their efforts continued, with multiple disruptive and potentially illegal actions carried out throughout 2017 and 2018.

The Ethics of Principled Disobedience

The justification of civil disobedience generally[4] takes place against the assumption that in near just societies there is a pro tanto duty to obey the law. Historically, there have been at least two major positions in grounding the duty to follow the law. First, the contractual or volunteerist position argues that we have a general duty to obey the law because we have consented to it. More or less, people establish themselves in a society and subsequently form government as this is better than the alternative, the "state of nature" (Locke, 2015).[5] Arriving at a similar conclusion, but for different reasons, non-volunteerists such as Hume (1971) take issue with the idea that we have consented to the law or more generally how society is governed, noting that because one chooses to remain in the country where they were born does not necessarily mean they consent to the law. For Hume (1971), the obligation to follow the law "derives not from consent or contract but from the straightforward utility of a system of laws that enables people to pursue their interests peacefully and conveniently" (Dagger & Lefkowitz, 2014). Drawing on these positions several further objections to disobedience have been proposed. Delmas (2018) provides an overview and response to a number of these, so I will not discuss them here in detail; however, beyond the obligation to obey the law, objections to disobedience generally relate to concerns about it sowing social discord or eroding democratic authority. These points have already been convincingly rebutted; however, some things are worth

---

[4] There is of course no consensus on whether there is an obligation to obey the law (e.g., Wolff, 1998).
[5] This is a term used by philosophers to refer to a hypothetical time when there was no organized society or government.

saying here. First, there are few who believe that the duty to obey the law is absolute, particularly when faced with egregious and persistent injustice. Second, other objections, namely in response to concerns about disobedience sowing social discord or eroding democratic authority, should be contrasted against a number of convincing arguments that civil disobedience can in fact strengthen and stabilize civic bonds (Arendt, 1970), contribute to the rule of law's integrity (Dworkin, 1968) and strengthen the laws legitimacy and efficacy (Scheuerman, 2015). As Delmas (2018) notes, as a whole, arguments against disobedience have failed to outline a convincing case for its prohibition, particularly when it comes to particularly egregious injustices.

It follows that if there is scope to disobey the law, when and how is this justified? Let's start with civil disobedience, where a number of criteria have been proposed in its justification. These generally relate to the action itself and its potential consequences, its use as a last resort, coordinating with others, the likely impact of action including its potential impact, its directness (or indirectness) and the non-violence of action. Importantly, the nature of the objection to the law and reasons behind the violation also matter (Brownlee, 2013). Traditionally, it has been these features of civil disobedience which have been seen as central to its status as being "civil", and thus a potentially justifiable breach of law, I will consider each below.

First, civil disobedience should be a last resort; that is, all other means of pursuing change have been shut off.[6] Second, Rawls (2013) suggests those engaging in civil disobedience should coordinate with other minority groups who may be facing similar injustices; this is so groups do not undermine each other's efforts. Third, consideration needs to be given to the likely impact of civil disobedience and its potential consequences. For Rawls (2013) civil disobedience should only be pursued if there is a reasonable chance of producing some kind of positive change. The potential harms of taking action also need to be weighed. Breaking the law may inconvenience people, on the one hand, but on the other hand, it could

---

[6] As noted, in relation to strike action, all options do not literally need to be attempted before resorting to civil disobedience; if legal or less disruptive alternatives are obviously futile, turning to civil disobedience may be justified (Greenawalt, 2002).

have more serious implications. Generally, the greater the likelihood of action being successful and having some kind of positive impact, the easier it becomes to justify (Greenawalt, 2002). Further to this, the risk to those engaging in civil disobedience needs to be carefully considered, as even if civil disobedience meets all of the criteria outlined here, it may not be wise to pursue this type of action if the risks are too high. Fourth, consideration should also be given to the nature of the action and whether a close connection exists between the issues being protested and the law being broken. Action could seek to break the law that has caused the injustice, or it could seek to break other laws, which are unrelated. Generally, it is accepted that the more direct the relationship between the injustice and the law broken the easier it is to justify the action. This, however, is not always straightforward. There are a multitude of examples where some laws could be "entirely immune from law-violating protest" (Greenawalt, 2002, p. 182). The final two considerations, non-violence and accepting the consequences of action, are important and, for many, essential in justifying civil disobedience; however, these are not essential in justifying uncivil and principled disobedience more generally. I will discuss this below.

In addition to the criteria above, it is equally important that individuals or groups engage in civil disobedience for the right reasons. There are at least three things to consider in this respect. First, the cause of the action should be well founded. That is, while resistors may believe their cause it just, they may be mistaken about facts or evidence. Second, the reasons why resistors support the cause also need to be considered; that is, are resistors motivated by the cause or some kind of self-interest? As Brownlee (2013) notes, it "would be appropriate to judge negatively the character of a person who was improperly motivated to take praiseworthy action in defense of others' rights". Finally, the reasons for engaging in civil disobedience also matter; that is, thought should be given to the particular strategy that is most appropriate given the range of political and social factors in which the action is carried out. Finally, these criteria are not exhaustive; as Brownlee (2013) discusses, any justification for civil disobedience needs to take into account the broader social impact of civil disobedience, that is, whether it contributes positively to society more generally.

While a case can be made for civil disobedience, when could uncivil disobedience be justified? Delmas (2018) suggests that like civil disobedience, some types of uncivil disobedience can be defended against the more general objections to disobedience, which were outlined above. She goes on to argue that we shouldn't necessarily prefer civil disobedience over uncivil disobedience. While she doesn't deny the importance of civility, she argues that civility also serves to maintain social bonds which do not extend to the most marginalized and can even serve to maintain their oppression. She goes on to deal with three possible arguments that we should prefer civil over uncivil disobedience.

First, civil disobedience is more effective than uncivil disobedience. While there is a convincing empirical literature that suggests non-violent action is far more effective than violent action, particularly in liberal societies (Chenoweth & Stephan, 2011), we shouldn't make the mistake of assuming violence and incivility are equivalent. Uncivil acts can be non-violent, and furthermore, uncivil acts, such as whistleblowing, can also be used to fuel civil disobedience. Additionally, we need to be careful in defining what we mean by effective, as Delmas (2018, p. 59) notes, "food, shelter, and legal aid to unauthorized migrants—can directly frustrate injustice and benefit people in dire need in ways that are not available to civil disobedients". Second, civil disobedience demonstrates the changes we aspire to see in society; that is, if we seek a civil and just future, our action should be congruent with this. While this may be somewhat true, it doesn't follow that uncivil action, including violence, necessarily betrays the just ends that it seeks. Are refugees' claims to be treated fairly diminished if they protested conditions (uncivilly) within detention centres? Third, it has been argued that by acting civilly, individuals continue to demonstrate their commitment to mutual reciprocity or "civic friendship". Such civic friendship, however, is often an illusion for minorities and other marginalized groups. As Delmas (2018, p. 64) notes, uncivil disobedience forces the community to "confront the disconnect between its reality and its professed ideals … Incivility calls civility's bluff". Additionally, incivility questions the rules of engagement, "who gets to speak, as well as where, when, and how. In doing so, uncivil disobedience helps to isolate the deceptions of civic friendship" (p. 64). In summary, we shouldn't assume that civil disobedience should be preferred over uncivil action, and in fact, civility can, in certain circumstances, exacerbate the issues it is seeking to address.

In addition to defending civil disobedience against more general claims that we should obey the law and against arguments that law breaking should be civil, Delmas (2018) goes further to argue that principled disobedience, that is, both civil and uncivil disobedience, are a duty in many cases. I won't go into this in detail; however, she argues that principles such as justice and fairness, which are commonly used to ground obedience, can also provide reasons to resist injustice. This point has larger implications; not only does this provide a convincing case in arguing for uncivil disobedience, this justification suggests we need to move beyond the assumption that obedience to the law is our primary duty—as Delmas (2018) notes, it is only one obligation amongst many.

All of this, of course, doesn't mean that anything goes. Delmas (2018) proposes a number of constraints in relation to uncivil disobedience. First, "[r]esistors must act with respect for other people's interests, including, but not limited to, their basic interests in life and bodily integrity; their interests in non-domination and in choosing the values that shape their lives; and their interest in protection by a stable, secure system of rights … one should accept and seek to protect these basic interests when engaging in principled disobedience" (p. 49). Second, similar to past thinking on civil disobedience, it is important that the interests being pursued are just and that conflicting interests are carefully weighed; for example, "disobedience may affect the majority's interest in a stable legal system, but principled lawbreaking may sometimes be necessary to protect people's basic interests in life and bodily integrity" (p. 49). Third, the least harmful course of action should be pursued, among the possible options that have a reasonable chance of success. Success in this respect could be measured in a number of ways, from the consequences it brings about to whether it simply raises awareness of the issues in question.

Before moving on, there are a few other points worth making. The first is that there has been a growing literature that has been developed in parallel with the discussions above, which has dealt with the question of breaking unjust immigration law. While almost all of the above reasoning could be applied here, immigration law raises the further question of the scope of political authority and whether this extends to outsiders. Hidalgo

(2019) offers one of the most comprehensive accounts against complying with immigration law, following similar logic to many thinkers above, concluding that "[i]f immigration restrictions are sufficiently unjust, then this injustice arguably releases citizens from their obligations to comply with them" (Hidalgo, 2019, p. 8). There have also been some attempts to justify civil disobedience[7] as it relates to the healthcare community. These add little to what has already been said above; however, they are worth considering before moving on.

One of the earliest examinations of civil disobedience as it relates to the healthcare community was provided by Childress (1985). He argued that while there was a general duty to obey the law, civil disobedience could be justified in healthcare as long as it met a number of the criteria outlined above: that the law in question was unjust, that such action was a last resort, the impact of such action was carefully considered and the features of civil disobedience (i.e., non-violence, acceptance of consequences) were followed. Macauley (2005) calls for organized, open defiance in the pursuit of universal health coverage in the US. While focused on this one issue, this proposed justification for civil disobedience is relatively similar to Childress (1985) above. He essentially outlines three criteria: civil disobedience should be in response to genuine injustice, it should be a last resort, and there must be a reasonable chance of success. Gross (2005) discusses and attempts to justify uncivil disobedience or what he calls evasive non-compliance in relation to healthcare professional-aided draft evasion. He argues that to be justified, such action should be "a last resort, without which it is impossible to avert harm appeal to a higher or at least equally weighty moral principle pass the test of utility so that the physician's illegal act brings more benefit than harm" (p. 451). Gross (2005) does bring up a further interesting consideration, that is, when breaking the law also violates well-established professional and ethical norms, namely in assisting draft evasion doctors would often have to lie.

Most recently, Bennett, Macmillan, Jones, Blaiklock, and McMillan (2020) drew from Childress (1985) and Rawls (2013) to reformulate five criteria, for assessing the justifiability of health professionals' engaging

---

[7] None have dealt with uncivil or the broader concept of principled disobedience.

in civil disobedience. First, whether civil disobedience is proportionate to the injustice in question. Second, whether civil disobedience is a last resort. Third, whether there is a reasonable chance that civil disobedience will be effective. Fourth, whether the least harmful action is pursued. And finally, they argue that the obligation to participate is greater for those who are likely to face fewer risks or repercussions.

In summary, there is no convincing prohibition against breaking the law, particularly if this relates to major injustice. If we take the traditional view of civil disobedience, we need to consider a number of factors in justifying our response. These generally relate to the action itself and its consequences, its use as a last resort, coordinating with other resistors, the likely impact of action including its potential positive or harmful impact, its directness (or indirectness) and the non-violence of action. The nature of the objection to the law and reasons behind the violation also matter. Action needn't only be civil however, nor should we work on the assumption that civil action is preferable to uncivil action. Uncivil action, which includes law breaking that is deliberately offensive, covert and anonymous, can be justified on similar grounds to civil disobedience; however, those engaging in such action should still show restraint if action is to be justified. These restrains mainly relate to acting with respect for other people's interests, carefully considering the interests being pursued and how to balance these when in conflict and finally pursuing the least harmful course of action; among the possible options that have a reasonable chance of success.

Should the Healthcare Community Engage in Principled Disobedience?

Taking all of the above into account, the more general literature on principled disobedience and the broader literature that deals with unjust immigration law, how might we then apply this to Australian immigration detention? When it comes to principled disobedience, the devil is often in the details, and I believe we can learn from the literature on both civil and uncivil disobedience. While there is a case for civil disobedience, action needn't meet the rigid criteria often used to judge civility. Certain types of uncivil disobedience could be justified; it may be preferable to anonymously leak information, act covertly or even be deliberately offensive. The justification of either civil or uncivil disobedience, however, will depend on a range of contextual factors.[8] That is, while I believe there is a prima facie case for principled disobedience in response to Australian immigration detention, this needs a number of qualifications. First and foremost, we should act with the constraints proposed by Delmas (2018) in mind. That is, principled disobedience should be carried out with respect for other people's interests, it should carefully consider and weigh conflicting interests, and the least harmful course of action should be pursued. Beyond this, there are a number of more specific considerations that we need to think about if action is to be justified.

The impact of principled disobedience in response to Australian immigration detention needs to be considered carefully. Like other forms of action discussed in this book, if principled disobedience were to potentially have a negative, short- or longer-term impact on detainees, this is something that should weigh heavily. It is completely possible that illegal action would cause less harm than legal action (such as a strike), but it is also possible that illegal action could also promote substantial harm. Healthcare professionals will also need to carefully consider the risks to themselves, not just in relation to repercussions from the government or media, but professionally. The only author to discuss civil disobedience conflicting with professional obligations has been Gross (2005). There is far more that could be said about this; however, it should suffice to say that healthcare professionals should carefully assess whether principled disobedience clashes with other professional and ethical obligations.

The instrumentality of any potential action needs to be considered carefully and weighed against the other factors discussed here (such as the potential consequences of action). While healthcare professionals could engage in principled disobedience by blocking driveways, disrupting deportations or even protesting in parliament, I don't believe that such

---

[8] It is somewhat difficult to be as specific with principled disobedience as I was with strike action and whistleblowing as principled disobedience refers to a range of action that could take a number of forms and target a range of laws.

action would be as impactful as targeted leaks or whistleblowing from those who have worked within centres; this, however, is not to say that under the right circumstances that such action wouldn't be justified. A related question here has to do with the direct or indirect nature of action; that is, should action target policy and legislation that are largely responsible for these policies, or should we break other laws? In the case of Australian immigration detention, either form could be justified. While the example provided above of action in response to the Border Force Act is an example of a direct violation, other opportunities may be limited as Australian citizens will not be subject to many sections of the Migration Act (1958) and related legislation. In seeking to either directly or indirectly break the law, we should again be guided by the potential impact and instrumentality of action. On this point and in thinking about instrumentality, it may also be in many cases that the most effective course of action will be to obey the law. As history has shown, the government has been particularly reactive to a range of reasonable and civil criticism.

A final question relates to principled disobedience and its relationship to the "near just society", that is, a society that is close to being fair and just. Almost all writing and thinking about principled disobedience has been done with the idea of a "near just society" in mind, that is, majority of high-income western countries today. Can we safely say that Papua New Guinea or Nauru are nearly just? I don't want to speculate too much on this point; however, it should suffice to say that if one is seeking to break the law outside of Australia, this will change the above considerations substantially. If transparency is lacking or the law is administered unfairly, it may weigh in favour of anonymous, covert law breaking, or even obeying the law. It would also likely change the calculus of whether one should accept punishment.

References

Arendt, H. (1970). Reflections civil disobedience. *The New Yorker*. Retrieved from https://www.newyorker.com/magazine/1970/09/12/reflections-civil-disobedience

Aubusson, K. (2015). 'It's child abuse': Australian doctor brought to tears by treatment of Nauru detainees. *The Sydney Morning Herald*. Retrieved from https://www.smh.com.au/national/its-child-abuse-australian-doctor-brought-to-tears-by-treatment-of-nauru-detainees-20150813-giysx9.html

Australian Human Rights Commission. (2014). The forgotten children: National inquiry into children in immigration detention. Retrieved from https://www.humanrights.gov.au/our-work/asylum-seekers-and-refugees/publications/forgotten-children-national-inquiry-children

Bennett, H., Macmillan, A., Jones, R., Blaiklock, A., & McMillan, J. (2020). Should health professionals participate in civil disobedience in response to the climate change health emergency? *Lancet, 395*(10220), 304–308.

Benson, K. (2010). Doctor took the law into his own hands. *The Sydney Morning Herald*. Retrieved from https://www.smh.com.au/national/doctor-took-the-law-into-his-own-hands-20100613-y64t.html

Border Force Act 2015 (Cth) (Austl.).

Brownlee, K. (2013). Civil disobedience. *Stanford Encyclopedia of Philosophy*. Retrieved from https://plato.stanford.edu/entries/civil-disobedience/

Chapman, S. (1996). Civil disobedience and tobacco control: The case of BUGA UP. Billboard utilising graffitists against unhealthy promotions. *Tobacco Control, 5*(3), 179.

Chenoweth, E., & Stephan, M. J. (2011). *Why civil resistance works: The strategic logic of nonviolent conflict*. New York: Columbia University Press.

Childress, J. F. (1985). Civil disobedience, conscientious objection, and evasive noncompliance: A framework for the analysis and assessment of illegal actions in health care. *The Journal of Medicine and Philosophy, 10*(1), 63–83.

Dagger, R., & Lefkowitz, D. (2014). Political obligation. *Stanford Encyclopedia of Philosophy*. Retrieved from https://plato.stanford.edu/entries/political-obligation/

Delmas, C. (2016). Civil disobedience. *Philosophy Compass, 11*(11), 681–691.

Delmas, C. (2018). *A duty to resist: When disobedience should be uncivil*. Oxford: Oxford University Press.

Delmas, C. (2020). Uncivil disobedience in Hong Kong. *Boston Review*. Retrieved from http://bostonreview.net/global-justice/candice-delmas-uncivil-disobedience-hong-kong

Dworkin, R. (1968). On not prosecuting civil disobedience. *The New York Review of Books, 10*(11).

Essex, R. (2015a). Ethics, foreseeability, and tragedy in Australian immigration detention. *Journal of bioethical inquiry, 12*(4), 537–539.

Essex, R. (2015b). Time to tell the truth before I'm gagged: Australia's detention centres ruin lives. *The Guardian*. https://www.theguardian.com/commentis-free/2015/jun/30/time-to-tell-the-truth-before-im-gagged-australias-detention-centres-ruin-lives

Essex, R. (2016a). A community standard: Equivalency of healthcare in Australian immigration detention. *Journal of Immigrant and Minority Health, 19*(4), 974–981.

Essex, R. (2016b). Healthcare, clinical ethics and Australian immigration detention: A review of the literature. *The International Journal of Human Rights, 20*(7), 1039–1053.

Essex, R. (2016c). Torture, healthcare and Australian immigration detention. *Journal of Medical Ethics, 42,* 418–419.

Greenawalt, K. (2002). Justifying nonviolent disobedience. In H. Bedau (Ed.), *Civil disobedience in focus* (pp. 176–194). London: Routledge.

Gross, M. L. (2005). Physician-assisted draft evasion: Civil disobedience, medicine, and war. *Cambridge Quarterly of Healthcare Ethics, 14*(4), 444–454.

Hidalgo, J. (2019). The ethics of resisting immigration law. *Philosophy Compass, 14*(12), e12639.

Hume, D. (1971). *Of the original contract*. Alexandria: Library of Alexandria.

Isaacs, D. (2015a). Are healthcare professionals working in Australia's immigration detention centres condoning torture? *Journal of Medical Ethics, 42*(7), 413–415.

Isaacs, D. (2015b). Doctors should boycott working in Australia's immigration centres and must continue to speak out on mistreatment of detainees-despite the law. *British Medical Journal, 350,* h3269

Isaacs, D. (2015c). Nauru and detention of children. *Journal of Paediatrics and Child Health, 51*(4), 353–354.

Locke, J. (2015). *The second treatise of civil government*. Peterborough: Broadview Press.

Macauley, R. (2005). The hippocratic underground: Civil disobedience and health care reform. *The Hastings Center Report, 35*(1), 38–45.

Migration Act 1958 (Cth) (Austl.).

Rawls, J. (2009). *A theory of justice*. Cambridge: Harvard University Press.

Rawls, J. (2013). The justification of civil disobedience. *Arguing About Law,* 244–253.

Sanggaran, J.-P. (2015). Asylum seekers are being abused on our watch. It's time to put detention under surveillance. *The Guardian*. Retrieved from https://www.theguardian.com/commentisfree/2015/sep/12/asylum-seekers-are-being-abused-on-our-watch-its-time-to-put-detention-under-surveillance

Sanggaran, J.-P. (2016). First, do no harm. Why doctors should boycott working in Australian detention centres. *The Guardian*. Retrieved from https://www.theguardian.com/commentisfree/2016/mar/05/first-do-no-harm-why-doctors-should-boycott-working-in-australian-detention-centres

Sanggaran, J.-P., & Zion, D. (2016). Is Australia engaged in torturing asylum seekers? A cautionary tale for Europe. *Journal of Medical Ethics, 42*(7), 420–423.

Sanggaran, J.-P., Haire, B., & Zion, D. (2016). The health care consequences of Australian immigration policies. *PLoS Medicine, 13*(2), e1001960.

Scheuerman, W. E. (2014). Whistleblowing as civil disobedience: The case of Edward Snowden. *Philosophy & Social Criticism, 40*(7), 609–628.

Scheuerman, W. E. (2015). Recent theories of civil disobedience: An anti-legal turn? *Journal of Political Philosophy, 23*(4), 427–449.

Scheuerman, W. E. (2018). *Civil disobedience*. London: John Wiley & Sons.

Scott, S., & Robinson, N. (2016). Leading Australian doctor challenges Malcolm Turnbull, Bill Shorten over 'torture-like conditions' at detention centres. *Australian Broadcasting Corporation News*. Retrieved from https://www.abc.net.au/news/2016-01-26/doctor-challenges-pm-over-immigration-detention-centres/7113966

Stott, R. (2019). My arrest in support of Extinction Rebellion: the imperative for action. *Lancet, 395*(10220), 309–310.

The Guardian Australia. (2015). Open letter on the Border Force Act: 'We challenge the department to prosecute'. *The Guardian*. Retrieved from https://www.theguardian.com/australia-news/2015/jul/01/open-letter-on-the-border-force-act-we-challenge-the-department-to-prosecute

Wolff, R. P. (1998). *In defense of anarchism*. Oakland: University of California Press.

Young, P., & Gordon, M. S. (2016). Mental health screening in immigration detention: A fresh look at Australian government data. *Australasian Psychiatry, 24*(1), 19–22.

10

Conclusions

In this chapter I will offer a brief summary, some conclusions and directions for future inquiry. I want to first recap the central arguments in this book, namely that the Australian healthcare community should include non-violent resistance as part of a future strategy. I will then discuss some caveats, limitations and future directions in relation to the arguments I have advanced here.

In this book I argued that the healthcare community should engage in non-violent resistance in response to Australian immigration detention. My basic point is that when faced with an egregious injustice and particularly when playing a role in maintaining these policies (by working in detention centres), the healthcare community should take action to undermine and resist these policies. Given the circumstances in Australia, the exceptional nature of detention and the fact that other less contentious approaches are likely to have little impact, non-violent resistance is one means to seek redress. In Chap. 2, I outlined the harm created and perpetuated by Australia's policy of mandatory immigration detention and the related measures it has taken throughout the Asia-Pacific region. In Chap. 3, I outlined the healthcare arrangements within detention. Testimony from healthcare professionals, detainees and statements from professional bodies not only showed the futility in the delivery of

© The Author(s) 2020
R. Essex, *The Healthcare Community and Australian Immigration Detention*,
https://doi.org/10.1007/978-981-15-7537-2_10

healthcare but also showed the degree to which healthcare deviates from generally accepted standards. I also outlined the action taken by the healthcare community outside of detention, protesting these policies. In Chap. 4, I considered the ethics of Australian immigration detention and concluded that Australian immigration detention and regional policies of deterrence and denial cannot be justified; however, any reform would require careful consideration as it would also have implications throughout the Asia-Pacific region. With this in mind, in Chap. 5, I turned to what the reform of Australian immigration detention (and policies throughout the Asia-Pacific) should look like, arguing that at a minimum if we are to address the health and wellbeing of those detained, Australia would need to act consistently with the human rights commitments it has made. I considered the constraints on achieving such reform, outlining a range of historical, social and political factors that explain the Australian governments approach. I then argued that given all of this, present approaches to health and wellbeing are poorly equipped to challenge these constraints. Chapter 6 made a prima facie case for non-violent resistance. I defined this as a strategy in seeking the reform of Australia's policies, which recognizes that change will not come through consensus or collaboration alone and instead leverages the power of the healthcare community to demand change. I then argued that the healthcare community has a responsibility to engage in such action. I went on to consider three forms of action. In Chap. 7, I considered strike action, while Chap. 8 discussed whether whistleblowing could be justified. And finally, Chap. 9 discussed principled disobedience.

In saying all of this and while I hope this book challenges those in the healthcare community to carefully consider non-violent resistance in response to Australian immigration detention, such action is far from a guarantee of better treatment of refugees and asylum seekers in Australia. While such action stands a far better chance of having an impact when coupled with current efforts, there is much work to be done. Into the foreseeable future, it is likely that Australia will continue to pursue increasingly restrictive policies that deter and deny those seeking protection. What is likely to change are the numbers of people in detention. Boat arrivals have now stopped, and Australian continues to look to resettle those who remain offshore overseas. Shifts in policy will require shifts in strategy. In this respect, I hope this is the beginning of a conversation over the longer term about the role of the healthcare community in response to Australian immigration detention.

Looking ahead, one of the most important questions we need ask relates to why Australia does what it does. Why it has some of the harshest policies in the western world, why it reserves the worst treatment for asylum seekers who travel by boat and why these policies appear to continue to receive a slight majority of public support. While there have been a number of investigations into public attitudes toward refugees and asylum seekers in Australia, the most comprehensive exploration into these issues has been conducted by Nethery (2010), discussed earlier. A greater understanding of these issues will allow a more effective response.

There is also scope to further explore the role that the healthcare community should play in social and political change more generally. While professional bodies in Australia have generally been supportive or at least sympathetic to whistleblowers and others who have been attacked by the government, there is little guidance on such action. Serious conversations are needed to begin to outline what type of action is justified in response to Australian immigration detention and more generally what the role of the healthcare community should be in resisting injustice.

Perhaps, most obviously, there is also substantial work that could be done exploring non-violent resistance. We could turn to the literature or look to history. We can also learn from those in the healthcare community who have resisted, who have stood up to injustice and who, rather than compromise their principles, have taken a risk in speaking out. Many of these acts of resistance I discussed in earlier chapters deserve to be analysed in greater detail.

Further to what I have advanced above, there are alternative approaches to these issues. We should be open to these. We should be open to collaboration. We can and should look at less contentious forms of action, how these can be made more effective, and how we can collaborate across professions and disciplines. Legislative reform and a bill of rights have all been discussed for many years. These should continue to be pursued. I am somewhat hopeful in this respect that there is no shortage of ideas or good will. One thing we need to be cautious about, however, is simply outlining calls to action or articulating our ends. Future approaches should deal with the messy realities of actually getting these ideas in front of politicians, gaining public support and dealing with the complexities of social and political change.

Finally, research exploring and documenting the experiences of those in detention should continue. This includes both healthcare professionals and those detained. While this book called for a shift in how healthcare professionals respond to Australian immigration detention, research within detention remains important for a number of reasons. First, research is an integral part of the culture of healthcare institutions. Second, such research will continue to provide important information about how states are able to co-opt healthcare institutions and professions into activities which target vulnerable populations for purposes that are antithetical to their health, wellbeing, long-term security and human rights. Third, research provides a degree of external oversight. Much of what we know about detention today has come from research or former staff and detainees speaking out. Finally, there may well come a time when the Australian government is held to account for its policy of mandatory detention and for the death and human misery it has caused. If and when that time comes, findings of research that has been conducted by and/or with practitioners who have first-hand experience of the system could provide important evidence (Essex & Jordens, 2018).

References

Essex, R., & Jordens, C. F. C. (n.d.). The Border Force Act, research and Australian immigration detention, Unpublished manuscript.

Nethery, A. (2010). Immigration detention in Australia. Doctoral dissertation, Deakin University, Victoria, Australia. Retrieved from http://dro.deakin.edu.au/view/DU:30032385

Index

The manufacturer's authorised representative in the EU is Springer
Nature Customer Service Centre GmbH, Europaplatz 3, 69115 Heidelberg,
Germany. If you have any concerns regarding our products, please
contact ProductSafety@springernature.com

Printed and bound by CPI Group (UK) Ltd, Croydon, CR0 4YY
29/04/2026
02099460-0001